THE IDEA OF THE POSTMODERN

The question of what postmodernism actually means is not an easy one to answer: it has meant different things to different people at different times, rising from humble literary-critical origins in the 1950s to a level of global conceptualization in the 1980s. How does the student approaching the subject for the first time distinguish between the various conceptual levels at which the terms 'postmodern' and 'postmodernism' have been employed, or between the diverse interpretations of the postmodern that – sometimes consecutively and at other times simultaneously – have been put forward over the past thirty years?

In *The Idea of the Postmodern*, Hans Bertens clears up the confusion by tracing and analyzing the debate in an accessible way and witty style. He sets out the interdisciplinary aspects, the critical debates, and the key theorists of postmodernism, and discusses the relationship between postmodernism and poststructuralism, and postmodernism and modernism.

The Idea of the Postmodern is an enjoyable and indispensable introductory text for today's students.

Hans Bertens is Professor and Director of American Studies at the University of Utrecht, The Netherlands. He has written extensively on the subjects of postwar fiction, popular literature, mass culture, and postmodern theory.

FOR REFERENCE USE ONLY
Do not remove.
This item has been security tagged.

THE IDEA OF THE POSTMODERN

A history

Hans Bertens

London and New York

21 FEB 1996

DUNDEE DISTRICT
LIBRARIES
LOCATION Ref 068220
ACCESSION NUMBER
C90 011 839X
SUPPLIER Daw PRICE £37.50
CLASS No. 909.82 DATE 16.2.96

First published 1995
by Routledge
11 New Fetter Lane, London EC4P 4EE

Simultaneously published in the USA and Canada
by Routledge
29 West 35th Street, New York NY 10001

Reprinted 1995

© 1995 Hans Bertens

Phototypeset in Baskerville by Intype, London

Printed and bound in Great Britain by
Redwood Books, Trowbridge, Wiltshire

Printed on acid-free paper

All rights reserved. No part of this book may be reprinted or reproduced or utilized in any form or by any electronic, mechanical, or other means, now known or hereafter invented, including photocopying and recording, or in any information storage or retrieval system, without permission in writing from the publishers.

British Library Cataloguing in Publication Data
A catalogue record for this book is available from the British Library.

Library of Congress Cataloguing in Publication Data
A catalogue record for this book has been requested

ISBN 0–415–06011–7 (hbk)
0–415–06012–5 (pbk)

For Laura, Redmer, and Roland

CONTENTS

ACKNOWLEDGMENTS

A book of this kind inevitably builds upon numerous other books and the reader will come across them in my references. But books also have less visible debts. This one certainly does. I want to thank my old friend Theo D'haen, who, perhaps to contribute to my education, first got me interested in postmodernism, and I want to thank Douwe Fokkema, who institutionalized that interest by inviting me to participate in an early research project on the modern/postmodern divide. Gerhard Hoffman, still at Würzburg, and Alfred Hornung, now at Mainz, added me to the impressive roster of their Würzburg conferences, leading to a cycle of intellectually exciting and more generally rewarding experiences, both in Germany and in the US. Closer to home, Willem van Reijen joined me for inspiring walks in the woods and offered lucid and helpful commentary on part of my manuscript. Yet closer to home, Prisca Bertens, in spite of her hectic life as a doctor, still found time and energy to give invaluable support.

I wrote part of this book while enjoying the hospitality of the Netherlands Institute for Advanced Study in the Humanities and Social Sciences, and I would like to thank its director, Dirk J. van de Kaa, and the NIAS staff for a wonderful time.

Finally, I would, at a less personal level, like to thank the following authors and publishers for their generous permission to quote from the parenthesized titles: Zygmunt Bauman and Routledge (*Intimations of Postmodernity*), David Harvey and Blackwell (*The Condition of Postmodernity*) and Fredric Jameson and Duke University Press (*Postmodernism, or, the Cultural Logic of Late Capitalism*).

Part I
POSTMODERNISMS

1

INTRODUCTION

Postmodernism is an exasperating term, and so are postmodern, postmodernist, postmodernity, and whatever else one might come across in the way of derivation. In the avalanche of articles and books that have made use of the term since the late 1950s, postmodernism has been applied at different levels of conceptual abstraction to a wide range of objects and phenomena in what we used to call reality. Postmodernism, then, is several things at once. It refers, first of all, to a complex of anti-modernist artistic strategies which emerged in the 1950s and developed momentum in the course of the 1960s. However, because it was used for diametrically opposed practices in different artistic disciplines, the term was deeply problematical almost right from the start.

Let me offer an example. Clement Greenberg, for more than thirty years easily the most influential art critic on the American scene, defined modernism in terms of a wholly autonomous aesthetic, of a radically anti-representational self-reflexivity. For Greenberg, modernism implied first of all that each artistic discipline sought to free itself from all extraneous influence. Modernist painting had thus purged itself of narrative – the presentation of biblical, classical, historical, and other such scenes – which belonged to the literary sphere, and had turned to a necessarily self-reflexive exploration of that which could be said to be specific to painting alone: its formal possibilities. From this anti-representational, formalist point of view, postmodernism gives up on this project of self-discovery and is a (cowardly) return to pictorial narrative, to representational practices. Architectural postmodernism has clear affinities with this. For Robert Venturi, Denise Scott Brown, Charles Jencks and other theorists, modernist architecture is the purist self-referential architecture of the Bauhaus –

Mies van der Rohe, Gropius, and others – and of the corporate architecture of the postwar International Style. Postmodern architecture turns away from this self-absorbed and technocratic purism and turns to the vernacular and to history, thus reintroducing the humanizing narrative element that had been banned by the Bauhaus group and its corporate offshoots.

However, for many of the American literary critics that bring the term postmodernism into circulation in the 1960s and early 1970s, postmodernism is the move *away* from narrative, from representation. For them, postmodernism is the turn towards self-reflexiveness in the so-called metafiction of the period, as practiced, for instance, by Samuel Beckett, Vladimir Nabokov, John Barth, Donald Barthelme, the Surfictionists, the *nouveau romanciers*, and a host of other writers. For them this particular form of postmodernism rediscovers and radicalizes the self-reflexive moment in an otherwise representational modernism (the self-reflexivity of the later Joyce, especially of *Finnegans Wake*, of the experiments of Raymond Roussel and others). Seen from this perspective, postmodernism is a move towards radical aesthetic autonomy, towards pure formalism.

The other arts further complicate the picture. Sally Banes tells us that in dance criticism the term postmodern has been applied both to an early movement toward functionality, purity, and self-reflexivity ('analytic postmodern dance'; Banes 1985: 81) and to a later 'rekindling of interest in narrative structures' (91). Film presents its own specific problems – of periodization, for instance. Maureen Turim's persuasive periodization of the early history of film – primitive (1895–1906), early classical (1906–25), and classical (1925–55) – coincides largely with literary modernism, whereas her modernist (1955–75) and 'potentially' postmodernist (1975-present) periods coincide with the postmodern period in most of the other arts (Turim 1991). There is, moreover, the intermittent presence of avant-gardist film which in its 'anti-structural' manifestations of the later 1970s and 1980s – which reintroduce 'cultural content' – is Noël Carroll's 'likeliest nominee for the title postmodern film' (Carroll 1985: 103).

In photography, however, 'content' is associated with realism and modernism, and the pendulum swings the other way again. For Douglas Crimp, Abigail Solomon-Godeau and other theorists, writing in the late 1970s and early 1980s, it is the fiercely anti-representational, anti-narrative, deconstructionist photography of

Cindy Sherman, Sherry Levine, and Richard Prince that is postmodern, to the exclusion of everything else. Depending on the artistic discipline, then, postmodernism is either a radicalization of the self-reflexive moment within modernism, a turning away from narrative and representation, or an explicit return to narrative and representation. And sometimes it is both. Moreover, to make things worse, there are, as we will see, postmodernisms that do not fit this neat binary bill. Yet, there is a common denominator. In their own way, they all seek to transcend what they see as the self-imposed limitations of modernism, which in its search for autonomy and purity or for timeless, representational, truth has subjected experience to unacceptable intellectualizations and reductions. But at this level we again find complications. The attempt to transcend modernism follows two main strategies, which unfortunately do not coincide with the distinction that I have just made between a self-reflexive postmodernism and a postmodernism that reintroduces (some kind of) representation. Those who opt for the first strategy are content to question modernism's premises and its procedures from within the realm of art. Those who wish to break more radically with modernism do not only attack modernist art, but seek to undermine the idea of art itself. For them the idea of art, that is, art-as-institution, is a typically modernist creation, built upon the principle of art's self-sufficiency, its special – and separate – status within the larger world. But such an autonomy, these artists argue, is really a self-imposed exile; it means that art willingly accepts its impotence, that it accedes to its own neutralization and depoliticization.[1]

At a second level of conceptualization we find similar confusions. Here postmodernism has been defined as the 'attitude' of the 1960s counterculture, or, somewhat more restrictively, as the 'new sensibility' of the 1960s social and artistic avant-garde. This new sensibility is eclectic, it is radically democratic, and it rejects what it sees as the exclusivist and repressive character of liberal humanism and the institutions with which it identifies that humanism. Here the avant-garde attack on art-as-institution is broadened and raised to a socio-political level. Such an early politicized form of postmodernism was first identified in the mid-sixties by Leslie Fiedler and other critics who monitored the contemporary American scene.

In the course of the 1970s, postmodernism was gradually drawn into a poststructuralist orbit. In a first phase, it was primarily associated with the deconstructionist practices that took their inspiration from the poststructuralism of the later Roland Barthes and, more in particular, of Jacques Derrida. In its later stages, it drew on Michel Foucault, on Jacques Lacan's revisions of Freud, and, occasionally, on the work of Gilles Deleuze and Félix Guattari. The translation of Jean-François Lyotard's *La Condition postmoderne* (1984; original edition 1979), in which a prominent poststructuralist adopted the term postmodern, seemed to many to signal a fully-fledged merger between an originally American postmodernism and French poststructuralism. Like poststructuralism, this postmodernism rejects the empirical idea that language can represent reality, that the world is accessible to us through language because its objects are mirrored in the language that we use. From this empirical point of view, language is transparent, a window on the world, and knowledge arises out of our direct experience of reality, undistorted and not contaminated by language. Accepting Derrida's exposure, and rejection, of the metaphysical premises – the transcendent signifier – upon which such empiricism is built, postmodernism gives up on language's representational function and follows poststructuralism in the idea that language constitutes, rather than reflects, the world, and that knowledge is therefore always distorted by language, that is, by the historical circumstances and the specific environment in which it arises. Under the pressure of Derrida's arguments, and of Lacan's psychoanalysis, which sees the subject as constructed in language, the autonomous subject of modernity, objectively rational and self-determined, likewise gives way to a postmodern subject which is largely other-determined, that is, determined within and constituted by language.

One can, as I have suggested, distinguish two moments within this poststructuralist postmodernism. The first, which belongs to the later 1970s and the early 1980s, derives from Barthes and Derrida and is linguistic, that is, textual, in its orientation. The attack on foundationalist notions of language, representation, and the subject is combined with a strong emphasis on what in Derrida's 'Structure, sign, and play in the discourse of the human sciences' (1970) had been called 'freeplay' – the extension *ad infinitum* of the 'interplay of signification' in the absence of transcendent signifiers, of metaphysical meaning – and on intertextuality. This deconstructionist postmodernism saw the text, in the terms made famous by Roland Barthes's 'The death of the author' of 1968, as 'a multidimensional space in which a variety of writings, none of them original, blend and clash'; as 'a tissue of quotations drawn from the innumerable centres of culture' (Barthes 1977: 146). Intent upon exposing the workings of language – and especially its failure to represent anything outside itself, in other words, its self-reflexivity – this Derridean postmodernism largely limited itself to texts and intertexts. In its firm belief that the attack on representation was in itself an important political act, it was content to celebrate the so-called death of the subject – and thus of the author – without realizing that the end of representation had paradoxically made questions of subjectivity and authorship (redefined in postmodern terms, that is, in terms of agency) all the more relevant. If representations do not and cannot represent the world, then inevitably all representations are political, in that they cannot help reflecting the ideological frameworks within which they arise. The end of representation thus leads us back to the question of authorship, to such political questions as 'Whose history gets told? In whose name? For what purpose?' (Marshall 1992: 4). In the absence of transcendent truth it matters, more than ever, who is speaking (or writing), and why, and to whom. Deconstructionist postmodernism largely ignored these and other political questions that the demise of representation had given prominence to. As a result, with the increasing politicization of the debate on postmodernism in the early 1980s, its textual, self-reflexive, orientation rapidly lost its attraction.

The other moment within poststructuralist postmodernism derives from Foucault and, to a much lesser extent, Lacan. It belongs to the 1980s rather than to the 1970s, although it is difficult to pinpoint its appearance. Foucault's influence materializes almost imperceptibly until it is suddenly very much there, like a fine drizzle that to your surprise has managed to get you thoroughly wet after an hour's walk. Like the earlier deconstructionist postmodernism, this later poststructuralist postmodernism assumes a reality of textuality and signs, of representations that do not represent. Here, however, the emphasis is on the workings of power, and the constitution of the subject. From the perspective of this postmodernism, knowledge, which had once seemed neutral and objective to the positivists and politically emancipatory to the left, is inevitably bound up with power and thus suspect. Although it does not necessarily follow Foucault in his extreme epistemological skepticism, which virtually equates knowledge with power and thus reduces it to the effect of a social relation or structure, it fully accepts that knowledge, and language *tout court*, have become inseparable from power. This postmodernism interrogates the power that is inherent in the discourses that surround us – and that is continually reproduced by them – and interrogates the institutions that support those discourses and are, in turn, supported by them. It attempts to expose the politics that are at work in representations and to undo institutionalized hierarchies, and it works against the hegemony of any single discursive system – which would inevitably victimize other discourses – in its advocacy of difference, pluriformity, and multiplicity. Especially important are its interest in those who from the point of view of the liberal humanist subject (white, male, heterosexual, and rational) constitute the 'Other' – the collective of those excluded from the privileges accorded by that subject to itself (women, people of color, non-heterosexuals, children) – and its interest in the role of representations in the constitution of 'Otherness'. Drawing on the later Foucault's interest in the subject, it more generally investigates the ways in which human beings are constituted – and reconstituted – by discourses, that is, by language, and recognize themselves as subjects. Some, especially British, theorists sought to supplement this with Louis Althusser's analysis of ideology and its effects upon the subject. In the course of the 1980s this mostly Foucauldian postmodernism had a far-reaching democratizing influence within cultural institutions – and on the relations between them – and in the humanities at large (even if a new dogmatism followed on its heels). It is this 1980s redefinition of the postmodern that enabled the close links with feminism and multiculturalism that are now generally associated with postmodernism.

On this second level of conceptualization – postmodernism as a *Weltanschauung* – the term is also not without its problems. On the political left some commentators distinguish between a 'good' deconstructionism, which they refuse to call postmodern, and a 'bad' version, which they then contemptuously label 'postmodern'. Christopher Norris, for instance, obviously convinced of the political correctness of Paul de Man, Derrida, and those deconstructionists who work in their spirit, chooses to see their work within a politically constructive framework, as engaged in the necessary process of erasing the old, harmful intellectual structures of liberal humanism in order to make room for new ones that will admit the light and fresh air of a revamped Enlightenment. Others, the postmodernists, from his point of view, are merely engaged in the wanton destruction of intellectual property without the ultimate aim of rebuilding on the scorched earth they leave in their wake. For Norris and a good many others on the left, postmodernism, rather idiosyncratically defined, is thus merely intellectual vandalism. There are, as I will argue below, good reasons to make a distinction between deconstructionism proper and postmodernism, but not along such evaluative lines.

In any case, no matter how one would want to draw such lines, in the later 1970s a broad complex of deconstructionist/poststructuralist practices became firmly associated with postmodernism. In some artistic disciplines, the new theoretical interest more or less absorbed the departures from modernism that had characterized the 1960s, leading to works of art in which artistic practice and theoretical argument became indistinguishable. On the theoretical level, these practices made themselves felt all over the humanities, first in the field of literary criticism, which had, after all, brought French theory to the US, and then in adjacent fields. Nowadays often called 'theory' – although it goes against all theory in a more traditional, say Popperian, sense – it has in the course of the 1980s filtered into and affected a large number of disciplines, in which its intellectual premises are usually simply called postmodern or postmodernist. It is this recent wide proliferation of the postmodern, in ethnology, sociology, social geography, urban planning, economics, law, and so on, that is responsible for the ever more frequent use of its terminology outside its original core area, the humanities, and that has increasingly led people to speak of the postmodern world that we inhabit. But that merely adds to the confusion. It's not the world that is postmodern, here, it is the perspective from which that world is seen that is postmodern. We are dealing here with a set of intellectual propositions that to some people make a lot more sense than they do to others. Although the omnipresence of the postmodern and its advocates would seem to suggest otherwise, not everybody subscribes to the view that language constitutes, rather than represents, reality; that the autonomous and stable subject of modernity has been replaced by a postmodern agent whose identity is largely other-determined and always in process; that meaning has become social and provisional; or that knowledge only counts as such within a given discursive formation, that is, a given power structure – to mention only some of the more familiar postmodern tenets.

I emphasize this because at again another conceptual level one can indeed speak of the postmodern world, or at least argue that the world as such has become postmodern, that is, entered a new historical era, that of postmodernity. Such arguments restrict themselves in practice to developments in the US, Western Europe, and some less prominent bulwarks of western capitalism such as Canada and Australia, and tacitly assume that the rest of the world will have to follow suit. To some critics postmodernity is still limited to certain areas of contemporary culture – usually to mass culture as mediated by television or to the more elitist yuppie life style promoted by designer magazines – or to certain sociologically definable groups within the western world. Others, casting a wider net, see postmodernism, both as a complex of artistic strategies and as a loosely coherent set of theoretical assumptions, as a sign of the times, as emblematic of a cultural shift of epistemic proportions. That new 'cultural logic' (Fredric Jameson's term) may then in turn be seen as a corollary of the changed nature of western capitalism. A key factor in this interpretation of postmodernism as the superstructure of the current socio-economic order is the ever-increasing penetration of capitalism into our day-to-day existence, or, to put it differently, the ever-increasing commodification of both the public and the private. The onslaught of commodification that is characteristic of late capitalism has, in the view of theorists such as Jameson and Jean Baudrillard, even managed to obliterate the classically Marxist distinction between the economic and the cultural. The causal relationship between base and superstructure that obtained in capitalism's earlier stages has given way to an indeterminate situation in which the economic and the cultural – representations, signs – create and feed each other. Industrial production has given way to Baudrillard's 'semiurgy': the sinister production of signs.

Postmodernism, then, means and has meant different things to different people at different conceptual levels, rising from humble literary-critical origins in the 1950s to a level of global conceptualization in the 1980s. The result was, and still is, a massive but also exhilarating confusion that has given important new impulses to and opened new territories for intellectual exploration. If there is a common denominator to all these postmodernisms, it is that of a crisis in representation: a deeply felt loss of faith in our ability to represent the real, in the widest sense. No matter whether they are aesthestic, epistemological, moral, or political in nature, the representations that we used to rely on can no longer be taken for granted. Whatever its origins, which are diagnosed in different ways by Daniel Bell, Lyotard, Jameson, and other theorists, this crisis in representation has far-reaching consequences. Some would seem to be debilitating. For example, now that transcendent truth seems forever out of reach, hermeneutics must replace our former aspirations to objectivity. Not surprisingly, Marxists like Jameson find this particularly hard to accept because it undermines the conceptual basis of Marxist politics. Other consequences are positively enabling. If all representations are constructs that ultimately are politically informed, then it should be possible, for instance, to break away from our current ones and really confront the Other. Still other effects have changed the map of the humanities: postmodernism has for instance led to a spectacular upgrading of cultural studies. Since the awareness that representations create rather than reflect reality has taken hold of contemporary criticism, representations have been endowed with an almost material status. Culture, long seen by many as determined, either directly or indirectly, by a more fundamental mode of production, has now become a major constitutive power in its own right. In fact, for many theorists signs (a term which of course includes all forms of representation) are the most important constitutive element in the contemporary world, if not, indeed, the only one, as for instance in the later work of Baudrillard. Inevitably, this revaluation of culture has led to an interest in the origins and history of specific representations and has thus stimulated historical projects that to the deconstructionist, self-reflexive, postmodernism of the late 1970s and early 1980s seemed pointless exercises in reigning in the play of textuality. In the wake of Foucault, postmodernism has with increasing frequency visited the past in order to illuminate the present.

UTOPIAS AND DYSTOPIAS

Only a ripple in the tranquil literary-critical pond of the 1950s, postmodernism turned in the course of the 1980s into a tidal wave that now even breaks against the office buildings of the highbrow press. As Lance Olsen informs us, '[i]n 1980 21 articles appeared in major American newspapers such as *The New York Times, The Washington Post,* and *The Los Angeles Times* that used the word "postmodern." In 1984 there were 116. In 1987 there were 247' (Olsen 1989: 277).

There is unmistakable satisfaction in Olsen's observation that the increase of the term's frequency is not matched by a similar increase in the intelligence with which it is used. Such sentiments, often voiced more stridently than Olsen's, have accompanied the rise of postmodernism practically right from the start. Frank Kermode, Gerald Graff, Daniel Bell, Hilton Kramer, Charles Newman, Terry Eagleton, and a host of others have offered at first dismissive, later rather more alarmed commentary. Especially the left, which, as Andreas Huyssen has rightly pointed out, took its time in taking seriously what was initially deemed far below its intellectual dignity, made up for its initial slowness in no uncertain terms.[2] There is, as is no doubt clear by now, indeed ground for such dismissive attitudes. The introduction of postmodernism has given rise to epochal confusions.

Right from the start of the debate, postmodernism has been a particularly unstable concept. No single definition of postmodernism has gone uncontested or has even been widely accepted, except, perhaps, in the field of architecture where the modernist enemy could be clearly identified as the Bauhaus vision and its later evolution into the International Style. Such instability is of course the inevitable fate of all critical concepts that try to delineate movements and/or periods, but the case of postmodernism is surely excessive. A major reason for postmodernism's extraordinary elusiveness, for its resistance to attempts to make it manageable from a conceptual point of view, lies surely in the temptations it has offered to those who were politically inspired to either condemn or welcome the new artistic and – somewhat later – social configurations that were inaugurated in the 1960s. Many of the postmodernisms and postmodernities that have been brought into circulation in the last thirty years have either described a new art in an eagerly awaited new age or have sought to describe the symptoms of what was and is diagnosed as the cultural, or even general, malaise of the late twentieth century. In other words, postmodernism is a term that has served to accommodate a number of critico-political utopias and dystopias, varying from visions of liberation and emancipation (of both the Enlightenment and the anti-Enlightenment varieties) to equally sincere visions of the apocalypse.

As an additional complication, postmodernism would actively seem to follow – be it at a certain distance – the utopian strain in contemporary culture, attaching itself to new utopias as these are formulated. Let me offer an example. In 1981 Andreas Huyssen, in discussing postmodernism's affinities with the historical avant-garde, very perceptively spoke of 'the temporal imagination of postmodernism, the unshaken confidence of being at the edge of history which characterizes the whole trajectory of American postmodernism since the 1960s' (Huyssen 1981: 30). In Huyssen's view being at the edge of history here, in 1981, implies a wholesale rejection of the past: 'The problem with postmodernism is that it relegates history to the dustbin of an obsolete epistémè, arguing gleefully that history does not exist except as text, i.e., as historiography' (35). Huyssen, who believes in history, was relieved to note that this (deconstructionist) postmodernism had not yet completely cornered the market:

> There is indeed an alternative search for tradition and history going on today which manifests itself in the concern with cultural formations not dominated by logocentric and technocratic thought, in the decentering of traditional notions of identity, in the search of women's history, in the rejection of centralisms, mainstreams and melting pots of all kinds, and in the great value put on difference and otherness. This search for history is of course also a search for cultural identities today, and as such it clearly points to the exhaustion of the tradition of the avant-garde, including postmodernism.
>
> (35–6)

However, within five years after the publication of Huyssen's article postmodernism had actually become identified with what he in 1981 saw as an oppositional, anti-postmodern 'search for tradition and history'. Instead of nearing its exhaustion, as Huyssen foresaw, it had remade itself to ride the crest of the explosively increased interest in feminism, multiculturalism, and whatever had been marginalized by mainstream culture. (I should, for the sake of fairness, add that Huyssen was also one of the first to recognize this development.) Refocusing on the politics of representation, postmodernism had become thoroughly politicized.

This investment in the political goes a long way towards explaining why the relatively few serious attempts to come to terms with postmodernism along formalist lines have had so little impact after the very first stages of the debate. Christopher Butler's *After the Wake: An Essay on the Contemporary Avant-Garde* (1980), Gerhard Hoffmann's 'The fantastic in fiction: its "reality" status, its historical development and its transformation in postmodern narration' (1982), Allen Thiher's *Words in Reflection: Modern Language Theory and Postmodern Fiction* (1984), Douwe Fokkema's *Literary History, Modernism, and Postmodernism* (1984), or Brian McHale's *Postmodernist Fiction* (1987) have all received less attention than they deserved in an intellectual climate that had turned away from formalist concerns and was increasingly inclined to see formalism as a throwback to an outmoded modernism.

APORIAS

This study seeks to chart the history of the debate on postmodernism from its tentative beginnings in the 1950s to its overwhelming self-confidence in the early 1990s. I am assuming, for better or for worse, that it is possible to construct a plausible history of the debate and to talk about its continuities and reorientations. That does not mean that there are no aporias or undecidables. In fact, one rather traditional aporia presents itself right at the outset: where should one place the beginning of such a history? The terms postmodern and postmodernism have a respectable history, much longer than that of the new art forms to which they became attached in the 1960s. I will, on the whole, leave those early uses for what they are. I situate the 'true' beginnings of the debate, which is of course the debate about contemporary, that is, post-mid–1950s culture, in the early 1960s. There a second problem immediately presents itself: the first stage of the debate quite clearly antedates the actual introduction of the term(s) in question. Susan Sontag, for instance, never uses 'postmodern' or 'postmodernism' in such seminal essays as 'Against interpretation' (1964) or 'One culture and the new sensibility' (1965), yet the art and the sensibility that she discussed were widely called postmodern by the late 1970s. The same is true for the criticism that

Ihab Hassan introduced in his 'The dismemberment of Orpheus' (1963) and then further developed in the course of the 1960s in such essays as 'The literature of silence' (1967). The literature that Hassan discusses in these essays is not necessarily postmodern – indeed, most of it is not, as we will see – but his intellectual frame of reference already is, at least according to his own later definitions.

The early responses in the other arts to the cultural upheavals of the 1950s and 1960s present us with the same problem of locating the origins, and determining the scope, of the debate. In the field of architecture Robert Venturi argued in 1965 in favor of a 'pop architecture', and in a later article, co-authored with Denise Scott Brown, introduced the eminently postmodern concept of the 'decorated shed' (Venturi and Scott Brown 1971). But even their immensely influential *Learning from Las Vegas* (1972, with Steven Izenour), which is in many ways canonically postmodern, never uses the term. Discussions of the visual arts present a similar picture. Erich Kahler published *The Disintegration of Form in the Arts* (1968), Harold Rosenberg wrote somewhat earlier about the 'anxious object' (1966), Calvin Tomkins perceptively grouped Duchamp, Tingüely, Cage, and Rauschenberg together in *The Bride and the Bachelors* (1965), countless other art critics offered views of Pop, Op, Conceptual, and Minimal Art, all without invoking the postmodern. Only the most intrepid critics (like Leslie Fiedler) truly adopted the term before the early 1970s, even though by then what would later be seen as the discourse of postmodernism was already firmly underway.

It is not just the 1960s that present us with this sort of problem. All through the 1970s we find critics who openly recognize and welcome postmodern art, but still resist, or are unaware of, the term. When in 1977 Douglas Crimp began to theorize the new deconstruction in photography, he did not use the term postmodernism, and only introduced it in the revised version of 1979. In 1980, Linda Hutcheon, later an important theorist of postmodernism, still preferred 'narcissistic' to 'postmodernist' because the latter term seemed to her 'a very limiting label for such a broad contemporary phenomenon as metafiction' (Hutcheon 1980: 3). The list of texts that in the 1960s and 1970s made attempts to come to grips with postmodernism without naming it as such is impressive, at least from a quantitative point of view.

If there is no clearly marked starting-point for a history of the debate, there is also no consensus about its scope. For a good many, mainly American, critics, French poststructuralism and its American deconstructionist offshoot are practically identical with postmodernism, a view that has induced some of them to take extraordinary liberties.[3] For other, mainly British, critics, there is a marked difference between Derridean poststructuralism, which from their point of view is radically cognitive and thus politically constructive, and postmodernism, which they scorn as reactionary or even nihilist. Typically, Anthony Easthope's brilliant *British Post-Structuralism Since 1968* of 1988 hardly ever mentions postmodernism in its detailed account of the British poststructuralist scene.

I will keep poststructuralism and postmodernism mostly apart. For one thing, it is not until the late 1970s that poststructuralism, which at that point had been around in the US for a good decade, was actually brought to bear upon postmodern art. The first generation of American deconstructionists – the so-called Yale School and its immediate followers – was decidedly modernist and even pre-modernist in its literary focus, just like its French masters. Huyssen usefully lists the interests of the French theorists: 'Flaubert, Proust and Bataille in Barthes; Nietzsche and Heidegger, Mallarmé and Artaud in Derrida; Nietzsche, Magritte and Bataille in Foucault; Mallarmé and Lautréamont, Joyce and Artaud in Kristeva; Freud in Lacan; Brecht in Althusser and Macherey, and so on *ad infinitum.*' French theory, Huyssen adds, 'provides us primarily with an *archeology of modernity*, a theory of modernism at the stage of its exhaustion' (1984: 39), a view that has since been repeated by other commentators.[4] There is no doubt that poststructuralism seemed overwhelmingly innovative to critics only familiar with the Anglo-American modernist tradition, but from a continental point of view the attack on representation and the rejection of the liberal humanist view of the subject and of history was a far less spectacular radicalization of (continental) modernist concerns, especially those of what Peter Bürger has termed the historical avant-garde. Although such concerns have indeed been incorporated by most postmodernisms and although there was a brief period in the early 1980s when a particularly vociferous version of postmodernism seemed identical with Derridean poststructuralism, the fact that questions of subjectivity and authorship feature prominently on the postmodern agenda is enough to suggest a substantial distance between postmodernism and poststructuralism. The postmodernist *Weltan-*

schauung borrows freely from all available poststructuralist positions but cannot be identified with any single one of them, transcending them in its openly political orientation. The work of Derrida, Foucault, Lacan, Deleuze and Guattari, and others can, in Meaghan Morris's words, 'only be part of a debate about postmodernism when "effectively situated" in relation to it by subsequent commentary and citation' (Morris 1993: 378).[5]

It would, in any case, not make any sense to present Barthes, Derrida, Foucault, and other poststructuralists as *theorists* of the postmodern. No matter how we evaluate the significance of their contributions to that ever expanding intellectual/artistic complex that is postmodernism, they have not involved themselves in those attempts to define and theorize the postmodern that are my subject here. The exception, of course, is Jean-François Lyotard, the only poststructuralist who has played a major role in theorizing the postmodern, and who will therefore have to come under close scrutiny.

A history of the debate on the postmodern is a doubtful enterprise. There is no doubt, however, about the particular place from which I will depart. The debate on postmodernism as it has been variously defined since the 1960s has its origins in American literary and cultural criticism and it is from there that it moves into all the other fields and disciplines where it has in the last twenty-five years manifested itself. Charles Jencks, who since 1975 has indefatigably theorized postmodern architecture, acknowledges the literary debate as his source, declaring that Ihab Hassan has both 'christened' and 'provided a pedigree' for postmodernism (Jencks 1987a: 18). Jean-François Lyotard, who in 1979 with his *La Condition postmoderne* brought philosophy into the debate, also mentions Hassan's work as his immediate source. Criticism is the only discipline in which there is an unbroken continuity of anti-modernist – that is, anti-humanist – theorizing from the early 1950s right up to the present, even though the anti-modern revolt had initially more force in some of the other arts than in literature itself (John Cage in music; Jasper Johns and Robert Rauschenberg in painting). But there are, apart from that continuity, more reasons to see American criticism as the proper point of departure. The initial confusions surrounding the debate on postmodernism, for instance, have everything to do with its origins in the American critical scene, with American criticism's specific, and narrow, idea of modernism.

But this is not a study of postmodern (literary) criticism. My aim is to follow the general debate on the postmodern as it has developed in the course of the last three decades and has drawn more and more disciplines into its orbit. In doing so, however, I will allow myself some restrictions. The continued Anglophone character of the debate has persuaded me to focus entirely on contributions presented in English, although I'm aware of the lively and stimulating discussions that are conducted in German and in other languages. Experience tells us, however, that contributions presented in German or French have to wait for a translation to make themselves internationally felt. Lyotard's *La Condition postmoderne* is a case in point. Picked up by only a few Americans after its original publication in French (one of them of course Ihab Hassan, who knows his French, another Richard Rorty), it immediately became one of the most widely quoted texts in the field after the English translation had been published. Another restriction is that I will not offer exhaustive critiques of the numerous positions that I will sketch. There simply is no room for detailed critiques next to detailed analyses. I will, finally, let my theorists speak for themselves, as much as possible, with the inevitable drawback that my text will be a minefield of quotations. There is much to say for the art of graceful summary, but I'd rather convey an impression of the different voices that have contributed to the debate.

NOTES

1 See Andreas Huyssen's 'Mapping the postmodern' (Huyssen 1984) for a brilliant discussion of these strategies and of their affinity with the historical avant-garde.

2 If it addressed the 'question of postmodernism' at all, the left's intentions were less than honorable, according to Huyssen: 'The Left's ridiculing of postmodernism was of a piece with its often haughty and dogmatic critique of the counter-cultural impulses of the 1960s' (1984: 28).

3 Emma Kafalenos, for instance, simply inserts 'postmodern' in a Roland Barthes quotation: ' "The pleasure of the [Postmodern] text is not the pleasure of the corporeal striptease or of narrative suspense" ' (Kafalenos 1985: 87).

4 Andrew Ross would even seem to speak for all of us in claiming that '[m]ore and more . . . we have come to see poststructuralism as a belated response to the vanguardist innovations of high modernism' (Ross 1988: ix).

5 Mark Poster makes the interesting, and to my mind valid, point that even poststructuralism is an American construct: ' "poststructuralist theory" is a uniquely American practice. Americans have assimilated Foucault, Derrida, and the rest by turning their positions into "poststructuralist theory" ' (Poster 1989: 6).

2

ANTI-MODERNISMS

Since Michael Köhler published his ' "Postmodernismus": ein begriffsgeschichtlicher Überblick' in 1977, a wide range of early uses of the terms postmodern and postmodernism has come to light. Wolfgang Welsch tells us that 'postmodern' was used as early as the 1870s (Welsch 1987: 12) and 'postmodernism' made its first appearance in the title of a book in 1926.[1] 'Postmodern' resurfaced in 1934, in 1939, and in the 1940s. From then on sightings begin to multiply. There is, however, very little continuity between these early uses and the debate on postmodernism as it gets underway in the course of the 1960s. The only discipline in which one finds real continuity is literary criticism, at least from the early 1950s onwards, when Charles Olson picks up the term and begins to use it to identify an anti-modernist strain in contemporary poetry (mostly his own work and that of other so-called Black Mountain poets) and a specific anti-rationalist position. Olson's orientation upon Heidegger, and the impact of the French *nouvelle critique* on American literary criticism in the early 1960s, created an identification of postmodernism with a set of polemical anti-Enlightenment positions that is still with us.

FIRST SIGHTINGS

Olson was right from the start involved in the anti-modernist cultural revolt that gradually gained momentum in the 1950s. The most famous of all the early anti-modern manifestations, staged by John Cage, took place in the summer of 1952 at Olson's Black Mountain College. Cage, Olson, the painter Robert Rauschenberg, the dancer Merce Cunningham, and some lesser-known artists, performed in an event that experimented with chance and improvisation. Its course was determined by the throwing of I Ching coins, while the participants were unaware of each other's intentions.

More important is that Olson repeatedly used the term 'post-Modern' in his writings and his lectures. To Olson, western culture willfully closes itself against true experience, against life's authenticity, because of its orientation on (originally Greek) rationalism, with its obsessive and relentless intellectualization of all human experience. In 'Human universe', written in 1951 during a stay in Yucatán, Olson seeks to develop an 'alternative to the whole Greek system' (Olson 1967: 5) in order to recapture at least the possibility of pristine experience. The absolute condition for reaching back beyond the 'Greek system' to that pre-rationalist, utopian space, is a radical parting of the ways with the 'old controlling humanism' that keeps us locked in rationality. In his 'Projective verse' of 1950, Olson had already proposed an anti-humanistic view, a *Weltanschauung* that involves 'the getting rid of the lyrical interference of the individual as ego, of the "subject" and his soul, that peculiar presumption by which western man has interposed himself between what he is as a creature of nature . . . and those other creations of nature which we may, with no derogation, call objects' (Olson 1967: 59–60). To free oneself from the straightjacket of rationalistic liberal humanism, Olson proposes what would seem to be a Heideggerian poetic practice that breaks with the western rationalist tradition and its compulsive and arrogant urge to make reality subservient to itself. Such a practice, in which language does not function as the expression of an essentialist, transcendent subject, but allows a primordial experience of the world, must paradoxically retrieve a more authentic humanism from the subjectivistic humanistic tradition. It must restore to experience the immanentist, authentic, sacramental character that it once possessed.

It is clear that this has affinities with Heideggerian existentialism and Heidegger's views of the function of art. In truly poetic language, the real speaks for itself, and is allowed to do so by the poet who merely functions as a mediator. Through poetry, the real represents itself. It is less clear whether Olson is indeed as close to Heidegger and more in particular to certain aspects of Derrida's reading of Heidegger as later commentators such as William Spanos have suggested. But the question of Olson's closeness to Heidegger and Derrida is not all that important. More relevant is that in the early 1970s he was reconstructed within a Heideggerian framework by a number of critics who developed a distinctly Heideggerian postmodernism in *boundary 2: a journal of postmodern literature and culture*, the first issue of which appeared in 1972. These critics, led and inspired by William Spanos, the journal's editor, constructed an existentialist postmodernism in which, after some initial misgivings on Spanos's part, Olson played a major role. As Wallace Martin put it in a 1980 retrospective: 'another American postmodernism emerged from the oral poetry of Olson, Creeley, David Antin, and Jerome Rothenberg. As represented by William Spanos, it signaled the end of logocentric metaphysics and the rebirth of the spoken word as conceived by Heidegger' (Martin 1980: 144). This existentialist postmodernism, which I will examine in more detail in the following chapter, would be a substantial influence on the American critical scene, until, in the late seventies, the impact of poststructuralism, combined with an updated Marxism, pushed it to the margins.

Another early contribution that still merits our attention is Irving Howe's 'Mass society and post-modern fiction' of 1959. Whereas Olson saw postmodern poetry as more authentic and therefore as not only experientially but also morally superior to modernist art, Howe was far less sanguine. Howe noted a breakdown of social and intellectual categories in the fiction of the 1950s and was not happy with what he saw as the 'increasingly fluid' nature of experience and the 'increasingly shapeless' character of the contemporary world (Howe 1959: 428). The authors he considered postmodern – Saul Bellow, Norman Mailer, J.D. Salinger, Bernard Malamud – were content to simply reflect the malaise and lacked the moral courage to impose the order and shape that were so sadly lacking. Even worse were those – 'the young men in San Francisco', that is, the Beats – who 'in their contempt for mind' (434–5) positively reveled in this amorphousness.

Howe's postmodern canon is now only of literary-historical interest, but his article is worth mentioning because it inaugurates a leftist analysis of postmodernism that places it within the social context of postwar consumer society:

> By the mass society we mean a relatively comfortable, half welfare and half garrison society in which the population grows passive, indifferent and atomized; in which traditional

> loyalties, ties and associations become lax or dissolve entirely; in which coherent publics based on definite interests and opinions gradually fall apart; and in which man becomes a consumer, himself mass-produced like the products, diversions and values that he absorbs.
>
> (426)

Following Adorno and Horkheimer's criticism of mass society and consumerism in their *Dialectic of Enlightenment* (1979), Howe offers a diagnosis that in the 1970s and after would be echoed by most critics on the left. Moreover, in far-sighted anticipation of positions that Fredric Jameson and Jean Baudrillard would formulate in the 1980s, Howe suggests that postmodernism arises in the wake of what is in reality a breakdown of representational schemes, broadly defined. As he put it some years afterwards: 'How can one represent malaise, which by its nature is vague and without shape?' (Howe 1970: 200). For Howe the end of the social, as Baudrillard would call it much later, is already a fact of life in the 1950s. It is, with hindsight, tempting to entertain the notion that Olson and Howe are talking about related developments – as, for instance, in the case of the Beat poets, who for Olson sometimes approach his idea of authenticity – with Howe, in good social democratic fashion, clinging to traditional representation and to the demands of the Enlightenment project, and Olson attempting to transcend both. With a little imagination we may see Olson and Howe as early contestants in a struggle over the heritage of the Enlightenment that still dominates our intellectual agenda.

THE SOUNDS OF SILENCE: THE 1960s

Between 1963 and 1967 the debate on what would later be called postmodernism really took off, in response to the anti-modernist trends in literature, the arts, and, more hesitantly, architecture. In 1963 Leonard B. Meyer published his 'The end of the Renaissance?' and Ihab Hassan started his inquiry into the 'literature of silence' with 'The dismemberment of Orpheus'. In 1964 Susan Sontag made herself the most prominent theorist of the new developments with 'Notes on "camp" ', 'Godard's *Vivre Sa Vie*', and the seminal 'Against interpretation', followed in 1965 by the equally influential 'One culture and the new sensibility'. That same year saw the publication of Leslie Fiedler's 'The new mutants' and of Robert Venturi's 'A justification for a Pop architecture'. By the time that Frank Kermode felt compelled to point out – quite correctly – that the developments in the various arts could 'be seen as following from palaeo-modernist premises without any violent revolutionary stage' (Kermode 1966: 68), the new agenda was firmly on the table. As is usual in such cases, that agenda was not only determined by the advocates of the new, but in practically equal measure by its declared enemies. 'What we witness all round', Erich Kahler said in one of the lectures collected in *The Disintegration of Form in the Arts*, 'is a veritable cult of incoherence, of sheer senselessness and aimlessness. We find it in writings, in paintings and decorations, in "chance" or "aleatory composing," in the mad contortions of the latest dances' (Kahler 1968: 96). Such misgivings can only whet the appetite and stimulate critical interest.

Let me begin this survey of the 1960s with Leonard B. Meyer's 'The end of the Renaissance?' There is, Meyer tells us, a new poetics at work in music, in painting, in fiction, in the theater:

> What is involved is a radically different set of ends, whether these ends be achieved by careful calculation as in the music of Stockhausen, the paintings of Tobey or Rothko, and the writings of Beckett and Alain Robbe-Grillet, or by random operations as in the music of Cage, the paintings of Mathieu, or the chance theater of McLow's *The Marrying Maiden.*
>
> (Meyer 1963: 173–4)

The art that results from either (over)calculation or randomness – much later the subject of detailed analysis in Christopher Butler's *After the Wake: An Essay on the Contemporary Avant-Garde* (1980) – is 'directionless'; it is, in Meyer's phrase and with his emphasis, '*anti-teleological* art' (173). Underlying this 'new aesthetic' that implies 'a denial of the reality of cause and effect and of traditional "meaning" ' (178–80) is a revolutionary new view of man, a view that Meyer, given his title, might have called posthumanist if the term had been available to him:

> Man is no longer to be the measure of all things, the center of the universe. He has been measured and found to be an undistinguished bit of matter different in no essential way

> from bacteria, stones, and trees. His goals and purposes; his egocentric notions of past, present, and future; his faith in his power to predict and, through prediction, to control his destiny – all these are called into question, considered irrelevant, or deemed trivial.
>
> (186)

Just like Olson, Meyer sees in this decentering of 'man' new possibilities rather than a cause for despair:

> It is to the naive and primitive enjoyment of sensations and things for their own sakes that these artists seek to return. We must rediscover the reality and excitement of a sound as such, a color as such, and existence itself as such.
>
> (175)

In an interesting aside, Meyer places the American contribution to the new sensibility in a nativist tradition, suggesting that 'the anti-teleological position with its emphasis on the value of naive, direct experience and upon the natural goodness of man, seems characteristically American' (176). In the years to follow Meyer's claim that the new anti-humanism belonged in at least one of its guises to a peculiarly American tradition – deriving from Emerson – would often be echoed.

Meyer's utopian assessment of the new anti-humanist aesthetic was shared by Ihab Hassan. In his 'The dismemberment of Orpheus: reflections on modern culture, language and literature', also of 1963, Hassan argues that modern literature may be 'extreme and its dreams outrageous', but it is always 'conceived in the interests of life' (Hassan 1963: 463). The movement toward disorder and the attack on form are 'intended to recover a kind of human innocence' (464). Within this literature of resistance Hassan, like Meyer, discerns two strategies – a 'dual retreat from language' – in, respectively, the ironic and self-effacing manner of Mallarmé, and the indiscriminate and surrealistic manner of Rimbaud. In the first, minimalist, mode, 'language aspires to Nothing'; in the second one, which is a mode of excess, 'it aspires to All' (474). This difference, however, is deceptive: 'Both are manners of silence, formal disruptions of the relation between language and reality. It is these two modes . . . that account for the development of antiform in modern literature from Kafka to Beckett' (474). As Hassan's examples make clear, his 'manners of silence' have a long pedigree, going back to the very origins of modernism. Indeed, he is almost exclusively concerned with modernism. In his early criticism, Hassan tries to create an anti-representational, anti-modernist canon of silence – that is, anti-modernist from an Anglo-American perspective – out of widely different modernist texts. It is a canon that is, very loosely, held together by what is certainly the most pertinent claim of the entire essay: 'Nietzsche is indeed the crucial figure in the intellectual history of our time' (466).

This is what Hassan is after: in a period dominated by the New Criticism and by moral criticism of the Eliot/Leavis variety, he seeks to promote the Nietzschean strain in modern literature. Like Olson and Meyer, Hassan advocates an anti-humanist art that acknowledges and sometimes even glories in its representational impotence and avoids the grand gestures of a modernism that, from this point of view, was the product of an authoritarian, elitist, and complacent humanism.

However, in a strategically significant move, Hassan soon abandoned the typological approach that had enabled him to find Nietzschean silences at the very sources of literary modernism. Only four years later he finds them only in fairly recent and contemporary writers. In 'The literature of silence' of 1967 we find him speaking of the 'new literature', a term that is a good deal more suggestive of contemporaneity than the vocabulary of 'The dismemberment of Orpheus' and that in fact excludes most of the writers he had discussed in the earlier article. With the obvious aim of creating a chronologically post-modernist, anti-modern literature Hassan now proposes Henry Miller and Samuel Beckett as the most prominent practitioners of the new literature of silence. His themes of indeterminacy and silence have not changed, it is just the period in which he finds them that has been drastically shortened. Curiously, the historical (and from Hassan's point of view anti-modernist) avant-garde is virtually ignored and mentioned only to highlight the new literature's innovative character: 'whatever is truly new in it evades the social, historical, and aesthetic criteria which defined the identity of the *avant-garde* in other periods' (74). One gets the impression that Hassan resolutely keeps the avant-garde out of the picture to emphasize the originality of the tradition of silence that he is creating for an audience that is largely unaware of the similar project of the *nouvelle critique*. It is only in the course of the

1970s that Hassan's literature of silence, then rechristened as postmodernism, once again becomes less exclusively contemporary.

FORMALISM AND ANTI-FORMALISM

Hassan's later travels with postmodernism will have to wait, however. Let me return to the earlier 1960s. With some critical license one can see Meyer's two anti-humanist strategies of (over)calculation and chance as a formalist mode and an anti-formalist mode and one can see how these two modes also inform the minimalism and the excess of Hassan's literatures of silence. William Burroughs's cut-ups (a fixed point of reference in these early discussions), John Cage's aleatory music (its inevitable companion piece), Robert Rauschenberg's collages of found objects, and Henry Miller's associative 'babel of noises' might be seen as exemplary for the anti-formalistic mode. The *nouveau roman*, the minimalism of the later Beckett, or the music of Stockhausen would then belong to the formalist mode.

Susan Sontag and Leslie Fiedler each single out one of these modes for critical attention. In her 'Against interpretation' of 1964, Sontag, too, shares in that late 1950s and early 1960s feeling of often angry alienation: 'The world, our world, is depleted, impoverished enough. Away with all duplicates of it, until we again experience more immediately what we have' (Sontag 1967: 7). We must, she urges us in true nativist fashion, 'recover our senses. We must learn to *see* more, to *hear* more, to *feel* more' (14). This sounds like Olson, Meyer, or Hassan. But Sontag is less interested in 'the world' than in art; consequently, what she has in mind is not so much an authentic experience of life through art, but an authentic experience of art itself. Such authenticity is disastrously hindered by 'the project of interpretation' which, she tells us, 'is largely reactionary, stifling' (7). Interpretation, then, should be avoided: 'It doesn't matter whether artists intend, or don't intend, for their works to be interpreted. . . . the merit of these works certainly lies elsewhere than in their "meanings" ' (9). Indeed, what matters in, for instance, Resnais and Robbe-Grillet's *Last Year at Marienbad* is 'the pure, untranslatable, sensuous immediacy of some of its images, and its rigorous if narrow solutions to certain problems of cinematic form' (9). In order to appreciate such art and discuss it in its own terms, we must 'cut back on content so that we can see the thing at all.... In place of a hermeneutics we need an erotics of art' (14). Shifting her focus from an anti-representational critical reception to an equally anti-representational artistic production, Sontag goes on to claim that 'a great deal of today's art may be understood as motivated by a flight from interpretation. To avoid interpretation, art may become parody. Or it may become abstract. Or it may become ("merely") decorative. Or it may become non-art' (10). We are dealing with what she too would later call the aesthetics of silence: 'The art of our time is noisy with appeals for silence' (1969: 12).

'Godard's *Vivre Sa Vie*' (1964b) gives us a good idea of the anti-representational strategies of the new art. The point of Godard's movie, she tells us, 'is that it does not explain anything. It rejects causality' (Sontag 1967: 199) and employs 'techniques that would fragment, dissociate, alienate, break up' (200). The film offers 'no longer a single unified point of view ... but a series of documents (texts, narrations, quotations, excerpts, set pieces) of various description. These are primarily words, but they may also be wordless sounds, or even wordless images' (202). With Sontag's approval, Godard ironizes and undercuts meaning, coherence, and homogeneity. But in spite of all this, Sontag still believes in at least some modernist views of form and in art's autonomy. She does not only find an unexpected unity in Godard's film – unexpected in the light of her earlier analysis – but takes offense when Godard disrupts it by crossing an ontological boundary, letting the 'real' world interfere with the fiction of the film: 'The one false step in *Vivre Sa Vie* comes at the end, when Godard breaks the unity of his film by referring to it from the outside, as maker.' Godard thus 'mock[s]' his own tale, which is unforgivable' (206–7).

Sontag's formalism and her professed (but not always equally acute) disinterest in meaning enable her to appreciate the new anti-representational art of the early 1960s, and to foresee a far more form-conscious general culture in the immediate future. Thus, in 'One culture and the new sensibility', published in the same year that Robert Venturi went public with his campaign for a pop architecture, she speaks of a 'new sensibility' that 'is more open to the pleasure of "form" and style' and that 'does not demand that pleasure in art necessarily be associated with edification' (303). From such a form-conscious vantage point, 'the beauty of a machine or of the solution to a mathematical problem, of a painting by Jasper Johns, or a film by Jean-Luc Godard, and of the personalities and music of the Beatles is equally accessible' (304). Indeed, if art 'is understood as a form of discipline of the feelings and a programming of the sensations, then the feeling (or sensation) given off by a Rauschenberg painting might be like that of a song by the Supremes' (303). It is not surprising that the sociologist Scott Lash, who defines postmodernism in terms of a cultural de-differentiation – a general weakening of the once so rigid cultural laws that kept the various genres and, more in particular, high and low culture, apart – should see Sontag as an important early theorist of the postmodern.[2]

The most interesting aspect of Sontag's position is that it is interdisciplinary and manages to be equally anti-modernist in the various fields that she covers. From the perspective of modernist literary criticism, for instance, her insistence on form at the expense of representation, that is, meaning, is unacceptable, the more so since it undercuts the modernist distinction between high and low art. That same formalism would seem to qualify Sontag as eminently modernist from a Greenbergian point of view. Yet, unlike Greenberg, she is not at all interested in a self-contained 'purity' as the ultimate aim of every single artistic discipline. Her eclecticism and her suggestion that art might be understood as a 'programming of the sensations' go right against what Greenberg defines as central to the modernist project.

Whatever her intentions, Sontag's formalist eclecticism is wholly apolitical – in other words, affirmative of the status quo. The commercialized postmodernism that began to flood the market in the course of the 1970s – in the form of rock videos, television commercials, and so on – often brilliantly programs the sensations, to use Sontag's phrase again, while it simultaneously promotes the consumer capitalism that has enabled its existence in the first place. It was the left's early (and wholly creditable) aversion to this consumer postmodernism that made it so reluctant to enter the debate and that for a long time conditioned its reactions.

Whereas Sontag privileged the formal in her discussions of the new artistic scene, Fiedler privileged anti-form and widened his scope to include more general cultural developments. Of those who used the term postmodern in the 1950s and 1960s Fiedler was the most outspoken enemy of modernism, that is, modernism defined as an unwholesome combination of a specific, narrow and self-satisfied rationalism, and an equally narrow and imperious liberal humanism. In his 'The new mutants' of 1965 Fiedler offers an analysis of the new flower power generation that brilliantly anticipates the postmodernism of the later 1980s, with its redefined humanism and its inclusion of feminism and ethnic minorities: 'To become new men, these children of the future seem to feel, they must not only become more Black than White but more female than male' (1965: 516). Young men, Fiedler tells us, are already creating a 'post-humanist, post-male, post-white, post-heroic world' (417). These new barbarians – Fiedler's term – announce the end of man, that is, 'the very notion of man which the universities sought to impose upon them: that bourgeois-Protestant version of Humanism, with its view of man as justified by rationality, work, duty, vocation, maturity, success' (511). Although Fiedler does not yet present the typical 1980s view of Enlightenment humanism as deeply prejudiced against women and people of color, he anticipates the Enlightenment critique that would be imported with the work of the French theorists. He is, with qualifications such as 'post-white' and 'post-male', arguably even closer to the spirit of the later 1980s and early 1990s than the French theorists who are now generally seen as the champions of posthumanism.

'Cross the border – close that gap: post-modernism' of 1969 again sees postmodernism in terms of a general cultural reorientation, but also focuses on the new literary art that tries to transcend modernism. 'We are living, have been living for two decades,' Fiedler argues, 'through the death throes of Modernism and the birth pangs of Post-Modernism' (1975: 344). The essay, first published in Hugh Hefner's *Playboy Magazine*, perhaps to make clear which side Fiedler was on, tells us that we have entered a new, 'apocalyptic, anti-rational, blatantly romantic and sentimental' age. It is an age 'distrustful of self-protective irony and too great self-awareness' (345) – the sins of modernism. Prophetically dismissive about the *nouveau roman* as a postmodern category – 'Robbe-Grillet . . . is still the prisoner of dying notions of the *avant-garde*' and his 'anti-novel is finally too arty and serious' (350) – Fiedler foresees a postmodern novel that will close the gap between elite and mass culture. To do so it turns 'High Art into vaudeville and burlesque' (359) and incorporates elements from subliterary genres like the western, science fiction, and even pornography. Such 'anti-artistic' and 'anti-serious' art, Fiedler argues, is political. The creation of such a willfully anti-representational art 'closes a class, as well as a generation gap' (359). It is, however, not an entirely negative art. The anti-rationalist, anti-modernist orientation of the new art will lead to new myths – not the essentialist ones of modernism – that will 'recapture a certain rude magic in its authentic context' (364). It will contribute to a magical tribalization in an age dominated by technology, creating 'a thousand little Wests in the interstices of a machine civilization' (365). What Fiedler here prophetically foresees is an art that has given up on representations with essentialist pretensions and instead offers local narratives that are aware of their own provisional status. In the terms of Brian McHale, the epistemological orientation of modernism – its overriding interest in knowing – gives way to the ontological orientation of postmodernism – an interest in modes of being. Modernist self-reflexiveness, its urge to question itself and its own foundations in its search for essential, timeless meaning, is replaced by a postmodern view of meaning as inevitably local, contingent, and self-sufficient – Fiedler's diagnosis of its 'tribal' character will resurface in sociological accounts of postmodernity of the late 1980s – and does not represent such an underlying realm of transcendent truth.

OTHER VOICES: GRAFF, BELL AND WASSON

It is especially Fiedler's anti-rationalist and anti-humanist postmodernism that was attacked in the early period, both by representatives of the traditional left (Gerald Graff, for instance) and by those of the traditional right (Daniel Bell and others). Graff and Bell, writing in the early and mid–1970s, saw Fiedler's countercultural postmodernism as a deplorable letting-go, a willful surrender to the forces of chaos and the id. Graff, who rather indiscriminately also includes Sontag in his attack, sees not much more than a worshipping of energy at the basis of this 1960s postmodernism, 'a celebration of *energy* – the vitalism of a world that cannot be understood or controlled' (1979: 58). He finds the same aimless energy in 'the poetry of the Beats, the "Projective" poets, and other poetic continuators of the nativist line of Whitman, Williams and Pound, in the short-lived vogue of the

Living Theatre, happenings, and pop art, and in a variety of artistic and also musical experiments with randomness and dissonance' (1979: 58). All these anti-intellectual and hedonistic manifestations of the postmodern refuse 'to take art "seriously" in the old sense'; they reject analysis and political awareness; and they reflect 'a generally less soberly rationalistic mode of consciousness, one that is more congenial to myth, tribal ritual, and visionary experience, grounded in a "protean," fluid, and undifferentiated concept of the self as opposed to the repressed, "uptight" Western ego' (1973: 384). Adopting a position that echoes that of Irving Howe, Graff argues that the postmodern manifestations of the 1960s are the product of an 'amorphous mass society that has lost contact with . . . earlier traditions and beliefs' (1975: 308).

Daniel Bell, writing somewhat later, repeats this diagnosis. For Bell, modernity is characterized by the spiritual crisis brought on by capitalism's destruction of the Protestant ethic, a crisis that becomes acute in the postmodern radicalizations of modernist art and theory:

> In the 1960s a powerful current of post-modernism developed which carried the logic of modernism to its farthest reaches. In the theoretical writings of Norman O. Brown and Michel Foucault; in the novels of William Burroughs, Jean Genet, and, up to a point, Norman Mailer; and in the porno-pop culture that is now all about us, one sees a logical culmination of modernist intentions'.
>
> (Bell 1976: 51)[3]

Modernism, Bell tells us, 'is exhausted and the various kinds of post-modernism (in the psychedelic effort to expand consciousness without boundaries) are simply the decomposition of the self in an effort to erase individual ego' (29). In its privileging of the instinctual and its denial of the subject, postmodernism functions as 'the psychological spearhead' for a general onslaught on traditional values and motivations. In postmodernism the narcissism and hedonism of modernist art have spilled over to create a virtually nihilistic life style.[4]

That it was possible to see all this in a more sympathetic light had somewhat earlier been illustrated by Richard Wasson's 'From priest to Prometheus: culture and criticism in the post-modern period' of 1974. Wasson saw a number of influences converging to create the countercultural dynamic described by Graff. Important in that dynamic are Norman O. Brown's and Herbert Marcuse's revisions of Freudian psychology and Northrop Frye's insistence on the erotic potential of art. In different ways, Wasson argues, Brown and Marcuse both attack what they see as Freud's repressive and finally alienating acceptance of the present reality system as final. Wasson's analysis attempts to show how the postmodernism that Fiedler had identified with the forces of the American counterculture was part of a larger context of revolutionary cries for liberation from the constraints – intellectual, social, and sexual – of a narrowly rationalist modernity. Wasson does not only make postmodern 'irrationalism' more respectable, his analysis also enables us to link it with intellectual events elsewhere, with, for instance, the anti-rationalist manifestoes that had somewhat earlier been published in France, by Barthes, Lyotard, Deleuze and Guattari, and others.

Earlier, in 1969, Wasson had already made a different postmodernism intellectually respectable. In his 'Notes on a new sensibility', the title of which surely not accidentally echoes Sontag's 'One culture and the new sensibility', Wasson had identified a postmodernism (although he does not yet use the term here) that shares the revolt against modernism and modernist assumptions with the counterculture, but is far more intellectual – not just more formal, as is sometimes the case with Sontag's new art – and also resolutely international. Wasson traces the new sensibility in four exemplary writers: Iris Murdoch, Alain Robbe-Grillet, John Barth, and Thomas Pynchon. What these writers have in common, despite significant differences, is a deep mistrust of modernist aesthetics. According to Wasson, they 'are skeptical of modernist notions of metaphor as a species of suprarational truth that unifies paradoxical opposites and modernist conceptions of myth which make it a principle of order for art and of discipline for the subjective self' (1969: 460). (Modernism is here defined in typically Anglo-American fashion as a combination of New Critical poetics and the privileging of myth that one finds in Yeats or Eliot, as in the latter's famous review of *Ulysses*.) Rejecting such notions, Wasson's four writers set out to subvert metaphor and myth as instruments of representation and order, as attempts to transcend the contingency and inaccessibility of the object world. For them, the world must be restored in all its object-ness, to its total inaccessibility, and must cease to be part of the subjective consciousness of the writer as was implicitly the case in modernist writing. The difference and distance between subject and object must be accepted, not denied through metaphorical or mythical means; unity of self and world through transcendental knowledge is an illusion.

Wasson's new sensibility has little in common with Fiedler's vitalist post-Protestantism in which such a fusion of self and world is as often as not the explicit aim, although not via representational strategies. Fiedler's postmoderns have simply moved beyond the sensibility that Wasson here identifies and would denounce it as a new round in the same old rationality game, just as Fiedler himself saw Robbe-Grillet as still imprisoned by obsolete avant-gardistic notions. It has obvious affinities, though, with the more intellectualistic anti-humanism of Olson and Meyer, and it informs some of Hassan's silences. We are, however, still far removed from the far more radical anti-humanism that would later be imported from France, witness for instance Wasson's remark that his writers present 'a world of contingency, a world in which man is free to cope spontaneously with experience' (476). The self is still firmly in place, in Wasson's scheme of things, no matter how stripped of its capacities for ordering and representation.

In the first stages of the debate, modernism is identified with a liberal humanism that is then exposed as inadequate and even inimical to the world of real human needs and desires. Either by themselves or in combination, these early theorists (and advocates) of the 'new sensibility' accuse modernism of arrogant anthropocentrism or, as in Fiedler's case, of a narrow eurocentrism, of repressive and reductive rationalism, of elitism, and of intellectual self-deception. The new anti-modernisms that they seek to theorize are, on the other hand, presented as liberating, democratic, open, respectful to both the human and the nonhuman, and sensitive to desire. It is remarkable how much of what is now broadly seen as the postmodern agenda was already more or less in place by the end of the 1960s. Moreover, although some critics, more in particular Sontag and Hassan, were indebted to the earlier *nouvelle critique*, the more radical Meyer and Fiedler were not: both mobilized what they saw as an indigenously American radical democracy – represented by Charles Olson, John Cage, Robert Rauschenberg, the Beats, and so on –

against a modernism that had allowed its own intellectualism to alienate it from all social roots. To look at this from a slightly different angle, what Meyer and Fiedler theorized was an American rebellion – which they saw as a resurfacing of the nativist strain in American art and thought – that had nothing to do with developments in Europe. It is the emergence of this American anti-modernism in the 1950s that is primarily responsible for the debate on the postmodern. As Andreas Huyssen tells us, 'Pop in the broadest sense was the context in which a notion of the postmodern first took shape' (Huyssen 1984: 16).[5] It is important to note, then, that postmodernist theory arises primarily as a response to contemporary artistic innovation – and not, as is too often thought, to poststructuralist rereadings of the great texts of modernism. In fact, from this vantage point, the later influence of deconstructionist poststructuralism on postmodern theorizing led the debate away from its radically democratic origins and effectively managed to depoliticize it until it more or less returned to its political origins in the course of the 1980s, substantially enriched in theoretical sophistication by its encounter with poststructuralism, so that Fiedler's post-humanist, post-white, and post-male future could not only politically, but also theoretically, be defended.

NOTES

1 Bernard Iddings Bell, *Postmodernism and Other Essays*, Milwaukee, Morehouse Publishing, 1926. See for surveys of other early uses, apart from Köhler, Hans Bertens, 'The postmodern *Weltanschauung*' (1986), Margaret Rose, *The Post-modern and the Post-industrial* (1991) and Steven Best and Douglas Kellner, *Postmodern Theory: Critical Interrogations* (1991).

2 Lash's thesis will be discussed in Chapter 10, which will deal with sociological approaches of the postmodern.

3 Andreas Huyssen quite rightly objects to this view of modernism and situates it historically: 'It is easy to see how such a jaundiced view of modernism is quite under the spell of those "terrible" 1960s and cannot at all be reconciled with the austere modernism of a Kafka, a Schönberg or a T. S. Eliot' (Huyssen 1984: 33–4).

4 Sixteen years later, Bell more mildly sees postmodernism as a 'trendy term' that covers 'the jumbling of styles from past and present in architecture, the mixing of figurative and abstract in painting, the self-conscious use of pastiche and parody in the arts, and the exuberant use of all modes to explode any and all definitions of genre'

(Bell 1992: 97). By that time, however, he had found something else to lament: the decay of American intellectual life.

5 It is generally taken for granted that this anti-modernist rebellion was a replay of the continental avant-garde on American soil. Such an interpretation seriously underestimates the extent to which it indeed operates within an authentically American context.

3

MODERNISM, EXISTENTIALISM, POSTMODERNISM

The 1970s

IHAB HASSAN AND WILLIAM V. SPANOS

Ihab Hassan no longer plays a significant role in the debate on postmodernism. Hassan's contributions, however, were vital in keeping the debate alive in the early 1970s, when it was mostly William Spanos and his *boundary 2* group and Hassan who actively promoted the terms postmodern and postmodernism. It is obvious now that it was Hassan's, rather than Spanos's, use of the term that gave it wider circulation, as has been duly acknowledged by Lyotard, Jencks, and others. Moreover, Hassan's formative influence on especially the literary-critical debate has been immense: there is virtually no article or book on literary postmodernism published between the mid–1970s and mid–1980s that does not refer to Hassan's work.

In 1980, looking back on the earliest days of postmodernism, Hassan noted that

> [i]t remained for Leslie Fiedler and myself, among others, to employ the term during the 1960s with premature approbation, and even with a touch of bravado. Fiedler had it in mind to challenge the elitism of the high modernist tradition in the name of pop. I wanted to explore that impulse of self-unmaking which is part of the literary tradition of silence.
>
> (Hassan 1980b: 118)

Hassan's claim as a trail-blazer is indeed well-founded, but that he actually used 'the term' during the 1960s is doubtful. It would in fact seem to enter his critical vocabulary – at least his published vocabulary – with his 'POSTmodernISM: a paracritical bibliography' of 1971 and *The Dismemberment of Orpheus: Toward a Postmodern Literature* of the same year.

This would be irrelevant if the aim was only to correct an innocent rewriting of literary history. There are, however, good reasons to insist that Hassan was right in *not* using the term postmodern for the literature that he discussed in the 1960s, even if he himself later thought that he had done so. As he pointed out in his retrospective of 1980, his main interest in the 1960s had been the 'impulse of self-unmaking' that he found in his literature of silence. That literature was most certainly not postmodern. On the contrary, most of it is definitely modernist, or even pre-modernist. What Hassan discovers and discusses, in 'The dismemberment of Orpheus' and all those later publications of the 1960s, is what from an Anglo-American point of view might be called the subversive strain within European modernism. In the 1960s, Hassan challenges what he sees as the hegemony of a conservative, elitist, and authoritarian modernism by promoting an alternative, anti-representational, and sometimes overtly political modernism. Around 1970 he begins to use postmodernism for the same purpose. Hence, Hassan can tell us in the original version of 'POSTmodernISM: a paracritical bibliography' of 1971 that 'it is already possible to note that whereas Modernism created its own forms of Authority, precisely because the center no longer held, Postmodernism has tended toward Anarchy, in deeper complicity with things falling apart' (29). However, in his desire to promote the postmodern, he forgets here that he had earlier actively promoted a similarly anarchic modernism. As a result, he finds himself forced to redress the balance in the (marginally) revised version of the same article in *Paracriticisms* (1975), where he speaks of a 'Modernism – *excepting Dada and Surrealism* – [that] created its own forms of artistic Authority precisely because the center no longer held' (Hassan 1975: 59; emphasis added). This (re)admission of Dada and surrealism to the discussion leads of course to problems of periodization: Hassan must distinguish between an earlier, anti-representational and subversive, modernism and postmodernism if he wants to use postmodernism as a periodizing term. Let me briefly review how Hassan deals with this and other problems and sketch a critical trajectory that set the agenda for much contemporary American criticism in the 1970s and early 1980s.

MODERNISM, AVANT-GARDE, POSTMODERNISM

During the 1960s Hassan works with a broad concept of modernism that includes the European avant-garde and its sources in the nineteenth century. In his earliest articles he is by no means under the illusion that he is writing about postmodernism. 'The dismemberment of Orpheus' of 1963 is subtitled 'Reflections on *modern* culture, language and literature' (emphasis added), and tells the reader that its purpose is 'to reflect on a strain of modern literature' (463). Those early reflections, including the books of that period, *The Literature of Silence* of 1967 and *The Dismemberment of Orpheus: Toward a Postmodern Literature* of 1971, however, imply an important distinction within modernism, between a traditional modernism and a 'silent', anti-representational one. Concentrating on the 'silent' strain within modernism, *The Dismemberment* offers chapters on de Sade, Hemingway, Kafka, Genet, and Beckett, counterpointed with 'interludes' on surrealism and existentialism. By 1967, however, Hassan begins to suggest that the postwar variants of the literature of silence are qualitatively different from their prewar precursors and, thus, by implication, that we are dealing with a post-modernist version of 'silent' modernism: 'whatever is truly new in [the new literature] evades the social, historical and aesthetic criteria which defined the identity of the *avant-garde* in other periods' (1967b: 74). But defining what is 'truly new' is clearly problematic. Hassan's claims for the new literature are very similar to those he had made for the older literature of silence. It 'strives for silence by accepting chance and improvisation; its principle becomes indeterminacy. By refusing order, order imposed or discovered, this kind of literature refuses purpose. Its forms are therefore non-telic; its world is the eternal present' (78). If there is any difference at all between the old and the new literature of silence it is presumably that the new variant is more radically self-reflexive: 'Silence in the new literature is also attained through radical irony, a term I apply to any statement which contains its own ironic denial' (77).

The problem of distinguishing between an older (modern) and a newer (postmodern) literature of silence returns in *The Dismemberment of Orpheus* of 1971, in which Hassan simultaneously moves backwards and forwards. He moves forwards by adopting the term postmodernism for what he earlier called the new literature, thus suggesting a decisive break between modernism and postmodernism, but he also suggests more continuity between the two than he did in 'The literature of silence'. Whereas he had earlier told us that his new literature went beyond the various avant-garde movements of the interbellum, he now tells us that '[Duchamp's] paradoxes take us to the heart of postmodern life' (1971a: 256). In fact, postmodernism has been with us for a long time: 'The postmodern spirit lies coiled within the great corpus of modernism. . . . It is not really a matter of chronology: Sade, Jarry, Breton, Kafka acknowledge that spirit' (139). This a-chronological, typological definition of the postmodern is obviously awkward in terms of periodization. Postmodernism would seem to be para-modern rather than post-modern. Hassan seeks to solve this problem by introducing another sort of periodization, located in the history of American criticism. What is postmodern about postmodern literature is the new awareness of the postmodern. The 'Prelude' to *The Dismemberment* makes clear that what is new is not so much the postmodern literature of silence, but its discovery by American criticism: 'it is time, perhaps, to make a new construction of literary history. A different line has emerged *within* the tradition of the modern. It leads more directly, through the present, to a literature to come' (4). In his 'Postlude', Hassan once again emphasizes that he sees postmodernism in terms of typology, in terms of a continuity between the older, prewar literature of silence and its postwar, postmodern version: 'the two accents of silence, heard throughout this study, persist in postmodern literature: (a) the negative echo of language, autodestructive, demonic, nihilist; (b) its positive stillness, self-transcendent, sacramental, plenary' (248). With *The Dismemberment of Orpheus* Hassan establishes a postmodernism that includes, first of all, the 'discovery', by a new generation of American critics, of an almost exclusively European tradition of silence. That postmodernism further includes contemporary versions of the literature of silence and manifestations of an even more radical silence in the other arts:

> But literature lags, as usual, behind other expressions. The arts of silence show greater exuberance in random music, concrete poetry, computer verse, electronic dance, guerilla theatre, deliquescent sculpture, autodestructive media, packaged nature, psychedelic spectacles, blank canvases,

> and plain happenings. Pop, Op, Funk, Concept, Topographic, and Environmental art proliferate, interpenetrate, even as new kinds of anti-art generate newer styles.
> (254)

It is not an unkindness to Hassan, who is, after all, tentatively exploring new territories with great erudition, to say that his modernist postmodernism has caused a good deal of confusion about the nature of literary postmodernism. It has also, not surprisingly, drawn a good deal of criticism from scholars working in the various European literatures in which this postmodernism is virtually indistinguishable from at least one version of modernism itself.[1] Hassan's problem is that he seeks a way to match the experimental art of the American 1950s and 1960s with the continental avant-garde while he simultaneously wants to distinguish between the two. Like the *nouvelle critique* – from which part of his terminology derives – and the then developing poststructuralism, he offers a critique of modernism, but unlike the French he soon turns, in what one is tempted to call typically American fashion, to contemporary art and the contemporary social scene. It is his attempt to create continuity between the modern avant-garde and the new art that runs into the problems that I have just sketched.

Up till 1971 Hassan's critical career does not present any problems of interpretation. 'Frontiers of criticism: metaphors of silence' of 1970, however, did already sound an ominous note, be it in passing: 'Criticism should learn about discontinuity and become itself less than the sum of its parts. It should offer the reader empty spaces, silences, in which he can meet himself in the presence of literature. This is the new anti-criticism; or better still, paracriticism' (1970a: 91). Taking his own admonition seriously, Hassan devoted much of the following decade to paracritical activities, beginning with 'POSTmodernISM: a paracritical bibliography' of 1971. In the revised version of that first paracritical effort Hassan defined paracriticism as 'an attempt to recover the art of multi-vocation' (1975: 25), and it is this multi-vocational practice that makes charting Hassan's position(s) during the 1970s a somewhat hazardous enterprise. Association and aphorism – for which he always had a not-so-secret predilection – tend to replace argument; 'digressions', 'frames', and 'counterpoints' abound; and some essays – 'Fiction and future: an extravaganza for voice and tape', 'Joyce–Beckett: a scenario in 8 scenes and a voice', 'Prometheus as performer: toward a posthumanist culture? A university masque in five scenes' – take multi-vocation very literally indeed ('Prometheus as performer' confronts, multivocationally, Pretext, Mythotext, Text, Heterotext, Context, Metatext, Postext, and Paratext with each other).

In any case, Hassan keeps wrestling with problems of periodization, that is, with distinguishing convincingly between modernism and postmodernism. As we have seen, *The Dismemberment of Orpheus* claims that the 'postmodern spirit. . . . is not really a matter of chronology' (1971a: 139). However, 'POSTmodernISM: a paracritical bibliography', published practically simultaneously, argues for a perhaps almost imperceptible but definitive break: postmodern artists 'are closer to "zero in the bone" ' than their modernist precursors (1971c: 23). 'The change in Modernism may be called Postmodernism,' Hassan tells us here, adding with a great show of conviction that 'without a doubt, the crucial text is *Finnegans Wake*' (11). It is true that he modifies this again in the revised version of 1975 – '*Query*: But is not *Ubu Roi* itself as Postmodern as it is Modern?' (1975: 44) – but still he gradually delimits his postmodernism to the postwar period. The periodization that was derived from the new internationalism of American criticism is now dropped and replaced by a periodization that is internal to literary history itself. One result is that Hassan's postmodernism becomes much more American. The older, European, literature of silence is now seen in terms of 'antecedents' (1980b: 121) and postmodernism is now a firmly contemporary phenomenon with only two or three exceptions – the work of Borges, Beckett and, perhaps, *Finnegans Wake* – and it now tends exclusively towards 'decreation', that is, towards anti-representation and anarchy, since Hassan has also decided to drop the Heideggerian 'sacramental' strain that in earlier publications had belonged to the literature of silence.

Simultaneously Hassan's postmodernism leaves the exclusively literary field and manifests itself into contemporary (American) culture at large. Already in 'POSTmodernISM' of 1971, where he supplies 'postmodernist notes' to a number of 'modern rubrics', Hassan moves towards a cultural rather than a literary postmodernism, although it is not until 1978 that he adopts the term 'postmodernity' (perhaps borrowed from Richard E. Palmer's

'Toward a postmodern hermeneutics of performance' (1977)). As so much of Hassan's writing during the 1970s, those postmodernist notes are endlessly suggestive but equally inconclusive. They make mention of McLuhan's Global Village, of Buckminster Fuller's Spaceship Earth, of ecological activism, prison riots, the computer as 'substitute consciousness', anti-elitism and anti-authoritarianism, of the diffusion of the ego, of radical irony, of the found object, Environmental Art, the Hippie movement, of the culture of *The Whole Earth Catalogue*, the repeal of censorship, the new sexuality, the homosexual novel, pornography, the counter culture(s), Zen, the widespread cult of apocalyptism, and so on (see 1971c: 24–8).

Hassan's postmodernist notes offer a reasonably exhaustive catalogue of non-mainstream American culture in the later 1960s, and what he misses here – feminism, 'Black, Red, and Chicano Power' – is added in the version printed in *Paracriticisms* of 1975. This identification of postmodernism with the democratizing urge of the 1960s would eventually lead Hassan to play down postmodernism's continuity with the purely 'decreative' avant-garde and to give more attention to its utopian political impulses: 'we can not simply rest – as I have sometimes done – on the assumption that postmodernism is antiformal, anarchic, or decreative' (1980b: 121). Although Hassan never exactly predicts Fiedler's post-male, post-white, and post-Protestant postmodernism, he too in the course of the 1970s theorizes a far-reaching cultural revolt that partly continues the avant-gardist revolt against the liberal humanism of the high bourgeoisie and partly is inspired by utopian politics.

In the 1970s Hassan also adds another important element to his postmodernism. The postmodern is not simply a major cultural shift, it also involves a new relationship between humankind and their environment. In the visionary 'The new gnosticism: speculations on an aspect of the postmodern mind' of 1973, Hassan suggests that 'we are witnessing a transformation of man more radical than anything Copernicus, Darwin, Marx, or Freud ever envisaged' (1973: 567). In this age of the new gnosticism, 'Mind' is becoming 'its own reality. Consciousness becomes all' (548). This notion that consciousness has absorbed the world plays a central role in what Hassan begins to see as the new postmodern episteme, a term which he first uses in 'Culture, indeterminacy, and immanence: margins of the (postmodern) age' of 1978 (1980c). In his 'Desire and dissent in the postmodern age' of 1983, where the absence of qualifying brackets confirms his adoption of an epistemic scheme of things, Hassan gives as good a summary of his neo-gnosticism as anywhere else (it is now called immanence, perhaps because of gnosticism's inevitable religious associations). Immanence, he declares, is 'the capacity of mind to generalize itself in the world, to act upon both self and world, and so to become more and more, immediately, its own environment' (1983: 10). It 'depends, above all, on the emergence of human beings as language animals, *homo pictor* or *homo significans*, gnostic creatures constituting themselves, and increasingly their universe, by symbols of their own making' (10). The idea of immanence is in fact the generalization of Hassan's earlier claim, implicit already in his writings on the literature of silence, that 'the postmodern endeavor in literature acknowledges that words have severed themselves from things, that language can now only refer to language' (1975: 90). But there is also another tendency that characterizes the postmodern age: that of indeterminacy, defined in the same essay as

> compounded of subtendencies that the following words evoke: heterodoxy, pluralism, eclecticism, randomness, revolt, deformation. The latter alone subsumes a dozen current terms of unmaking: decreation, disintegration, deconstruction, decenterment, displacement, difference, discontinuity, disjunction, disappearance, decomposition, de-definition, demystification, detotalization, delegitimation.
>
> (1983: 9)

Indeterminacy and immanence together characterize the postmodern age: 'The play of indeterminacy and immanence is crucial to the episteme of postmodernism' Hassan declares in 1978, and coins a new phrase in calling that episteme the 'age of "indetermanence"' (1980c: 91). One does not need such Derridean neologisms to see that Hassan has by now moved close to a poststructuralist position, just as one does not need the names of de Saussure, Lacan, Derrida, Foucault, Deleuze, Barthes, or Kristeva in his list of writers who have contributed to the postmodern episteme (1980b: 123). But there is an important difference. In suggesting a prelapsarian time when words had not yet severed themselves from things, and in presenting the emergence of man as a self-constituting 'gnostic creature' as a virtually contemporary phenomenon, Hassan adopts a rather more traditional scheme of things that leaves open the possibility of a return to an older, representational order.[2] Such a position is of course not unproblematical. However, Hassan does not question it. He is, with Leslie Fiedler and Charles Jencks, the least theoretical of all major theorists of the postmodern. Although he is obviously familiar with French poststructuralism long before the average American critic, Hassan's temperament has too much of the humanist to accept its propositions on a more than superficial level. For all his seeming radicalism, Hassan never pursues his own position to its potentially radical conclusions.

As always, Hassan is fully aware of this. Already in his January 1974 preface to *Paracriticisms* we find him warning us about himself: 'In my own temperament, I know, at least three persons quarrel: an Existentialist, a Utopian, and an Orphist' (1975: xiv). And by 1980, when poststructuralism and its American version, deconstruction, have firmly established themselves as the cutting edge of contemporary criticism, Hassan feels compelled to register his dismay with what he sees as their emotional sterility:

> The (post)structuralist metaphysic of absence and its ideology of fracture refuse holism almost fanatically. But I want to recover my metaphoric sense of wholes. . . . Everything collapses inward on language itself, on structures within/without structures. But I long for a concept of literature that is also explosive.
>
> (1980a: 56)

He has, of course, been a closet humanist all along: 'The (post)structuralist temper requires too great a depersonalization of the writing/speaking subject. Writing becomes plagiarism; speaking becomes quoting. Meanwhile, we do write, we do speak' (1980a: 56). The first to link postmodernism and deconstruction, Hassan is also the first to be disenchanted with its impact. Remarkably, Hassan's disenchantment is not so much with deconstruction's depoliticizing effects – the reason why a good many others would abandon it in the course of the 1980s – but because he still expects so much from literary language. In spite of the fifteen years that he has devoted to the literature of silence, he still expects it to be eloquent. Almost against his own better judgment, Hassan never loses his faith in art, even if that art must turn against itself. For Hassan, art still constitutes a separate and transcendent realm.

In a final irony, Hassan's critical career, for so long fueled and inspired by European thinkers, comes home to rest in his adopted country. In 'Making sense: the trials of postmodern discourse' of 1987 Hassan turns to the American pragmatic tradition. Once again reviewing his postmodernism, Hassan moves beyond it. His postmodernism has not much changed, but his lingering humanism now demands more than silence and decreation. Nietzsche may still be 'key to any reflection on postmodern discourse' and Barthes may 'surely' be 'the preeminent critical intelligence of our moment, perhaps of our century' (1987b: 444), but with Rorty, and even more with William James, Hassan feels 'on native ground' (447) and thus at home. The time has come, he declares, 'for provisional reconstructions, pragmatic remythifications' (451), and pragmatism is an experienced guide: 'pragmatism is intimate with all the uncertainties of our postmodern condition without quiescence, sterility, or abdication of judgment' (452). As we will see later, Hassan might also have found a new spirit of commitment in the repoliticization of the postmodern in the mid–1980s, but he chooses to ignore it, just like he kept his distance from the socio-political events of the 1960s. In the pragmatism of William James Hassan finds 'balm to the crisis of postmodern discourse, balm enough' (454).[3]

EXISTENTIAL POSTMODERNISM

With Hassan, William Spanos and his *boundary 2: a journal of postmodern literature and culture* were the most active promotors of postmodernism in the early 1970s. Although Spanos, unlike Hassan, has kept the faith – witness an interview in 1990 (Bové 1990) – he too no longer plays a role of importance in the debate. Still, he is one of the most important early theorists of postmodern literature and *boundary 2* in the course of the 1970s significantly contributed to the ever-increasing acceptance of the term.

Spanos's early uneasiness with the dominant position of the New Criticism had led him to European existentialism long before French poststructuralism arrived in the US. His Heideggerian/Sartrean existentialism would later be influenced by his reading of Derrida – whose terminology gradually enters his essays –

but he never abandoned it. As he argued in the interview with Bové, his existentialism led him to a broadly political reading of a poststructuralism that most critics saw in far more narrow terms:

> It was my existential orientation that compelled me to read the discourse of difference – the discourse of French critics such as Derrida and Foucault and the poststructuralists in general – as a discourse that makes or is capable of making a difference in the world; whereas, most of the academics who welcomed the importation of poststructuralism in the United States (at least this is my sense of it) had bypassed Sartre's and Heidegger's existential analytic.... As a consequence, they tended to reduce the poststructuralist discourse to just another academic or institutional discourse.
> (Bové 1990: 17)

What Spanos demands from criticism is that it can make 'a difference in the world'. The political commitment that such criticism in turn demands from the critic is for Spanos impossible without an existential subject. His existentialism, as Bové quite rightly notices, prevents him effectively from traveling the road suggested by poststructuralist critics like Paul de Man, the road towards rhetoric, towards the unconditional surrender to language, towards the 'end of man'. Spanos's increasing marginality in the postmodern debate in the later 1970s and early 1980s was the direct result of this refusal to accept the priority of language in a period in which at least the literary-critical debate was dominated by the idea of textuality.

Modernist spatialization and postmodern temporality

Let me return to the early 1970s, when Spanos and other contributors to *boundary 2* followed Charles Olson in trying to forge a connection between an anti-humanist Heideggerian existentialism and the developing idea of the postmodern. In 'The detective and the boundary: some notes on the postmodern literary imagination', Spanos first develops his claim that 'the postmodern imagination ... is an existential imagination' (Spanos 1972: 148). This imagination, which he sees at work in Sartre, Beckett, Ionescu, Genet, Frisch, but also in Thomas Pynchon, is governed by the impulse 'to engage literature in an ontological dialogue with the world on behalf of the recovery of the authentic historicity of modern man' (166). This 'postmodern anti-literature of the absurd' employs an 'aesthetic of de-composition' that reveals to us 'the primordial not-at-home, where dread, as Kierkegaard and Heidegger and Sartre and Tillich tell us, becomes not just the agency of despair but also and simultaneously of hope, that is, of freedom and infinite possibility' (156). It confronts us, either thematically or formally (by way of self-reflexivity, for instance), with the radical temporality that is our inevitable fate after the breakdown of metaphysics. Because of his insistence on Heideggerian historicity and temporality, Spanos rejects not only the 'early modern imagination' but also a whole range of contemporary art that, following Hassan, he is willing to call 'postmodern' (his quotation marks), but that, from his perspective, still 'spatializes' time. Such art repeats modernist gestures and strategies in that it ultimately tries to escape from temporality in its attempt to create an autonomous realm of transcendent timelessness:

> In the past decade or so there have emerged a variety of 'postmodern' modes of writing and critical thought that, despite certain resemblances to aspects of the existential imagination, are ultimately extensions of early iconic modernism. I am referring, for example, to the structuralist criticism of Roland Barthes, the phenomenological criticism of consciousness of Georges Poulet and Jean-Pierre Richard, and the neo-Imagism of Marshall McLuhan; the 'field poetry' of Charles Olson and the concrete poetry of Pierre Garnier, Ferdinand Kriwet, and Franz Mon; the *roman nouveau* of Robbe-Grillet and Michel Butor; the 'Happenings' of Allan Kaprow and Claes Oldenburg; and the Pop Art literature advocated by critics such as Leslie Fiedler. . . . These modes of creativity and critical speculation attest to the variety of the postmodern scene, but this pluralism has also tended to hide the fact that, in tendency, they are all oriented beyond history or, rather, they all aspire to the spatialization of time.
>
> (165–6)

Instead of confronting the reader with his or her existential temporality, such art serves to keep alive the illusion of timelessness – through, for instance, its conscious acceptance of a separate realm of art – and thus of metaphysics. As this quotation makes clear, Spanos includes contemporary criticism in his strictures. Much criticism similarly evades the confrontation with temporality and continues the traditional attempt to fix texts in time, that is, to see them in terms of timeless meaning.

In the course of the 1970s Spanos further develops his existential postmodernism in essays such as 'Heidegger, Kierkegaard, and the hermeneutic circle: towards a postmodern theory of interpretation as dis-closure' (1976) – which rehabilitates Olson's postmodernism – and 'The un-naming of the beasts: the postmodernity of Sartre's *La Nausée*' (1978). In 1976, Spanos still equates 'postmodern' with 'post-modern,' suggesting a periodized postmodernism that has its roots in Kierkegaard and Heidegger and emerges, roughly speaking, with French existentialist literature in the 1930s. Increasingly, however, Spanos would come to see postmodernism in typological terms and the postmodern literary imagination as a time-honored alternative to the logocentric 'onto-theological' western tradition. There has been, he tells us in 'De-struction and the question of postmodern literature: towards a definition' of 1979,

> a 'postmodern' literature, albeit marginal, throughout the literary history of the West, texts, for example, like Euripides' *Orestes*, the *Satiricon* of Petronius, Cervantes' *Don Quixote*, Rabelais' *Gargantua and Pantagruel*, Swift's *Gulliver's Travels*, Lawrence Sterne's *Tristram Shandy* [sic], Dickens' *Bleak House*, etc. . . . postmodernism is not fundamentally a chronological event, but rather a permanent mode of human understanding.
>
> (Spanos 1979: 107)

Although this mode of understanding has obvious deconstructionist aspects in its radical rejection of metaphysics in the interest of temporality, it is different from Derridean deconstruction which is too indiscriminate in its critique of language. Its 'critique of speech (*parole*) as logocentric' is therefore partly misguided. Spanos is willing to support that critique in so far as it is a 'critique of a philosophical idea, an abstraction, of language,' but not if its target is 'the real speech – the engaged and thus utterly uncertain dialogic process, however "prejudiced," however inscribed by culture, of historical men speaking to each other in the real world' (114). In other words, Spanos refuses to follow Derrida in equating speech and writing and in seeing both as marked by 'absence', by the endless play of signification. For Spanos, 'oral speech' is still suffused with presence. He has, as he tells us, no quarrel with 'the voice as such' (114), hence his promotion of oral poetry and improvisations. Implicitly Spanos distinguishes between a written language that inevitably tends towards timelessness and metaphysics and that must therefore unceasingly undermine itself through self-reflexivity, through the destruction of the representations that it offers – so that its authenticity lies in its negation of itself – and a spoken language that has at least the potential of speaking authentically.

However, by 1979 Spanos's hope that the 'authentic postmodern imagination' would be able to effect 'something like a Copernican revolution' (119) was clearly an illusion. After the mid–1970s what Spanos saw as the only true postmodernism had been increasingly marginalized by the impact of Derridean poststructuralism. Derrida's presentation at the famous Baltimore conference of 1966, his appearance in English in Richard Macksey and Eugenio Donato's *The Structuralist Controversy: The Languages of Criticism and the Sciences of Man* of 1970, and the work of Paul de Man and others, occasioned a massive swing to the deconstructionist poststructuralism that Spanos saw as politically inadequate.

The power of the spell exerted by the sirens of poststructuralism is illustrated by the intellectual career of one of Spanos's early allies, Charles Altieri. In 'From symbolist thought to immanence: the ground of postmodern American poetics' of 1973, published in one of the earliest issues of *boundary 2*, Altieri rejects a modernist poetics and poetic practice that is 'informed almost entirely by the symbolist tradition' (Altieri 1973: 608). The 'postmoderns', on the other hand, 'seek to have the universal concretized, to see the particular as numinous, not as representative' (611). Informed by this Olsonian perspective, 'postmodern poets have been seeking to uncover the ways man and nature are unified, so that value can be seen as the result of immanent processes in which man is as much object as he is agent of creativity' (608). In some of his formulations, Altieri is perhaps even closer to a mystical celebration of authentic presence than to Spanos's thoughtful existentialism: 'God for the contemporaries manifests himself as energy, as the intense expression of immanent power' (610). (It is perhaps this attitude, no matter how anti-essentialist, that would much later move Spanos to refer somewhat ungracefully to Altieri's article as a 'failure' [Bové 1990: 21]). This mystically immanentist version of postmodernism lasted, by the way, well into the 1980s, especially in the field of performance art and in poetry criticism, witness the introduction to Donald Allen and George Butterick's 1982 anthology *The Postmoderns: The New American Poetry Revisited*, which sees postmodern poetry as 'marked by an acceptance of the primordial, of spiritual and sexual necessity, of myth, the latest understandings of science, chance and change, wit and dream' (Allen and Butterick 1982: 11). But to return to the point: Altieri's essay seems blissfully unaware of any spoke that poststructuralism might put in its immanentist wheel.

By the late seventies, however, Altieri had radically reversed his position on postmodernism. As he put it in a paper presented at a symposium on postmodernism that also featured, among others, William Spanos and Gerald Graff: 'In post-modern writing there is very little that allows any direct application to existential situations except as ironic stances for negotiating a world so full of signifiers it must be empty of beliefs' (Altieri 1979: 98). Poststructuralist themes (and terms) have replaced the former existentialist concerns and politics have disappeared from sight. For Spanos, ironically, politics had become even more crucial during the same decade. Influenced by his reading of Foucault, and able to reconcile, at least to his own satisfaction, Foucault's thought with that of Heidegger – 'Foucault's historically specific or, if you will, "ontic" critique of the panopticon and panopticism is consonant with Heidegger's ontological critique of the onto-theo-logical as fundamentally and radically metaphysical' (Bové 1990: 27) – Spanos began to see postmodernism as 'a fundamentally and radically disruptive impulse, undermining that which has become official, that is, the cultural value system the State relies on to maintain its authority without having to resort to force' (23). It must be said, though, that this is the Spanos who looks back from the vantage point of the late 1980s and that for him, too, the past has come to look more like the present than it actually did. In his actual writings of the time (for example, 'Heidegger, Kierkegaard, and the hermeneutic circle' of 1976) he is only implicitly political and reads Heidegger in terms that are not really different from those offered by another *boundary 2* critic, Richard Palmer, in the latter's 'The postmodernity of Heidegger' of the same year. As Cornel West noted in 1989, '[i]n [William

Spanos's and Paul Bové's] neo-Heideggerian readings of American poets like Robert Creeley and Charles Olson, postmodern notions of temporality, difference, and heterogeneity loomed large, yet still it remained at the level of philosophic outlook and artistic enactment' (West 1993: 392). Still, Spanos and his *boundary 2* authors worked hard at keeping a political postmodernism going in a period that is now mostly known for its political passivity.

The rapid marginalization of Spanos's existentialist postmodernism in the late 1970s is an indication of the strength of the deconstructionist onslaught at the end of the decade. Following Hassan's lead in connecting postmodernism and poststructuralism, a generation of newly converted deconstructionists brought postmodernism within a deconstructionist orbit in which there was no place for a politically motivated promotion of presence or for an existentialist subject that seemed to belong to the benighted 1950s rather than to the enlightened 1980s. But that story will have to wait until a later chapter.

NOTES

1 See, for instance, the objections raised in Andreas Huyssen's 'Mapping the postmodern' of 1984, or in Susan Suleiman's and Helmut Lethen's contributions to Fokkema and Bertens's *Approaching Postmodernism* of 1986.

2 Jean Baudrillard and Fredric Jameson subscribe to a similar history of increasing textuality, as we will see later. Theories of a gradual loss of referentiality rightly or wrongly usually associate that loss with the rise of capitalism. Hassan, however, seems wholly uninterested in a possible socio-economic scenario underlying the cultural upheavals that he is charting. For Hassan the realm of aesthetics would seem to be autonomous and to follow its own laws, although he is also not really interested in how and where those laws might originate.

3 In 'Prospects in retrospect' which concludes *The Postmodern Turn* of the same year, Hassan is somewhat more willing to acknowledge the latest shifts in the trajectory of postmodernism. Yet, here too, deconstruction, which had in fact already lost much of its impact, still 'threatens to engulf postmodernism in its ironies, threatens to neutralize its utopian will' (1987a: 216). And here, too, pragmatism is the guide that will lead us out of the sterile aporias of the postmodern: 'Neither the indeterminacies of postmodernism nor its ghostly immanences will deter the Jamesian "will to believe" ' (229).

4

THE 1970s CONTINUED

Architecture, the visual arts, postmodernisms

POSTMODERN ARCHITECTURE

Public dissatisfaction with what Robert Venturi in 1966 called 'the puritanically moral language of orthodox Modern architecture' (Venturi 1977: 16), and with an equally austere and technocratic modernist urban planning, already had a respectable history when the term postmodernism was actually introduced in the architectural debate, in the mid–1970s. The attack on modernism can be traced through Jane Jacobs's *The Death and Life of Great American Cities* (1961), Robert Venturi's *Complexity and Contradiction in Architecture* (1966), Robert Stern's *New Directions in American Architecture* (1969), *Learning from Las Vegas* by Venturi, his wife Denise Scott Brown, and Steven Izenour (1972), and Peter Blake's *Form Follows Fiasco* (1974), to mention some of the more consequential salvoes in that battle. While Jane Jacobs's book initiated a long overdue discussion on urban planning, Venturi's work was mainly responsible for getting the debate on the inadequacies of modernist architecture underway. When he was awarded the prestigious Pritzker Architecture Prize, in 1991, the jury could indeed say that he is 'generally acknowledged to have diverted the mainstream of architecture away from Modernism' (Ketcham 1992: 91).

Venturi and others

Complexity and Contradiction in Architecture expresses Venturi's preference for 'the difficult unity of inclusion' over what he sees as modernism's 'easy unity of exclusion' (1977: 16). What Venturi has in mind is 'a complex and contradictory architecture based on the richness and ambiguity of modern experience' (16). 'I like', Venturi writes,

> elements which are hybrid rather than 'pure', compromising rather than 'clean', distorted rather than 'straightforward', ambiguous rather than 'articulated', perverse as well as impersonal, boring as well as 'interesting', conventional rather than 'designed', accommodating rather than excluding, redundant rather than simple, vestigial as well as innovating, inconsistent and equivocal rather than direct and clear. I am for messy vitality over obvious unity.
>
> (16)

Preferring ' "both-and" to "either-or" ', Venturi promotes an architecture that 'evokes many levels of meanings and combinations of focus' (16). In anticipation of the double coding that Charles Jencks will later see as central to postmodern architecture, he at one point suggests that those levels of meanings come in pairs in which a new meaning is superimposed upon, or merges with, an older one. One way to achieve such a double meaning is to use conventional or 'vestigial' elements in new ways. Such elements will then 'contain in their changed use and expression some of their past meaning as well as their new meaning' (38). Venturi, who in the course of his career has repeatedly expressed his admiration for modernist architecture, does not seek to break completely with the immediate architectural past. The achievements of modernism may be integrated in the new architecture that he envisions.

While *Complexity and Contradiction*'s promotion of pre-modernist architectures, mainly those of Mannerism and the Baroque, still stayed within the parameters of the academic architectural debate, the publications leading up to and including *Learning from Las Vegas* did not. 'A significance for A&P parking lots, or learning from Las Vegas' (1968), 'Co-op city: learning to like it', and 'Ugly and ordinary architecture, or the decorated shed' (1971), all with Denise Scott Brown, created heated controversy because of their shameless interest in, and even appreciation of, popular commercial architecture (Venturi had already preluded on this with his brief 'A justification for a Pop architecture' of 1965). Venturi and Brown claim that architecture can learn from pop art, which 'has shown the value of the old cliché used in a new context to achieve new meaning: to make the common uncommon' (1968: 91). Gleefully admitting that 'I.M. Pei will never be happy on Route 66' (37), they don't hide their fascination with the commercial landscape's inclusiveness (an echo of Venturi's earlier book):

> the order of the Strip *includes*: it includes all levels, from the mixture of seemingly incongruous advertising media plus a system of neo-Organic or neo-Wrightian restaurant motifs in Walnut Formica. It is not an order dominated by the expert and made easy for the eye. The moving eye in the moving body must work to pick out and interpret a variety of changing, juxtaposed orders, like the shifting configurations of a Victor Vasarely painting.
>
> (91)

Order and unity are here in the eye of the beholder; they are not the prerogative of the expert. As a result, they are subjective and shifting; in fact, different orders, always subject to revisions, can coexist simultaneously. Instead of conforming to the ahistorical timelessness of modernist architecture, the order of the Strip is thoroughly historical. As important as their revaluation of commercial architecture is Venturi and Brown's insistence on architecture's communicative function, a function largely ignored by the purist modernism of the International Style: 'Modern architects abandoned a tradition of iconology in which painting, sculpture and graphics were combined with architecture' (37). Such communication can serve commercial purposes, as in Las Vegas – 'The desert town is intensified communication along the highway' (39) – but it can also serve to convey individual visions of the good life, no matter how clichéd. Discussing the much despised American suburban landscape, with its 'Regency, Williamsburg, New Orleans, French Provincial, or Prairie-Organic modes', they argue in *Learning from Las Vegas* that 'the symbolic meanings of the form in builder's vernacular also serves to identify and support the individualism of its owner' (1977: 153). What architecture can learn from such examples and from Las Vegas is inclusiveness, allusion, comment; it is the importance of communication; it is 'the particular significance of the decorated shed with a rhetorical front and conventional behind . . . architecture as shelter with symbols on it' (90). Both *Complexity and Contradiction* and *Learning from Las Vegas* present the case for a multiplicity of architectural languages that should replace the single, intimiditating language of self-sufficient power employed by modern architecture, and they further introduce the idea, more fully developed by Jencks, that architecture collectively constitutes only one of the languages that create the cityscape. Architecture can therefore not isolate itself from the other languages of the city, as the language of modern architecture sought to do in order to maintain its purity.

A similar respect for what has 'organically' evolved – in other words, for history – and a similar desire to substitute (postmodern) multivalence for modernism's univalence, marks the rejection of modernism by the European Neo-Rationalists, according to Heinrich Klotz 'the most successful response to functionalism in Europe' (1988: 210). In his *L'Architettura della Città* (1966) Aldo Rossi argued that contemporary architecture should build on, rather than replace, the historical character of the traditional European city. New forms should be suggested by analyses of traditional architecture and urban elements – the street, the square, the monument – and not dictated by functionalism and utilitarianism. Urban designers such as the originally Luxembourgian Krier brothers, Rob and Leon, embraced similar contextualist principles, advocating a regional historicism without, in Charles Jencks's terms, 'approaching too close to traditional syntax' (1981: 135), or reverting to a wholly premodern concept of the city. Rob Krier's proposals for the restoration of city centers, for instance, leave modernist architecture in place and do not ignore the demands of modern traffic. Other well-known projects, such as Lucien Kroll's buildings for the new University of Louvain and Ralph Erskine's Byker Wall project, both the product of close cooperation between architect and inhabitants, similarly tried to avoid the mistakes of modern architecture while respecting the modernist heritage. In the course of the 1970s, both in the US and in Europe, architects began to revisit the past, not simply to raid it for ideas, but, in Matei Calinescu's words, 'also as a "dialogic" space of understanding and self-understanding, a space in which complicated problems had been inventively solved, in which recurrent questions had received diverse creative answers' (Calinescu 1987: 282). In response, critics have been ambivalent about the new historicism, especially in its later versions, warning against the thin line between historicism and nostalgia. There is no denying that in some of its manifestations it is as closed off from the real world as modernism ever was. Leon Krier's project to rehabilitate the Nazi architecture of Albert Speer (*Albert Speer: Architecture 1932–1942*) is offensive in its historical myopia. There is, more in general, a tendency to ignore historical architecture's original languages and to accept at face value the – usually arcadian – language that has become attached to it. Historicism can easily turn into an attitude that is as anti-historicist as that of the modernists, but is more reprehensible, because it deceptively suggests otherwise.

Introducing the postmodern

After it had been used occasionally by Sir Nikolaus Pevsner and Philip Johnson in the course of the 1960s, postmodernism unofficially entered the language of architectural criticism in 1974, when it was brought into circulation by a number of New York-based architects and critics (Robert Stern, Paul Goldberger, Douglas Davis, and others).[1] The following year they were joined by Charles Jencks, who within the next five years would become, in Ada Louise Huxtable's words, 'the acknowledged guru of Post-Modernism' (1981: 10). Jencks first used the term in an article called 'The rise of Post-Modern architecture' (1975), and has since then defended and promoted it in countless publications, expanding his interests in the mid-1980s to include painting. His first landmark publication – at least as far as his interest in postmodernism goes – was his *The Language of Post-Modern Architecture* of 1977, which, at the time of writing, has gone through four revisions. By the second edition of 1978 Jencks had already developed his characteristic concept of a double coded postmodernism and he has since then not really shifted his theoretical base, even if he has considerably widened his horizon. Of all the theorists of architectural postmodernism Jencks is easily the most influential. It is tempting to think that this has to do with the fact that his model is eminently accessible – as is his style – while it simultaneously seems intellectually respectable (his introduction of a semiotic vocabulary into the architectural debate certainly is a masterly coup). In comparison, Robert Stern's 'The doubles of Post-Modern' (published in 1980 to improve upon his earlier 'At the edge of Post-Modernism' of 1977) seems too academic an exercise, while other important contributions to the debate such as Paolo Portoghesi's *Postmodern: The Architecture of the Postindustrial Society* (1983) or Heinrich Klotz's *History of Postmodern Architecture* (1988) lack Jencks's clear focus and could in any case only add to his original achievement. This account of architectural postmodernism will then concentrate on Jencks's work, with occasional reminders that his is not the only game in town.

Charles Jencks

'The rise of Post-Modern architecture' (1975) is a plea for a postmodern pluralism that is obviously influenced by Venturi and Scott Brown. Among the alternatives to modernism Jencks lists the restoration of old buildings; what he calls 'ersatz' architecture; a consumer-oriented architecture; a new 'social realism'; and radical traditionalism. The first edition of *The Language of Post-Modern Architecture* (1977) is similarly inclusive. Let me quote the summary that Jencks himself published in 'The genealogy of Post-Modern architecture' of the same year:

> For my purposes a strong postmodernist would have all seven attributes I show in the chart. . . . This multiple definition immediately shows that there is no single strong postmodernist at work. If there were he would have to design mixed metaphors like Utzon, indulge in historicism and eclecticism like Venturi, be regionalist like Neo-Liberty and the Barcelona School, adhocist like Goff, Erskine and Kroll, use a different style for each job like Saarinen and Kikutaka, use them semantically like Kurokawa, incorporate the pluralism of various codes like Takeyama, be sensitive to urban context like Jane Jacobs and Leon Krier, indulge in ironic parody like Mozuma Monta or Thomas Gordon Smith, and commit travesty and traditionalesque – like the Madonnas of Madonna Inn.
>
> (1977b: 269)[2]

At this point Jencks's postmodernism is not much more than a ragbag of anti-modernist overtures. This is not to say that other early attempts to describe postmodern architecture were notably more precise, although they are still of interest because they all prefigure the turn towards a modest, ironic, and playful humanism that would come to define one of the major postmodernisms of the 1980s. C. Ray Smith's *Supermannerism: New Attitudes in Post-Modern Architecture* (1977), which uses 'post-modern' only in its title, notes a new interest in 'social considerations' on the part of architects, a striving for 'a new humanism', even if supermannerism is still, 'very strongly, a formal style' (1977: 325–31). Paul Goldberger, who like Smith argues that '[i]f the formal roots of post-modernism are anywhere they are in Mannerism' (1977: 259), focuses on postmodernism's 'tendency to let image determine form rather than vice versa' (1977: 260), a tendency which involves 'a choice of certain social and even emotional values over intellectual ones, a choice that post-modernism, as a rule, tends to make' (260). Philip Johnson makes a similar point: 'Post-modernism is then a legitimization of some feelings that reach beyond the puritanism of modern architecture' (1977: 18).

Of all the early discussions, Robert Stern's 'At the edge of Post-Modernism' is probably the most precise. Also published in 1977, when with Jencks's *Language* and the special postmodernism issue of *Architectural Design* the debate on postmodern architecture really took off, Stern's article offers three 'principles, or at least attitudes' that characterize postmodern architecture: 'contextualism', or the recognition that an individual building always is a 'fragment of a larger whole'; 'allusionism', or 'architecture as an act of historical and cultural response'; and, finally, 'ornamentalism', or 'the wall as the medium of architectural meaning' (1977: 275). Interestingly, Stern makes an early distinction between allusionism and a 'simplistic eclecticism' (which substitutes 'pre-digested typological imagery for more incisive analysis' (275)), a distinction that parallels the one that Jencks would make somewhat later, in the second edition of *Language*, between a 'weak eclecticism' and 'a stronger more radical variety' (1978: 128). This distinction, which is basically that between a 'responsible' and a commodified eclecticism, is never adequately worked out, even though Jencks will later return to it, apparently stung by the leftist critique of the supposedly commodified postmodern architecture of the early and mid–1980s (articulated by Jürgen Habermas, Kenneth Frampton, Hal Foster, Fredric Jameson and others).[3] The problem of 'authenticity' versus commodification, which becomes a major theme after Fredric Jameson's equation of postmodernism with consumer capitalism in 1983 and 1984, remains largely unresolved in the architectural debate.

It is in the second edition of *The Language of Post-Modern Archi-*

tecture (1978) that Jencks begins to find his stride and that a clearer sense of his postmodernism emerges. We see now that Jencks seeks to steer a middle course with his postmodernism and marks his distance from the deconstructionist postmodernism that Douglas Crimp and others were developing around the same time (see the following chapter) and from the postmodern sublime that Jean-François Lyotard would formulate in 1982. As Jencks put it in characteristically strong terms in 1986, 'it is clear that Lyotard continues in his writing to confuse Post-Modernism with the latest avant-gardism, that is Late-Modernism. It's embarrassing that Post-Modernism's first philosopher should be so fundamentally wrong' (1986: 36).[4] For Jencks architectural postmodernism 'is committed to engaging current issues, to changing the present', but is not interested in avant-gardist principles of 'continual innovation or incessant revolution' (1981: 6).[5] Jencks's postmodernism 'takes a positive approach towards metaphorical buildings' and 'the vernacular' (6); it favors 'historical memory' and 'local context', even if it simultaneously indulges in modernist strategies such as irony and parody. In the second edition of 1978, this double focus now serves the 'Post-Modern building' to

> speak[] on at least two levels at once: to other architects and a concerned minority who care about specifically architectural meanings, and to the public at large, or the local inhabitants, who care about other issues concerned with comfort, traditional building and a way of life. Thus Post-Modern architecture looks hybrid and, if a visual definition is needed, rather like the front of a Classical Greek temple. (6)

In its attempt to reach out to the public, postmodern architecture is

> trying to get over [modernist] elitism not by dropping it, but rather by extending the language of architecture in many different ways – into the vernacular, towards tradition and the commercial slang of the street. Hence the double-coding, the architecture which speaks to the elite and the man on the street.
>
> (8)

Modernism, then, is not 'dropped' but 'extended' and is not

quite as dead as Jencks will a little later suggest.[6] It has, in fact, a new lease of life – although admittedly a different kind of life – through postmodernism. Jencks, for all his contempt for Mies van der Rohe and his 'universal grammar of steel I-beams' (15), or for the 'nasty' and 'brutal' buildings that are 'produced for profit by absentee developers, for absentee landlords for absent users whose taste is assumed as clichéd' (14), never completely jettisons modern architecture. His postmodernism wants to improve upon modernism, not replace it.

This reluctance to throw out modernism altogether is tied up with his semiotic view of architecture. Since Jencks sees architecture as a language, no new architecture can from his point of view afford to break completely away from the modernist idiom: 'All developed languages must contain a high degree of conventional usage, if only to make innovations and deviations from the norm more correctly understood' (22). Postmodernism must thus inevitably build upon the conventions of modernism. Moreover, it also 'accepts' modernism 'for semiotic balance, for its place within a system of meaning', for 'reasons of signification and richness' (106). In spite of the narrow range of its own language, modernism must have its place in a postmodern system of architectural communication in which meaning is generated by difference, by the 'play' of contrasts and similarities between the various elements that go to make up architecture's semiotic 'structures'.

It is in the earlier editions of *The Language of Post-Modern Architecture* by no means clear exactly what role Jencks has in mind for modernism. However, in the 'Postscript – towards radical eclecticism' that he adds to the third edition of 1981, Jencks develops firmer ideas about the place of modernism within contemporary architecture: postmodern architecture 'is double-coded, an eclectic mix of traditional or local codes *with Modern ones*' (133; emphasis added). In other words, modernism is always one of the two codes that go to make up the various double codes of postmodernism. It is the inclusion of modernism that gives Jencks's definition of postmodernism its distinctive flavor and that, by the way, also partly contradicts his claim that postmodernism is not committed to 'incessant innovation'. For Jencks, too, postmodernism must go beyond the modern, and cannot simply revive pre-modern styles (the 'straight revivalist' category of 1977 has no place in this new scheme of things).

There must, moreover, exist a palpable tension between the modernist code and the code with which it is combined, which, given the fact that such tensions always deteriorate into clichés and thus into invisibility, implies a demand for continual innovation. The notion that the codes that make up postmodernism should always be conflicting also takes some time gestating, although it is already implicit in Jencks's earlier idea that the truly postmodern building 'attempt[s] to set up a discourse between different and opposed taste cultures' (132). By 1987, in a discussion of James Stirling's *Neue Staatsgalerie* in Stuttgart, with its artful blending of modern and classical codes, Jencks will insist that 'we enjoy the resultant hybrid aesthetic for its continuity with our daily life. By contrast, integrated systems can seem artificial and constricting' (1987a: 271). Instead of demanding a deconstructionist, political, strategy from postmodern architecture – along the lines of Kenneth Frampton and others – Jencks here sees it in essentially representationalist terms. In its double coding, postmodern architecture reflects the unspecified tensions of everyday experience.

In the early 1980s, then, Jencks's postmodernism is taking its definitive shape. It is characterized by eight so-called 'ideological definers', by thirteen stylistic variables, and by nine 'design ideas'. The ideological definers include double coding, pluralism, a preference for semiotic over functional form, active involvement, and encouragement of participation; the stylistic variables include hybridism, complexity, eclecticism, representation, ornamentalism, interest in metaphor, historical reference, symbolism, and humour; the 'design ideas', finally, include 'contextual urbanism and rehabilitation', 'functional mixing', 'collage/collision', and a wonderfully open category that in fact makes all the others superfluous, simply called 'all rhetorical means' (1980: 32). Beginning in 1980, with the *Late-Modern Architecture* from which I have just quoted, Jencks makes a sharp distinction between 'Late Modern' and 'Post-Modern' architecture.[7] 'Late Modern' architecture – the Westin Bonaventure hotel in Los Angeles that Fredric Jameson will later see as the architectural embodiment of postmodernism, the Centre Pompidou, the new Lloyd's building in London, the Hongkong and Shanghai Bank in Hong Kong – is 'an exaggeration of several Modern concerns such as the technological image of a building, its circulation, logic and structure' (1981: 133). Late modern architecture, which for Jencks emerges simultaneously with postmodernism, flaunts its high-tech character while sometimes allowing itself ironic gestures in the direction of postmodernism (as in the case of Philip Johnson's AT&T skyscraper). It is, in Jencks's 1986 'essential definition', 'pragmatic and technocratic in its social ideology and from about 1960 takes many of the stylistic ideas and values of Modernism to an extreme in order to resuscitate a dull (or clichéd) language' (1986: 32). Like its modernist parent, late modern architecture is thus single coded; it is, moreover, self-referential in its exposed technology, or in its mocking gestures, or in both.

While Jencks developed his distinction between 'Post-Modernism' and 'Late Modernism', Robert Stern proposed a similar distinction between 'traditional post-modernism' and a deconstructionist, 'schismatic post-modernism'. For Stern 'traditional' postmodernism – which I will focus on here – relies increasingly on representational as opposed to 'abstract or conceptual modes' (1980: 84), and it 'opens up artistic production to a public role which modernism, by virtue of its self-referential formal strategies, had denied itself' (85). Stern sees in traditional postmodernism a 'genuine and unsentimental humanism' which expresses itself in a deeply felt sense of 'social and cultural responsibility' (85).

Stern's essay is important because it casts a wider net than Jencks's early work and brings already into focus what Jencks would add to his position in the course of the 1980s. Showing himself aware of Rackstraw Downes's seminal discussion of postmodern painting (which I will discuss in the second section of this chapter), Stern argues that postmodernism signifies a widespread return to humanism in the arts in general:

> The fundamental nature of this shift to post-modernism has to do with the reawakening of the artists in every field to the public responsibilities of art. Once again art is being regarded as an act of communication as opposed to one of production or revelation (of the artist's ego and/or of his intentions for the building or his process of design).
>
> (87)

From the early 1980s onwards, architectural postmodernism becomes closely identified with Stern's 'unsentimental' humanism, while both post–1960 high tech or ultra-modernism (initially also called postmodern by Paul Goldberger, Douglas Davis, and others) and deconstructionist architecture (Stern's schismatic postmodernism) are gradually moved from the postmodern to the late (or, as the case may be, a neo-) modern category.[8] Although Heinrich Klotz is not uncritical of that distinction (at least as proposed by Jencks), his postmodernism, too, supports a more humane, consumer-friendly orientation, given his defining characteristics, which include 'fictional representation', 'poetry', 'improvization and spontaneity', 'history and irony', and 'contextualism' (see Klotz 1988: 421 for the complete list). Paolo Portoghesi, one of the earliest and strongest advocates of the new historicism, likewise turns away from a modernist architecture that had reduced itself to 'pure material production' and sees 'the postmodern in architecture' as 'a reemergence of archetypes, or as a reintegration of architectonic conventions, and thus as a premise to the creation of an *architecture of communication*' (Portoghesi 1993: 310–11). For Portoghesi, after the aberrations of modernism, postmodern architecture returns to time-honored basics in its 'appeal to conventions of universal value corresponding not to ideological superstructures, but to permanent characteristics of the perception and appropriation of space' (Portoghesi 1983: 42).

Such a return to a universal style was indeed in the air in the 1980s. Even Jencks, who in 1980 had still suggested that postmodern architure was moving '[t]owards radical eclecticism', would in the course of the 1980s come to privilege a 'universal' language, that of 'Free-Style Classicism'. By 1987 he felt so sure of his case that he could title his new book *Post-Modernism: The New Classicism in Art and Architecture.* After a pluralist and an eclectic phase, postmodernism had now entered its 'classical stage'. As Jencks explained in an interview of the same year:

> The argument of my book is to say that Free-Style Classicism underlies both the art and architecture of the third phase of Post-Modernism, starting roughly from the 1970s and continuing until the present. And it is more or less a consensus, a world consensus, though it has many sub-styles, like the International Style had. . . . the general reason for all this happening is the need for a universal language, a public language.
>
> (1987b: 45)

Jencks has a point, and *Post-Modernism: The New Classicism in Art and Architecture* does indeed make a case for this development. It is, however, also an exercise in renaming. Jencks may now present postmodernism as a 'radical investigation of the classical language that revives, simultaneously, every single period of Classicism', but it revives, indeed, all periods, that is, 'Egyptian architecture', 'Mannerism', '1900', 'rationalism', and so on (1987b: 45–6). Likewise, Jencks's list of 'rules' may have changed (and shrunk) and the names of the various postmodern sub-styles may have changed, but those of the architects involved have remained the same.

In *What is Post-Modernism* (1986) Jencks had in the meantime widened his horizon to include painting.[9] What is true for postmodern architecture is also true for postmodern painting (and even for postmodern fiction), Jencks now argues. Postmodern painters abandon self-reflexivity and autonomy and 'focus on the semantic aspect': 'the so-called "return to painting" of the 1980s is also a return to a traditional concern with content' (25). This was, by 1986, unexceptional. However, here too Jencks sees an almost inevitable return to classicism: 'We can see in this return to the larger western tradition a slow movement of our culture, now worldwide, back to a "centre which could not hold" (to misquote Yeats)' (38). But here Jencks is on uncertain ground. *What is Post-Modernism* and *Post-Modernism: The New Classicism in Art and Architecture* are a good deal more convincing on architecture than on painting. One would not want to deny that many of the most exciting contemporary architects work in what Jencks calls the classicist mode. Outstanding examples are Charles Moore's Piazza d'Italia in New Orleans, Michael Graves's Humana Building in Louisville, Kentucky, James Stirling's *Neue Staatsgalerie* in Stuttgart, Norman Neuerburg's Getty Museum in Malibu, much of the work of Aldo Rossi and Leon Krier, and so on (even Philip Johnson's AT&T building is now included). Jencks's painters, however, present a different picture, so to speak. Some of them may last, but one is strongly inclined to agree with Anne Gregory's verdict that the art that Jencks presents as postmodern classicism is 'simply unworthy of serious critical attention'.[10] Historicism with 'quotation marks', with a 'self-conscious artificiality' (1987c: 61), just is not enough.

Jencks in the course of the 1980s gradually drifted towards a *laisser faire* position. Although he still insists on irony and on double coding, there is little irony or tension between incommensurable codes in his postmodern classicism. There is, on the contrary, nothing that would offend the bourgeois eye in, for instance, the paintings reproduced in *What is Post-Modernism?* and there is, indeed, very little evidence of internal tension in the blandness that characterizes most of them. His latest postmodernism can accommodate virtually all contemporary architecture, except straight modernism and the deconstructionist architecture that became prominent in the later 1980s and that in its attempts to inflict formal violence upon architectural basics is more radically self-undermining than the double codes of Jencks's postmodern classicism, which, in the manner of the New Criticism, seek to keep tension and paradox in precarious and ultimately transcendent balance. Postmodern classicism's ironies are as often as not so faint that its historicism seems merely arcadian, an exercise in nostalgic anti-historicism rather than a confrontation with historical realities. The always precariously thin line between a critical, radical eclecticism and a weak one seems to have disappeared and radical eclecticism with it.

OTHER ARTS, OTHER VOICES

By 1980 the terms postmodernism and postmodern had become firmly established in literary criticism and in the discussion of contemporary architecture. But in the second half of the 1970s they had also begun to appear in discussions of recent art in various other disciplines, such as painting, sculpture, photography, and film, and in discussions of contemporary drama and performance art. This section will look at these early attempts to theorize the postmodern in art forms other than architecture and literature (although it will finally return to literary criticism). It will not do so by way of a grand tour of the various arts, which would involve a good deal of repetition, but by way of the different postmodernisms that emerge in the second half of the 1970s and that go on to dominate the debate, with those of Hassan and Jencks, until the impact of the grand theorizers of the postmodern, Jean-François Lyotard, Jean Baudrillard, and Fredric Jameson, coupled with the ever-increasing influence of Foucault, cause a major reorientation in the mid-1980s. In a sense, the discussion that follows will disentangle the various strains within the all-inclusive postmodernism that Ihab Hassan had created in the early 1970s and had since regularly expanded.

It is possible to distinguish three major postmodernisms in the theorizing of the later 1970s and early 1980s, even if we keep architecture out of the picture. In some disciplines there is a sort of consensus about what qualifies as postmodern, in other disciplines critics theorize two, or even three postmodernisms simultaneously. There is, first of all, the return of representation and narrative, which for obvious reasons is only possible in those art forms – such as painting – where representation and narrative had been repressed. Diametrically opposed to this is the attack on representation and narrative, which we find in practically all the arts, and which betrays the impact of deconstructionist poststructuralism, which in the course of the 1970s had increasingly made itself felt. This is not the rejection of representation that one finds in the modernism theorized by Clement Greenberg in which artistic disciplines achieve complete autonomy by purging themselves of all foreign elements and focus self-reflexively on their own formal possibilities. The postmodern rejection of narrative and representation follows Barthesian/Derridean deconstruction in its denial of presence, of origins, of the coherent subject, and so on. Many of its later practitioners and theorists see this deconstructionist postmodernism as a political force. Since the politicized version becomes virtually an industry by itself in the early 1980s, at least on the level of theory, I will here only signal some early theorizations, and discuss it separately in the next chapter, which will deal with postmodern cultural politics. There is, thirdly, a number of scattered attempts to define postmodernism in terms of a (mostly) non-discursive immediacy, of a sacred fullness that in its theatrical manifestations is directly influenced by Artaud. In descriptions of this postmodernism the artist and his or her art is often seen in shamanistic terms. Finally, we find attempts to transcend some of the contradictions between these postmodernisms, not by simply lumping them all together, but by seeing the postmodern as a dialogic space rather than as a monolithic mode, not unlike the architectural postmodernism of Charles Jencks, although not necessarily inspired by Jencks's example. Indeed, the literary critic Alan Wilde conceived of his 'mid-fiction' before Jencks developed his concept of postmodernism's double codes.

The return of representation

In 1971, Brian O'Doherty, one of the very first to use the term postmodernism in print with reference to the visual arts, could see nothing more than 'angry dumbness' in postmodern art (O'Doherty 1971: 19). Around the same time, however, the idea began to crystallize that many of the recent departures from modernist art could be seen in terms of a new anti-formalism (see, for instance, Jack Burnham's *Great Western Salt Works: Essays on the Meaning of Post-formal Art* of 1974). The first explicitly to link the new anti-formalism with postmodernism was Rackstraw Downes, in a brief essay called 'Post-modernist painting', published in 1976. Modernism, Downes noted, had deteriorated into 'a painting capable only of admiring its own nature' (Downes 1976: 72). Postmodernism, by contrast, once again gave the act of painting 'something to do'. It reintroduced representation and reinstated illusion and modeling, but with a certain awkwardness that functioned as 'the stamp of authenticity which revealed that this was not a borrowed diction but a mode of vision' (72). More in general, postmodernism replaced modernism's 'compression, focus and specialization' with 'expansion, inclusion and wholes' (73).

Downes's equation of representation and illusion with postmodernism proved trendsetting. In 1980, Kim Levin's 'Farewell to modernism' saw a massive shift away from the 'purity' of a formalist, 'reductive and austere' modernism to an 'impure' postmodernism:

> The '70s has been a decade which felt like it was waiting for something to happen. It was as if history was grinding to a halt. Its innovations were disguised as revivals. The question of imitation, the gestural look of Abstract Expressionism, and of the words that had been hurled as insults for as long as we could remember – illusionistic, theatrical, decorative, literary – were resurrected, as art became once again ornamental or moral, grandiose or miniaturized, anthropological, archeological, ecological, autobiographical or fictional. It was defying all the proscriptions of modernist purity.
>
> (Levin 1980: 90)

This does not mean that postmodern art is straight revivalist, in Jencks's terms. It reintroduces representation, illusion, and narration, but does so 'with irony, whimsey, and disbelief' (91). Remarkably, Downes and Levin ignore the rebellious, anti-modernist experimentalism of the 1950s and 1960s, presumably because of its avant-gardist, largely anti-representational attitudes. Their postmodern painting is a product of the ironical 1970s, and signals a coming to terms with the painterly tradition, not through the iconoclastic suggestions of that tradition's obsoleteness of the 1950s (Mona Lisa's smile made even more enigmatic by a substantial mustache), but through a mildly ironical acceptance of the unavoidable points of reference that it presents. Like postmodern architecture, postmodernist painting combines historicist awareness, a new representational impulse, and an ironic self-reflexivity.

In the early 1980s more and more critics came to accept this view of the postmodern in painting. Donald Kuspit argued that in postmodern art 'content, rather than form, becomes crucial' (Kuspit 1931: 18), and Lawrence Alloway suggested that 'the term *Post-Modernism* assumes an end to formal innovation' and implies social and personal elements that were totally absent from modernist art (Alloway 1981: 9). In Europe, Achille Bonito Oliva noted similar developments. His 'international trans-avantgarde' also 'reintroduces the tradition of painting into art' (Oliva 1982: 36). It recovers 'languages, positions, and methodologies pertaining to the past' (38), and is not afraid of description and decoration. But this, too, is not straight revivalism. The international trans-avantgarde is ironical, it gives in to whims, and it deliberately avoids the heroic stances of the modernists: 'The work intentionally lacks character, it does not hold heroic attitudes, and it does not recall exemplary situations. Instead, it presents small events related to individual sensibility and circumscribed by adventures laced with irony and subtle detachment' (40). Like the 'mid-fiction' of Alan Wilde that I will discuss below, these views of the postmodern in the field of painting suggest the focus on the local and the provisional in the absence of essentialist representations that French poststructuralists such as Foucault and Lyotard were advocating. Still, given the fact that the vocabulary of the American art critics quoted here gives no sign of any encounters with French thought – Oliva is of course a different proposition – it is perhaps more to the point to speak of a separate, parallel, development and to link them with Fiedler and his early theorization of a postmodern turn towards small-scale, ironical mythologies.

The turn towards representation and its theorization in terms of postmodernism were most striking in the field of painting, where Greenberg's modernism represented a well-defined monolithic target, much like the International Style in architecture. But it was also noted in other disciplines. In 1979, Gene Thornton saw a similar, although still tentative, return of narration and content in the photography of the 1970s. One cannot help feeling, he wrote, that one is 'witnessing the birth of post-modernism in photography' (Thornton 1979: 67). (Thornton's representational postmodernism was short-lived, as we will see in the next chapter. In the same year, Douglas Crimp began his successful campaign for a fiercely anti-representational postmodern photography.) In the field of poetry, Marjorie Perloff defined postmodernism as being the urge to return to poetry that which had been excluded by the Romantic lyric: the political, ethical, historical, and philosophical. The lyric, then, gives way to a postmodern poetry that can, 'once again, accommodate narrative and didacticism, the serious and the comic, verse *and* prose' (Perloff 1985: 181). Here too, as she had noted in her 'From image to action: the return of story in postmodern poetry' of 1982, there is no question of a simple going back to historical forms. Narrative is reintroduced, but it is now 'fragmented, dislocated' (Perloff 1982: 425). (A literary critic, Perloff had not escaped being tarred with the deconstructionist brush.) In the field of avant-gardist film, Noël Carroll saw as postmodern the return to various narrative concerns that had followed upon the self-reflexive stance of structural filmmaking: 'in avant-garde film, the structural moment can be regarded as the celluloid correlate to painterly and sculptural minimalism. This, in turn, implies a certain loose appropriateness to employing the term "postmodernism" to the various anti-structural efforts' (Carroll 1985: 103). Finally, in postmodern dance, Sally Banes distinguished between an earlier, 'analytic', period – whose major concerns correspond to those of modernist painting – and a later 'metaphoric' period. By the end of the 1970s, she tells us, 'the clarity and simplicity of analytic postmodern dance had served its purpose and threatened to become an exercise in empty formalism' (Banes 1985: 89). The response was 'an urgent search for ways to reinstall meaning in dance' (90), leading ultimately to a 'rebirth of content' in the 1980s, to a postmodernism that had rediscovered representation.

Postmodernism as radical self-reflexivity

Sally Banes's 'analytic' postmodernism, which precedes the return to representation, is, as I have just suggested, not unsimilar to Greenbergian modernism. Her 'analytic postmoderns' emphasize choreographic structure and foreground movement. They seek to create dances in which the audience is confronted with the essentials of dance 'without expressive or illusionistic effects or reference' (87). The thematics of the dance are thus the dance itself and the art of dancing.

This movement towards complete self-reflexivity constitutes another postmodernism of the 1970s. Not surprisingly, it manifests itself primarily in those artistic disciplines where modernism had not been self-reflexive, or not sufficiently self-reflexive. In its initial stage, it usually takes a Greenbergian form, that is, it is anti-representational without being interested in the problematics of representation and asserts the autonomy of art. After the mid–1970s, its anti-representationalism is seen in deconstructionist terms, as engaged in an interrrogation of representation, of language, of the subject, and of the underlying liberal humanist ideology in general. According to its theorists, this postmodernism pursues across a range of artistic disciplines the same deconstructionist aims that the later Roland Barthes and Jacques Derrida pursue in their critical writings. In again a later phase, as I have already suggested, this anti-representational, deconstructionist postmodernism is increasingly seen from a Foucauldian perspective; the emphasis then shifts to its interrogation of the discourse of art itself and its supporting institutions (such as the museum), and how art can more broadly function as a political intervention. In the 1970s, however, Foucault was not yet a presence on the postmodern scene, and the poststructuralism that gradually begins to enter the vocabulary of the debate on postmodernism is that of Barthes and Derrida.

In the early 1970s poststructuralism was not yet in sight and even self-reflexivity or anti-representationalism did – as terms – not yet feature on the critical agenda. Critics that theorized postmodernism (or the 'new sensibility') did so in traditional terms. Richard Wasson's discussions are a case in point. So is Michael Holquist's description of the aesthetics of postmodernism as 'militantly *anti*-psychological' and radically '*anti*-mythical' (Holquist 1971: 148). In 1975, however, Bruce Morrisette's 'Postmodern generative fiction: novel and film' defined postmodernism in terms of radical self-reflexivity, although he did not yet call attention to its deconstructionist potential. In the same year, Michael Kirby's 'Post-modern dance issue: an introduction', the first attempt to theorize postmodern dance, saw postmodernism in similar terms. In postmodern dance, movement 'results from certain decisions, goals, plans, schemes, rules, concepts, or problems' (Kirby 1975: 3). Postmodern dance 'is not about anything' (4) except itself (corresponding to what Sally Banes would later call 'analytic postmodern' dance). In the field of fiction, Raymond Federman, of short-lived Surfiction fame, suggested that 'the primary purpose of fiction will be to unmask its own fictionality, to expose the metaphor of its own fraudulence, and not pretend any longer to pass for reality, for truth, or for beauty' (Federman 1975: 8). Fiction was not to be a representation of an exterior world, but 'self-representation' (11). All of this is difficult to distinguish from what in painting was defined as self-reflexive modernism, although with Federman we have a transitional case in the development towards the deconstructionist self-reflexivity that I have sketched above.

However, in the next years, self-reflexivity would increasingly come to be linked with Barthesian/Derridean deconstruction. Allen Thiher's 'Postmodern dilemmas: Godard's *Alphaville* and *Two or Three Things That I Know About Her*' of 1976 defined 'the postmodern canon' as

> the view that mimesis can be no more than a representation of itself, a laying bare of its own genesis, or a critique of those conventions that would claim to represent some substantial reality transcending the act of representation itself.
> (Thiher 1976: 947)

The next year Charles Caramello proposed that we 'take the range of postmodern performance activities . . . as analogical strivings toward the hypothetical *writerly text* that Barthes posits' (Caramello 1977: 225), and in 1979 Charles Altieri also hitched his wagon to Barthes: 'my imaginary postmodern . . . will be an imaginary practitioner of the Roland Barthes concept of the pure writerly text' (Altieri 1979: 94). Two years later, Frederic Jameson echoed Thiher's appraisal of Jean-Luc Godard:

> Godard's films are . . . resolutely postmodernist in that they

> conceive of themselves as sheer text, as a process of production of representations that have no truth content, are, in this sense, sheer surface or superficiality. It is this conviction which accounts for the reflexivity of the Godard film, its resolution to use representation against itself to destroy the binding or absolute status of any representation.
>
> (Jameson 1981: 111; quoted in Foster 1985: 220)

The equation of postmodernism with an anti-representational, deconstructionist self-reflexivity lasts well into the 1980s. Its classic statement is perhaps Allen Thiher's *Words in Reflection: Modern Language Theory and Postmodern Fiction* of 1984, which offers chapters on Wittgenstein, Heidegger, and de Saussure and Derrida before it discusses anti-representationalism and reflexivity in contemporary fiction. But there is also Hilary Lawson's significantly titled *Reflexivity: The Post-modern Predicament* (1985), or Patrice Pavis's analysis of postmodern theater, which, in his view, 'sets itself the task of effecting its own deconstruction as a way of inscribing itself, no longer in a thematic or formal tradition, but into an autoreflexive self-consciousness of its enunciation and this into its very functioning' (Pavis 1986: 15). In 1987, Philip Auslander's discussion of the Wooster Group's performances again appeals to Barthes's authority: 'In constructing their performance text, the Group seems to assume a poststructuralist idea of textuality like that advanced by Roland Barthes' (Auslander 1987: 33). Even in 1990, Paul Crowther argued that the 'Critical Super Realism' and the 'critical neo-Expressionism' that he had singled out in his discussion of contemporary painting gave art 'a deconstructive dimension'. Such a deconstructive art 'embodies the same kinds of strategy which inform contemporary poststructuralist approaches to discourse in general. They can, therefore, be defined as the definitive postmodern tendency' (Crowther 1990: 252).

In Thiher's *Words in Reflection* Heidegger and Derrida were all over the place. Foucault, on the other hand, only got two pages (in the 'Afterword', at that). In Lawson's *Reflexivity* Derrida again was continually invoked, while Foucault was mentioned only once. But the times were already changing. The Derridean attack on language and representation would in the course of the 1980s give way to a Foucauldian interrogation of the power inherent in representation and in the institutions that privileged certain forms of representation at the expense of others. As a result, issues of gender, race, ethnicity, and even class, which in the self-reflexive postmodernism that I have sketched here play no role of any significance, gradually find a place in the debate on postmodernism and eventually come to constitute one of its major themes. That shift, initiated by the left, will be examined in the next chapter.

The postmodernism of immediacy and presence

In 1974, Charles Russell remarked that a good deal of contemporary literature and thought expressed the desire for 'a mystic union of self and world, untarnished by language' (Russell 1974: 356–7). Although language is the enemy here, it is, if one accepts the possibility of such a union, by no means impossible to achieve a state of (temporary) grace through language, no matter how paradoxical that seems. In such cases language is used as a means to transcend itself. This is a not unimportant sub-theme in the Heideggerian postmodernism of the 1970s. We have already seen how Charles Altieri claimed in 1973 that 'postmodern poets have been seeking to uncover the ways in which man and nature are unified' (Altieri 1973: 608). Other contributors to *boundary 2* argued in similar terms. According to Robert Kern, postmodern poets sought 'a poetry that [would] embody the presence of living speech. Heidegger's "Saying" ' (Kern 1978: 216). Even Spanos himself was not immune to the promise of such a presence, as we have seen.

Still, although the problem of language is not insurmountable, immediacy is for obvious reasons easier to achieve in a non-discursive discipline than in the field of poetry. Not surprisingly, most attempts to formulate a postmodernism of immediacy and presence find it in performance art – as distinct from a more discursive theater – and in unclassifiable performances/installations such as those of Joseph Beuys. This postmodernism of immediacy takes two major forms. In one form it aims for the immediacy that Suzi Gablik describes as a process in which

> [t]he artist as shaman becomes a conductor of forces which go far beyond those of his own person, and is able to bring art back in touch with its sacred sources; through

> his own personal self-transformation, he develops not only new forms of art, but new forms of living'.
>
> (Gablik 1984: 126)

In discussions of this postmodernism, the shaman – in Gablik's words, a 'mystical, priestly, and political figure' who has become a 'visionary and a healer' (126) – is an important trope. Jerome Rothenberg sees the postmodern 'performance/ritual impulse' in 'a range of healing events as literal explorations of the shamanistic premise' (Rothenberg 1977: 12); for Michel Benamou the 'shamanistic' is one of the two 'visions' that frame the discourse of postmodern performance (Benamou 1977: 5); John Paoletti, in a discussion of postmodernism in the visual arts, speaks of 'those artists who assume the mysterious role of shaman in order to bring us closer to the verities of the complex and difficult-to-decipher environments that we inhabit' (Paoletti 1985: 66). The shaman's most utopian moment was voiced by Richard Palmer, who expressed the hope that a postmodern hermeneutics of performance might 'restore to the interpreter his ancient shamanic-hermeneutical powers to reveal the hidden, to transform the understanding, even to heal the soul' (Palmer 1977b: 31). This is what this postmodernism of shamanistic immediacy is all about and this is what the performer/artist – in the role of shaman, of visionary interpreter of the real – must ideally achieve. With hindsight, the shamanistic postmodern moment was a relatively brief interlude that was cut short by its internal contradictions and by the increasing politicization of the postmodern in the 1980s. Its search for 'intensities' (Benamou) that may be seen as a somewhat belated response to the search for spiritual healing of the later 1960s has, however, been an important force in contemporary theater.[11]

But in the 1970s we also find another theater of intensities, inspired by Antonin Artaud. The sacred theater of gesture that Artaud had preached was the goal of the Becks' Living Theater, of Richard Schechner's 'Performance Group', and of much avant-garde theater of the period (others, such as Herb Blau, were less sanguine about the possibilities of putting Artaud's exhortations into practice and sought sophisticated ways to go beyond traditional representation without surrendering to the lure of immediacy or falling into the abyss of infinite regress). For Richard Schechner, one of its major practitioners, postmodern performance 'abandons narrative as its foundation' (Schechner 1982: 97) and is non-political and non-ideological. Whereas the modern 'proposes the analytic, the critical, the narrative, the skeptical, the contentious – what used to be called the rational, intellectual, and humanist', the postmodern is 'the religious, the synthetic, the holistic, the ritualized, the uniform' (106). Such a theater of immediacy asserts, in Steven Connor's terms, 'the presence of performance against the inauthenticity of representation' (Connor 1989: 154). Since it pits moments of authenticity, no matter how fleeting, against inauthenticity, it has qualities that are inherently liberating. (It does of course not claim access to a realm of timeless truth, even if Schechner's account would seem to suggest otherwise. It rather suggests alternative, more rewarding, modes of experiencing reality.) Since this theater of immediacy must guard itself against its own inevitable tendency to aggrandize itself and its claims, it sometimes incorporates self-reflexive, deconstructionist elements.

What it cannot and, indeed, does not want to avoid is its own theatricality. In both versions, the postmodernism of immediacy continues modernism's insistence on the unique and healing qualities of the aesthetic experience and the introduction of a shamanistic role for all practical purposes even intensifies modernism's glorification of the artist, no matter if the shaman is supposedly anonymous, distinguished by a force rather than by a recognizable identity.

Hybrid postmodernism

Some of the postmodernisms of the 1970s repeated what they themselves saw as modernist gestures of exclusion. Self-reflexive postmodernism, for instance, rigorously excluded reference and representation. But there were also attempts to define a less exclusive, 'impure' postmodernism, a postmodernism that paradoxically combined features from different postmodernisms, that combined, for instance, a return to narrative and representation with reflexivity. Although one could argue that Oliva's 'international trans-avantgarde' theorized such a postmodernism for the visual arts, most theorizations outside the field of architecture of such an internally dialogic postmodernism were the work of literary critics and, occasionally, writers themselves.

The first critic who convincingly theorized such a hybrid postmodernism – which he called mid-fiction – was Alan Wilde. His 'Barthelme unfair to Kierkegaard: some thoughts on modern and postmodern irony' of 1976 described a postmodernism whose concerns are ontological rather than epistemological, that is, concerned with modes of being rather than with knowledge – a distinction that later, in a slightly modified form, would inform Brian McHale's *Postmodernist Fiction* (1987). For Wilde, postmodern writers do not so much seek to understand the world, as to accept it, in all its fragmentation and incoherence, without seeking to control its tensions by aesthetic means, as the (Anglo-American) modernists used to do. (Wilde's essay, published in *boundary 2*, had clear affinities with the journal's existentialist thrust.) Abandoning modernism's heroic stances in the face of the void because they are so many examples of self-dramatization, mid-fiction's 'suspensive' irony operates in 'the open, temporal field of the phenomenal' (1976: 65), guided by 'an ethic of subjectivity and risk' (68). Mid-fiction thus 'manages to combine the problematic *and* the assentive', although its assent is always 'strictly limited, qualified, and local' (1982: 182), a gesture of affirmation against a background that cannot be totalized or otherwise made amenable to understanding. Aware of the anti-representational impulse, the writer of Wilde's postmodern 'mid-fiction' yet avoids total reflexivity because of its 'ultra-formalism' (1976: 65) and instead tries to negotiate 'the oppositional extremes of realism and reflexivity' (1982: 192). There is some truth to Steven Connor's claim that Wilde 'underestimates the determinate forms of negation which create historical alienation' and that '[t]he alienation of modernist art and its anxious attempts to negotiate incoherence are not just the result of a failure of will, or elitist *hauteur*', but are 'the marks of actual struggles over meaning' (Connor 1989: 117). Wilde's examples of mid-fiction do indeed suffer from complacency. Mid-fiction is, however, an improvement upon modernism's dismissal of – inevitably compromised – political solutions to its alienation, upon its uncompromising clean hands policy.

In 1980 the novelist John Barth followed suit. Labelling the self-reflexive short stories collected in his own *Lost in the Funhouse* 'mainly late-modernist' – whereas much criticism of the time saw them as exemplary postmodern – he went on to describe his ideal postmodern author, who

> neither merely repudiates nor merely imitates either his twentieth-century modernist parents or his nineteenth-century premodernist grandparents. He has the first half of our century under his belt, but not on his back. Without lapsing into moral or artistic simplism, shoddy craftsmanship, Madison Avenue venality, or either false or real naivité, he nevertheless aspires to a fiction more democratic in its appeal than such late-modernist marvels (by my definition and in my judgment) as Beckett's *Stories and Texts for Nothing* or Nabokov's *Pale Fire.*
>
> (Barth 1980: 70)

A true postmodernist, like Italo Calvino, 'keeps one foot always in the narrative past . . . and one foot in, one might say, the Parisian structuralist present' (70). This is reminiscent of Jencks's double coding, except that for Barth the fixed pole is not modernist, but determined by the French intellectual scene. (Note, though, how Barth holds on to the democratizing impulse originally brought under the postmodern aegis by Leslie Fiedler.)

Alfred Hornung noted a similarly structurally ambiguous attitude in postmodern fiction, arguing that many postmodern texts had 'a firm basis in personal or public histories, which – in the context of a particular fiction – undergo a number of changes, which in turn affect their reality status' (Hornung 1983: 57). Allan Thiher, too, saw next to a purely self-reflexive postmodernism, a category of 'schizo-texts' that suggested that their language both could and could not reach the world, that is, could and could not represent. This concept of a structurally ambiguous postmodernism that we already see in Wilde's mid-fiction becomes in the later 1980s the basis for two major theorizations of postmodern fiction, Linda Hutcheon's *A Poetics of Postmodernism: History, Theory, Fiction* (1988) and Brian McHale's *Postmodernist Fiction* (1987). For McHale, postmodern fiction negotiates the tension between self-reflexivity and representation by abandoning the modernist emphasis on epistemology – which leads inevitably towards reflexivity – for an emphasis on ontology. Knowing loses its privileged position to pluriform, polyphonic being. The one world which the modernists sought to know is replaced by a plurality of autonomous worlds that can be described and the relations between which we can explore, but that can never be the objects of true knowledge. Whereas McHale sees postmodernism as the end of epistemology, in Hutcheon's work epistemology and ontology remain precariously balanced. Here, postmodern fiction ('historiographic metafiction') is self-reflexive and anti-representational, and simultaneously reinstates representation and narrative: 'Postmodernism is a contradictory phenomenon, one that uses and abuses, installs and then subverts, the very concepts it challenges' (Hutcheon 1988: 3). It does not unconditionally reject, as does the purely self-reflexive text – which Hutcheon sees as late modern – but it ironizes, through parody (the 'perfect postmodern form' (11)) and other strategies. Hutcheon's attractive (and immensely successful) model has the great advantage that it, in her own words, 'gives equal value to the self-reflexive and the historically grounded' (1989: 2) and can thus retain a political dimension (even if it simultaneously calls political commitments into question). Because of its refusal to surrender to sheer textuality, it can, with a certain amount of credibility, investigate the determining role of representations, discourses, and signifying practices. It can, in other words, address the matter of power.

It is clear that Foucault has definitely entered the picture. The orientation on anti-representational self-sufficiency that characterized some early attempts to theorize literary postmodernism has now given way to an overriding interest in how language, knowledge, and power are intertwined: 'The relation of power to knowledge and to historical, social, and ideological discursive contexts is an obsession of postmodernism' (86). The next chapter will examine how this new Foucauldian orientation gradually emerges out of the deconstructionist postmodernism of the late 1970s.

NOTES

1 Sir Nikolaus Pevsner used the term 'post-modern' in his 'The return of historicism' of 1961 which identifies a recent practice of imitating, and seeking inspiration in, various historical styles that belong to the not-so-distant past. Since he sees that practice as 'a sign of weakness', Pevsner is not much impressed with what he goes on to call the 'new post-modern anti-rationalism'. Nikolaus Pevsner, *Studies in Art, Architecture and Design, Victorian and After*, vol. 2, London, Thames and Hudson, 1968, p. 259. Pevsner returned to the question of postmodern architecture in two articles published in *The Listener* in 1966 (29 December) and 1967 (5 January). Even though one cannot say that

these are attempts to theorize the postmodern in architecture, Pevsner must be given credit for signaling 'post-modernist' architecture's 'eclecticism' and its non-modernist rejection of functional form.

2 The 'attributes' are: 'vernacular/popular', 'metaphorical', adhocist', 'historical/regionalist/pluralist', 'quasi pm', 'urbanist/activist', and 'straight revivalist' (270).

3 For Frampton, Jencks goes not far enough. Frampton champions a 'critical regionalism' which should 'mediate the impact of universal civilization with elements derived indirectly from the peculiarities of a particular place' (1983: 21). This would seem compatible enough with Jencks's postmodernism. However, Frampton places his critical regionalism within the wider context of cultural politics. It should also ' "deconstruct" the overall spectrum of world culture which it inevitably inherits' and 'has to achieve, through synthetic contradictions, a manifest critique of universal civilization' (21). Critical regionalism is thus part of the deconstructionist offensive that I will discuss in the following chapter. As we will see, Jencks moves in the course of the 1980s towards an affirmation, rather than a critique, of 'universal civilization'.

4 Jencks is not one to mince his words. In an earlier comment on Lyotard's seemingly paradoxical claim that postmodernism is modernism in the 'nascent state' (in 'Answering the question: what is postmodernism?' of 1983), he tells us that '[t]his crazy idea at least has the virtue of being original' (1986: 36). Whatever one would want to say about Lyotard's notion, which proposes postmodernism as that moment of flux, radical indeterminacy, and openness, before rigidification inevitably sets in, Jencks gives little evidence of having understood its significance.

5 For convenience's sake I will quote here from the 'third revised enlarged edition' of 1981, which is not so much revised (it is virtually identical with the second edition, to the point that even the page numbers correspond), but is indeed enlarged with a new 'postscript' entitled 'Towards radical eclecticism', which contains an interesting new departure.

6 Surely Jencks's most quoted statement is that 'Modern Architecture died in St Louis, Missouri in July 15, 1972 at 3.32 p.m. (or thereabouts) when the infamous Pruitt-Igoe scheme, or rather several of its slab blocks, were given the final *coup de grâce* by dynamite' (1981: 9). Later Jencks will discover that the Pruitt-Igoe embarrassment was not quite the first of its kind and will go back to Jane Jacobs's *The Death and Life of Great American Cities* of 1961 for the definitive diagnosis of modern architecture's terminal disease.

7 Matei Calinescu points out that Jencks's seeming completeness is largely rhetorical:

> Jencks fails to tell us how many of his thirty variables must be effectively taken into account as a minimum for determining that a specific structure is either late-modern or postmodern. In reality,

Jencks himself, when faced with individual cases, seems to use no more than five or six criteria, which he selects as he pleases from the total of thirty – a procedure that is statistically indefensible.

(Calinescu 1987: 287)

8 When Stern first signals his deconstructionist postmodernism there are just a few architects who qualify as deconstructionists (Peter Eisenman is the only one that Stern discusses). By the time that *Art & Design* devotes a special issue to the so-called 'New Modernism' (*The New Modernism: Deconstructionist Tendencies in Art*, 1988), we can speak of a fully-fledged movement, including prominent architects such as Bernard Tschumi (whose Parc de la Villette in Paris is seen as exemplary), Eisenman (who by then has cooperated with Jacques Derrida himself in an architectural project), Richard Meier, Coop Himmelblau, Rem Koolhaas and Daniel Libeskind. Although the theoretical assumptions underlying architectural deconstruction (or deconstructivism as it is sometimes called) are seen as eminently postmodern in several other disciplines, in architecture they constitute an anomaly. I have decided to follow David Kolb's sensible example and leave it out of this discussion:

> If we wished to include deconstructive architecture under the label postmodern we would have to extend that term even further. All the senses thus far considered involve some movement away from abstraction and towards representation.... Deconstructive architecture contests both sides of that duality. Thus I suggest that we distinguish between postmodern and deconstructive architecture, even though in philosophy and criticism the label postmodern is used by proponents of deconstruction to describe their own thought.
>
> (Kolb 1990: 90–1)

9 Perhaps in response to Portoghesi's criticisms Jencks even addresses the postmodern condition and will continue to do so in the later 1980s. Since he does not add anything new to the debate I will leave his views undiscussed.

10 Quoted in Rose 1991: 263.

11 We also find it in related disciplines. Sally Banes tells us that in the field of dance '[t]he appreciation of non-Western dance led to an interest in the spiritual, religious, healing and social functions of dancing in other cultures' and that dance 'became a vehicle for spiritual expression' (1993: 162).

5

POSTMODERN DECONSTRUCTION

The politics of culture

In the late 1970s the attack on artistic representation began to move out of the literary field to the other arts. That move was initiated and led by a small group of art critics: by Douglas Crimp, whose *Pictures*, a catalog for a photographic exhibition published in 1977, was probably the first American attempt to place recent developments in one of the visual arts in a deconstructionist framework; by Craig Owens, whose 'Earthwords' (1979) did the same with landscape sculpture; by Crimp's former teacher at New York's City University Rosalind Krauss ('John Mason and post-modernist sculpture: new experiences, new words', 1979); and by Hal Foster, who gave the poststructuralist approach wide currency with his *The Anti-Aesthetic: Essays in Postmodern Culture* of 1983, an enormously influential collection which, apart from Foster's important preface, included essays by Crimp, Krauss, and Owens. (*The Anti-Aesthetic* also included an essay by Jean Baudrillard and Fredric Jameson's first exploration of postmodernism, and it reprinted Jürgen Habermas's controversial 'Modernity versus postmodernity' of 1981, presumably to leave no doubt about its political affinities, even if most of the essays included were not exactly designed to win Habermas's approval.) In the late 1970s and early 1980s these critics, and the art journals with which they were associated (Crimp and Krauss with *October*, Foster and Owens with *Art in America*), gave the debate on the postmodern a new, political direction. The politics of these and other somewhat less prominent critics were based on the generally poststructuralist insistence on the inevitably 'coded' nature of the real and its representations and on the more specifically Foucauldian insistence on the interconnectedness of representation and power. Poststructuralism had made a leftist cultural politics a more promising project than it had ever been. Under the classical Marxist dispensation, cultural politics had been condemned to marginality because of the determining, fundamental, role of the economic basis. Now that real power was no longer exclusively tied up with the economic, but had instead become a function of all cultural production, cultural politics could really make a difference. As Michael Ryan put it in 1988:

> Rather than being expressive representations of a substance taken to be prior, cultural signs become instead active agents in themselves, creating and evoking new substances, new social forms, new ways of acting and thinking, new attitudes, reshuffling the cards of 'fate' and 'nature' and social 'reality'.
>
> (Ryan 1988: 560–1)

Representation had acquired a sort of materiality. To control representations, which now no longer reflected reality, but instead had come to actively constitute it, was to wield power; to attack representation was to attack that power. Furthermore, there was a point now to contesting power on a local basis and on the level of micropolitics. Whereas under the older dispensation power had always been conceived of as centralized, or at least concentrated in intimidating institutions, power tied up with representations seemed dispersed, local, easier to target for attacks, even if it still always operated within a larger capitalist network.

What must be emphasized is that Crimp *et al.*, notwithstanding their poststructuralist vocabulary, did indeed think of themselves as dealing with postmodernism. In Crimp's case the realization that there was already an appropriate label for the artistic practices that he discussed can be pinpointed fairly accurately. *Pictures*, of 1977, does not mention postmodernism. But the almost identical version that is reprinted under the same title in *October* 8 of 1979 explicitly places the photographic art that it examines in a postmodern context. Later that same year Owens argued that 'the eruption of language into the aesthetic field' that he discusses apropos of Robert Smithson's 'earthworks' is 'coincident with, if not the definitive index of, the emergence of postmodernism' (Owens 1979: 126), and around the same time we find Krauss speaking of John Mason's 'postmodernist' sculpture. That these critics situated poststructuralist artistic practices within a postmodernist framework says a good deal about the sort of poststructuralism that they work with. The 'eruption of language into the aesthetic field' that Owens signals is indicative: the emphasis is on language, on textuality, and the poststucturalist context derives largely from the work of Barthes and Derrida.

I am emphasizing this to highlight the differences with the British critical scene. In the UK the critical avant-garde had already from the early 1970s worked with a version of poststructuralism, but one that was deeply inimical to Derrida, and especially to the deconstructionist critical practice that de Man and others were developing on the basis of Derrida's work. Anthony Easthope succinctly summarizes these separate developments:

> Put at its simplest, [British] intellectuals who were already Marxists read texts by Louis Althusser in the 1960s and 1970s, and were led from there and the analysis of ideology to the psychoanalytic writings of Jacques Lacan. In North America, because of the 1966 Baltimore conference and the subsequent publication in 1970 of Macksey and Donato's *The Structuralist Controversy* (containing, quite out of sequence, Derrida's work in progress, the essay 'Structure, sign, and play in the discourse of the human sciences'), poststructuralism there went to Derrida first and then to the psychoanalytic theories of Jacques Lacan, so managing to by-pass almost altogether the work of the French Marxist theorist, Louis Althusser.
>
> (Easthope 1988: xiii)

Because Althusser was already firmly established by the time that Lacan began to be assimilated, 'Althusserianism', to quote Easthope again, 'is the culture in which British poststructuralism grew' (10). As a result poststructuralist criticism in the UK was from the beginning marked by its interest in questions of ideology and politics, its acceptance of the determining power of economic practice (in Althusser's modification of that position), and by its (often quite creative, even if dogmatic) use of such typically Althusserian concepts as 'interpellation', the 'subject position' constructed by such interpellations, and the 'speculary' structure of ideology. Much of this work took place in the area of film theory and first appeared in *Screen* (which for instance published Laura Mulvey's classic 'Visual pleasure and narrative cinema' in

1975), but the Althusserian influence was not limited to film criticism. In the field of literary criticism Colin McCabe, Catherine Belsey (who in her *Critical Practice* of 1980 readily acknowledges that she has 'drawn freely' on work published in *Screen*), and others adopted poststructuralist positions that derived from Althusser.

The British orientation upon Althusser and the American orientation upon Derrida explain why there was so preciously little interaction between the British and the American critical avant-gardes in the 1970s. As Easthope has noted, outside film journals *Screen*'s work went almost wholly unnoticed in the US until the early 1980s. It certainly does not inform the positions of Crimp, Owens, Krauss, or Foster as these developed in the late 1970s. It is only when the political potential attributed by the Americans to poststructuralist art begins to look doubtful that new positions, somewhat closer to the British one, are formulated. The difference in orientation still persists to this day, however, even though now that British poststructuralism has moved away from Althusser there is more reason to speak of British poststructuralist theorizing as postmodern. As a matter of fact, after offering occasional room to essays that theorized the postmodern, *Screen* in 1987 officially recognized postmodernism with a special issue (*Screen* 28, 2).[1]

THE POLITICS OF CULTURE: IMMANENT CRITIQUES

Authenticity, origins, representation

But to return to the late 1970s. In the fall of 1977 Douglas Crimp, who had just become managing editor of *October*, organized a show called 'Pictures' for the alternative gallery Artists Space in Lower Manhattan. Although, according to Michael Starenko, the show 'elicited little enthusiasm from art critics and gallery directors' (Starenko 1983: 4), it would prove seminal. In Starenko's words, 'the news was out. It spread quickly' (4). The news in question was not so much the work of the young photographers that Crimp had brought together as the theoretical framework that he provided in his catalog. With the publication of the expanded version of Crimp's essay in *October*, one-and-a-half years later, the news (now recast as the news about postmodernism) reached the larger art audience and rapidly acquired gospel status. As Linda Andre noted in 1984, 'within a mere 6–7 years, postmodernism has acquired all the weight of orthodoxy in the art-photography world. To take any other position as a photographer, or to argue for its viability as a critic, is to be ignored' (Andre 1984: 17).

Crimp argued that the artists he had selected for his show were guided by the notion that 'we only experience reality through the pictures we make of it.' At that point he still seemed to subscribe to the popular idea that we have gradually lost the ability to experience the real first-hand: 'To an ever greater extent our experience is governed by pictures, pictures in newspapers and magazines, on television and in the cinema. Next to these pictures, firsthand experience begins to retreat, to seem more and more trivial' (Crimp 1977: 3). Crimp's photographers are out to expose this second-hand quality of our perceptions. This does, however, not yet exclude the possibility of representation. In 1977 Crimp hesitates between a Baudrillardian reading of representation, according to which under the pressure of capitalism representation has become increasingly difficult and has finally disappeared altogether, and a Derridean reading according to which representation has always been an illusion since experience is inevitably mediated by language, and thus always coded.

By 1980, however, that hesitation has gone. Crimp has now fully assimilated the messages of Roland Barthes's 'The death of the author' and of Derridean deconstruction. In 'The photographic activity of postmodernism' Crimp's group of photographers – the most representative of which are Cindy Sherman, Sherrie Levine, and Richard Prince – is presented as having

> addressed photography's claim to originality, showing those claims for the fiction they are, showing photography to be always a *re*presentation, always-already-seen. Their images are purloined, confiscated, appropriated, *stolen*. In their work, the original cannot be located, is always deferred; even the self which might have generated an original is shown to be itself a copy.
>
> (Crimp 1980b: 98)

Postmodern photography is now fully identified with the attack on representation and originality. What Crimp somewhat misleadingly calls its 'presence' is paradoxically 'effected through absence, through its unbridgeable distance from the original, from even the possibility of an original. Such presence is what I attribute to the kind of photographic activity I call postmodernist' (94). Sherman's self-portraits in which she created a fantastic cast of characters that refer to stereotypical images of women, Levine's photographs (presented as her own) of the work of canonical photographers like Edward Weston and Walker Evans, and Prince's practice of rephotographing images he had found on the advertisement pages of glossy magazines all were supposed to bring home to us the truth that all visual perception is coded in one way or the other, that there is nothing outside pre-coded representation, that art is therefore always a copy of a copy, and that there is no subject in the traditional sense of the term. In his 'On the museum's ruins', published somewhat earlier in the same year, Crimp had in fact already made these claims for all postmodern art:

> The fantasy of a creating subject gives way to the frank confiscation, quotation, excerptation, accumulation, and repetition of already existing images. Notions of originality, authenticity, and presence, essential to the ordered discourse of the museum, are undermined.
>
> (1980a: 56)

If Crimp's first move was to create this Barthesian/Derridean postmodernism for the field of photography and, with photography as his basis, to claim a similar postmodernism for the other visual arts, his second move was to accord it an avant-gardist status. In 'Pictures' he explicitly identifies his photographers with those who courageously venture into the unknown (they 'remain', in his terms, 'committed to radical innovation') and dismisses the postmodernism 'which wishes to deny the possibility that art can any longer achieve a radicalism or avant-gardism' (1979: 87). By placing his photographers in the tradition of the avant-garde, Crimp, who assumes that the attack on representation and originality has political implications, seeks to underscore the political nature of their project.

At this point, Crimp's concerns are still primarily aesthetic. Crimp's photographers reject the unsound representational, humanist, poetics of modern photography and the institutions that embody those poetics. In 'On the museum's ruins', he notes with satisfaction that Rauschenberg's art 'enacts a deconstruction of the discourse of the museum, of its pretensions to anything we could possibly call knowledge' (1980a: 43). The attack on origins and representation in artistic practice is simultaneously an attack on the discourse of art history, which is predicated upon such notions, and on the museum, which has traditionally institutionalized art. The museum, Crimp tells us in 'The photographic activity of postmodernism', also of 1980, 'has no truck with fakes or copies or reproductions. The presence of the artist in the work must be detectable; that is how the museum knows it has something authentic' (1980b: 94). Crimp's description of the museum as an 'institution of confinement' (1980a: 45) leaves no doubt about the liberationist character that he attributes to strategies that seek to undermine the museum's power. But even if Crimp draws here on Foucault's critique of institutions, the politics of his postmodernism remain confined to the world of art, its discourses and its institutions. In spite of Crimp's later claims – for instance in 'The postmodern museum' of 1987 – in 1980 cultural politics were still firmly tied to a deconstruction of modernism and its supporting institutions.

Confinement and purity, expansion and hybridization

The example of Rauschenberg, in 'On the museum's ruins', introduces yet another attack on 'the museum' and its hallowed traditions. Crimp's photographers stayed with photography; Rauschenberg, however, had from the early sixties on moved away from what one might call pure painting and had come to incorporate photography and various reproductive techniques (silk-screens, transfer drawings) in his work. In 1979, Rosalind Krauss and Craig Owens had discussed similar 'impurities' in the work of John Mason and Robert Smithson. In 'John Mason and post-modernist sculpture: new experiences, new words' Krauss works with the notion of an 'expanded field' (as she also does in her 'Sculpture in the expanded field', published in the same year and reprinted in Foster's *Anti-Aesthetic*). Sculptural modernism, Krauss argues, had attempted to create a special form of art out of a 'set of negatives – the non-architecture plus the not-landscape', to create 'the monument as abstraction, as pure marker or base, logically placeless and largely self-referential' (1979a: 121). Postmodern sculpture problematizes these negations, ignores the space created by these negatives, and has instead turned its attention on the two opposing poles: architecture and landscape. It has, in other words, expanded the field of sculpture. In her discussion of John Mason's 'Hudson River Series', which employs (or is constituted by) firebricks (in other words, building material), Krauss argues that the firebricks make it possible

> to think the sculptural in relation to architecture without conflict. To think this relationship without conflict, and to think it moreover in a structure which also includes landscape, is to inhabit that expanded field that I have mapped out as post-modernist.
>
> (125)

That Krauss at this point still hyphenates the term indicates how new 'post-modernist' is to attempts to theorize the field. But she is well aware that in this particular field – as distinguished from Crimp's photography – the 'conception of post-modernism' is 'a response to a set of problems posed very generally by the work of many artists over the last ten to 15 years' (125). The expansion of the field through the substitution of 'both/and' for 'either/or', the farewell to sculptural purity, already has a substantial history of its own, beginning perhaps with Robert Smithson's *Mirror Travels in the Yucatán* and illustrated in various ways in the work of Dennis Oppenheim, Richard Long, Hamish Fulton, and many others.

Craig Owens's 'Earthwords', a review of Smithson's posthumous *Writings*, signals a different kind of impurity. Smithson's work (the most famous example of which is probably the *Spiral Jetty* in the Great Salt Lake) had already 'effected a radical dislocation of art, which was removed from its locus in the museum and gallery to remote, inaccessible locations' (Owens 1979: 122–3), but what Owens sees as 'perhaps the most significant displacement of them all' is 'that of art from the visual to the verbal field' (123). Smithson's *Writings* testifies 'to the eruption of language into the field of the visual arts, and the subsequent decentering of that field' (122). This eruption, signaled by the writings of Smithson himself, but also by those of other artists (Dan Flavin, Carl Andre, Robert Morris, Donald Judd, Sol LeWitt, and Yvonne Rainer), 'is coincident with, if not the definitive index of, the emergence of postmodernism' (126). Here, too, modernism's either/or gives way to postmodernism's both/and. What is more, these texts 'also reveal the degree to which strategies which must be described as *textual* have infiltrated every aspect of contemporary aesthetic production' (127).[2] Following Crimp's example in photography, Owens is claiming experimental work in the other arts for a Derridean, textual, poststructuralism. Offering a reading of a concrete work of art, the *Spiral Jetty*, Owens argues that at least one 'aspect of [Smithson's] practice coincides with the techniques of post-structuralist theory – Derrida's deconstructive reading, for example, of Foucault's archeology' (130). By situating Smithson's work in a deconstructionist framework, Owens, too, can suggest that it has a political dimension: 'Smithson's activity was a thoroughly *critical* one, engaged in the deconstruction of an inherited metaphysical tradition' (130). For a short while in the late 1970s and early 1980s deconstruction reigned supreme among avant-gardist critics. A fascinating example is provided by Craig Owens's influential 'The allegorical impulse: toward a theory of postmodernism' of 1980, in which Owens, as Foster would remark towards the end of the decade, 'rewrites Benjaminian allegory in terms of Derridean textuality and de Manian illegibility' (Foster 1988: 262). Owens sees allegory – as defined by Walter Benjamin – as the informing principle of a postmodern art that thrives on '[a]ppropriation, site specificity, impermanence, accumulation, discursivity, hybridization' (Owens 1980a: 75). After first establishing a link between allegorical activity and Crimp's 'photographic activity of postmodernism' – 'Allegorical imagery is appropriated imagery; the allegorist does not invent images but confiscates them' (69) – he then goes on to cast this in Derridean terms by claiming that allegory should be 'conceived as a *supplement*' (83). The next step is now predictable: 'If allegory is identified as a supplement, then it is also aligned with writing, insofar as writing is conceived as supplementary to speech' (84). We are back with textuality. It is only in 1988 that Foster noted with amazement that the word 'capital' did not appear once in Owens's two-part article (although it borrowed extensively from Benjamin) and that '[a]t this point the stake of postmodernism [was] aesthetic' (1988: 261). For that matter, Foster's own 'Subversive signs' of 1982, which discusses the art of Barbara Kruger and Jenny Holzer (although not in terms of postmodernism), is equally concerned with aesthetics. In his analysis Foster, too, leans heavily on Barthes – who is quoted frequently – and Derrida to place Kruger and Holzer's art in a similarly deconstructionist framework. Yet he does not hesitate to call their work political: 'Holzer and Kruger question stereotypes in work that, though it does not conform to political art conventions, is acutely critical, i.e., political' (92). Ironically, he concentrates so much upon its deconstructionist strategies, that he is virtually blind to its feminist politics. For Foster, Holzer's 'Inflammatory Essays' of 1979–82 are 'concerned with the *force* of language rather than with its truth value' (91), and with respect to Kruger's photo-texts he merely notes that 'neither photo nor text is privileged' while missing that photo and text *together* often make unambivalent political statements. The politics of this postmodern avant-garde, as theorized by Crimp, Owens, Foster, Abigail Solomon-Godeau, and others, are primarily aesthetic. Although the strategies involved, such as appropriation and hybridization, are supposed to open the eyes of the larger public to the fact that representation and culture are always political, they remain aesthetic with an impact that is limited to a small coterie of artists and critics whose eyes are open anyway (at least to the political character of culture). It is doubtful, moreover, that these politics would have shocked the American nation even if it had been aware of them. It is hard to imagine that an electorate that had given a former B-movie actor a comfortable majority in a presidential election would have been seriously unsettled by photographs in which a young woman presented herself as an actress in B-movie scenes.

Working to 'problematize the activity of reference', as Craig Owens put it, resurrects the classical strategy of the historical avant-garde. Unlike mainstream art, it does not seek to present the world as it is, but seeks to present it as it is not – in fact, from its point of view, the real can only be presented as it is not, since it is a priori unrepresentable. In such presentations of the world-as-it-is-not politics and aesthetics become indistinguishable, with the political and the aesthetic occupying the same moment. Ideally, such presentations will have the effect of disrupting (ideologically comforting) presentations of the world-as-it-is, and of introducing the complacent bourgeoisie to the exciting uncertainties and vast political potential of the world-as-it-is-not. Progress depends on ever new representations that do not represent the world – on process, not on resolution. I will return to this in my discussion of Habermas and Lyotard. In any case, in a world where aesthetics and the political meet in the presidency of Ronald Reagan, and where capital has so thoroughly penetrated the world of culture that every avant-garde strategy leads to the opening up of new markets rather than new worlds, to fall back on an avant-gardist stance is deeply problematical. Equally problematical is the avant-gardist cult of the artist, which even outdoes that of modernism. Whereas the modernist artist is our humane guide, leading us towards a realm of timeless knowledge, the avant-garde artist is our dashing heroine or hero, taking risks on our behalf in venturing into the aesthetic/political unknown. In the rejection of origins we find, paradoxically, a reckless and daring originality.

THE POLITICS OF CULTURE: BEYOND IMMANENCE

The feminist/postmodern crossing

Change, however, was already in the air. In an essay called 'Appropriating appropriation' that was published in an exhibition catalog in December 1982,[3] Crimp still stands by his earlier assessment of his most representative appropriator, Sherrie Levine (who had gone on to photograph German Expressionist paintings and drawings):

> Levine's appropriation reflects upon the strategy of appropriation itself – the appropriation by Weston of classical sculptural style; the appropriation by Mapplethorpe of Weston's style; the appropriation by the institutions of high art of both Weston and Mapplethorpe, indeed of photography in general; and finally, photography as a tool of appropriation.
>
> (1982: 30)

But Crimp is now painfully aware that the alternative to his deconstructionist postmodernism is not simply a new, postmodern humanism (as he seemed to think in 'Pictures'), but that there is a good deal of postmodern practice that makes use of appropriation without having what he would consider honorable political intentions:

> Over the past few years it has become increasingly clear that the strategy of appropriation no longer attests to a particular stance toward the conditions of contemporary culture. To say this is to suggest that appropriation *did* at first seem to

> entail a critical position and to admit that such a reading was altogether too simple. For appropriation, pastiche, quotation – these methods can now be seen to extend to virtually every aspect of our culture, from the most cynically calculated products of the fashion and entertainment industries to the most committed critical activities of artists, from the most clearly retrograde works (Michael Graves' buildings, Hans Jürgen Syberberg's films, Robert Mapplethorpe's photographs, David Salle's paintings) to the most seemingly progressive practices (Frank Gehry's architecture, Jean-Marie Straub and Danielle Huillet's cinema, Sherrie Levine's photography, Roland Barthes' texts). And if all aspects of the culture use this new operational mode, then the mode itself cannot articulate a specific reflection upon that culture.
>
> (27)

Crimp was shaken by his discovery of what had for quite a while been a widespread artistic practice. Although in a last-ditch attempt he tries to establish structural differences between politically progressive and politically reactionary appropriation – 'Graves appropriates from the architectural past; Gehry appropriates laterally, from the present' (28) – appropriation was a lost cause: 'The strategy of appropriation becomes just another academic category – a thematic – through which the museum organizes its objects' (34).

This time, too, the news traveled fast. In 1983 Abigail Solomon-Godeau could still speak of Sherrie Levine's 'critical stance' which manifested itself as a 'refusal of authorship, uncompromising rejection of all notions of self-expression, originality, or subjectivity' (1984b: 90) and of the 'social and political implications' (91) of such a refusal. But she was one of the last to do so (looking back in 1988 she noted that around 1983 the work of Levine and the others 'had now been fully and seamlessly recuperated under the sign of art photography' (1988: 201)). However, Solomon-Godeau also pointed at what seemed a way out of the impasse. In her 'Winning the game when the rules have been changed: art photography and postmodernism' of 1983, she noted, almost in passing, that 'the notion of the author is integrally linked with that of patriarchy; to contest the dominance of the one, is implicitly to contest the power of the other'

(1984b: 91). Sherrie Levine 'is thus a kind of guerilla feminist within the precincts of the art world – a position shared by a number of other artists using photography within the postmodernist camp' (92).

Crimp's reluctant abandonment of appropriation as a privileged political strategy and Solomon-Godeau's tentative turn toward feminism were symptoms of a larger shift. In 1981 Martha Rosler, herself a feminist photographer, had already warned that the persistence of the gallery system, even of the alternative galleries that exhibited deconstructionist art, suggested a 'still pervasively Modernist view of high art' (1981: 38). The next year, Hal Foster, who shortly before had been an enthusiastic champion of deconstructionist strategies, voiced similar reservations. Appropriation is seen as critical, Foster noted, but 'can a critique be articulated within the very forms under critique?' (Foster 1984b: 197). Benjamin Buchloh thought the whole deconstructionist effort misguided. In his 'Allegorical procedures: appropriation and montage in contemporary art', also of 1982, he lifted allegory and appropriation out of the narrowly textual, deconstructionist framework theorized by Owens and Crimp and reconstructed them as strategies that were deeply political in their institutional critique. Buchloh's artists, for instance Marcel Broodthaers, go beyond the aesthetic in their critique and reach for that which makes the museum possible; they do not so much question the museum's knowledge, as its socio-economical and political grounding, the enabling forces in its background.

By 1983 the time was ripe for a reorientation.[4] In his postscript to the reprint of his 'Re: Post' of 1982 in Brian Wallis's *Art After Modernism: Rethinking Representation* (1984), Hal Foster criticizes the deconstructionist criticism to which he himself had contributed as having failed to engage the 'social uses and discursive affiliations' (1984b: 201) of the art that it theorized. The 'very limits' of 'Re: Post', Foster tells us, 'pushed me to consider the problem of postmodernism more broadly (one result of which was the collection *The Anti-Aesthetic: Essays on Postmodern Culture*)' (201). *The Anti-Aesthetic*, published in 1983, is one of the milestones of the debate. Like Brian Wallis's just mentioned *Art After Modernism*, the other landmark collection of the early 1980s, *The Anti-Aesthetic* is a transitional collection. It does not disown the narrowly aesthetic cultural politics of the recent past (it reprints essays by Crimp and Krauss), but it simultaneously offers a much more encompassing and far more political approach in the contributions by Owens, Fredric Jameson, and Jean Baudrillard. *Art After Modernism* presents the same mixture of deconstructionist postmodernism and a new, more convincing politicization. Here, too, we find Crimp and Krauss (supplemented with Owens's 'Allegorical impulse', Solomon-Godeau, and Foster himself). At the other pole, we again find Jameson and Baudrillard, this time reinforced by Walter Benjamin, Martha Rosler, Michel Foucault, and even by Laura Mulvey's 'Visual pleasure and narrative cinema' (Mulvey's appearance was a sure sign that *Screen* had been definitively discovered).

Of the essays published by Foster and Wallis, those by Owens, Jameson, and Baudrillard had easily the most impact. Jameson's 'Postmodernism and consumer society', published by Foster, was his first effort to theorize the postmodern and would, in the expanded version that appeared the following year as 'Postmodernism, or the logic of late capitalism', open a wholly new line of debate. The same can be said of Baudrillard's 'The ecstasy of communication' (Foster) and especially his 'The precession of simulacra' (Wallis), which had already appeared in *Art & Text* in September 1983 and had in the same year, together with his 'The orders of simulacra', also been published by Semiotext(e) under the title *Simulations.* However, with Jameson and Baudrillard we leave the area of cultural politics and arrive at grand attempts to theorize postmodernity as a new epoch, postmodernity as distinctively different from an earlier modernity. I will therefore leave Jameson and Baudrillard waiting in the wings and deal here with Owens and some later attempts to create a more substantial postmodern cultural politics.

Craig Owens's 'The discourse of others: feminists and postmodernism' is one of the seminal essays of the 1980s. As Susan Suleiman would later note, 'Owens made one of those conceptual leaps that later turn out to have initiated a whole new train of thought' (Suleiman 1991: 115). Although others had occasionally remarked on the feminism implicit in some of the art that was theorized in deconstructionist terms, Owens was the first to link feminist politics explicitly with postmodernist artistic practice; in point of fact, he went even further to claim feminism *tout court* for the postmodern: 'I would like to propose that women's insistence on difference and incommensurability may not only be compatible with, but is also an instance of postmodern thought'

(Owens 1983: 61–2).[5] Owens is still bent on deconstructing representation – he speaks of 'the tyranny of the *signifier*, the violence of its law' (59) – but he is now aware that the signifier's power 'authorizes certain representations while blocking, prohibiting or invalidating others' and that '[a]mong those prohibited from Western representations, whose representations are denied all legitimacy, are women' (59). The representational systems of the West 'posit the subject of representation as absolutely centered, unitary, masculine' (58). Owens thus arrives at the 'apparent crossing of the feminist critique of patriarchy and the postmodernist critique of representation' (59).

This 'crossing' enables Owens to retheorize – and thereby provide with a new political edge – that work by women artists that was earlier theorized in generally deconstructionist, anti-representational terms:

> the affinities between poststructuralist theories and postmodernist practice can blind a critic to the fact that, when women are concerned, similar techniques have very different meanings. Thus, when Sherrie Levine appropriates – literally takes – Walker Evans' photographs of the rural poor or, perhaps more pertinently, Edward Weston's photographs of his *son* Neil posed as a classical Greek torso, is she simply dramatizing the diminished possibilities for creativity in an image-saturated culture, as is often repeated? Or is her refusal of authorship not in fact a refusal of the role of creator as 'father' of his work, of the paternal rights assigned to the author by law? Levine's disrespect for paternal authority suggests that her activity is less one of appropriation – a laying hold and grasping – and more one of expropriation: she expropriates the appropriators.
>
> (73)

Likewise, Cindy Sherman's photographs no longer merely deconstruct neutral cultural codes, but 'function as mirror-masks that reflect back at the viewer his own desire' (75) – Owens uses the male pronoun because the spectator posited by Sherman's work is 'invariably male'. And isn't Barbara Kruger speaking of the '*masculinity* of the look, the ways in which it objectifies and masters?' (77). Feminism thus offered one form of deconstructionist art a new lease of life, at least from the perspective of Owens and his associates. (From another perspective, they had been incomprehensibly slow in grasping that art's original intentions.) That Owens had brought feminist art effectively within the orbit of postmodern theory was in the course of the 1980s amply confirmed by the number of feminist responses. As Janet Wolff noted in 1990, '[t]he radical potential of an art practice which not only poses alternative images and ideologies, but refuses pre-existent and unitary categories of "woman" and "feminine", is clear' (Wolff 1990: 201). If Wolff – like many other feminist critics – ultimately chooses for 'a kind of modified modernism', that is, a modernism that no longer systematically excludes woman from its institutions and self-conception, she chooses in fact also for a modified deconstructionist postmodernism, which has abandoned the 'radical relativism and scepticism of much postmodern thought' that are 'incompatible with feminist (and indeed any radical) politics' (205).

The politics of anti-capitalism

If feminism was one way out of the deconstructionist impasse, a more rigorous institutional critique, involving questions of control and benefits, was the other. Such a 'resistant postmodernism' should, according to Hal Foster's preface in *The Anti-Aesthetic*, be concerned 'with a critical deconstruction of tradition . . . with a critique of origins' in order to explore 'social and political affiliation' (1983: xii). It should thus go beyond a merely aesthetic critique, and not merely 'destructure' representations but also 'reinscribe' them (xv). In the introduction to his *Recodings* of 1985, when Foster's postmodernism of resistance has taken firmer shape, we are told that 'any truly critical practice must transform rather than merely manipulate signification, (re)construct rather than simply disperse structures of subjectivity' (1985: 6). Although Foster in the essays collected in *Recodings* still invokes the Barthesian/Derridean vocabulary (with assists from Lacan, Adorno, Benjamin, and others) he has now moved away from a deconstructionism that is content to decenter and deconstruct. Instead, deconstructionist art – and criticism – should now expose the lamentable contemporary situation in which (cultural) signification is controlled by the ruling class, and in which art (at least in the United States) has become 'the plaything of (corporate) patrons whose relation to culture is less one of noble obligation than of overt manipulation – of art as a sign of power, prestige, publicity' (4). In other words, a deconstructionist postmodern art must now confront the inroads that capitalism has made into the world of high culture.

There is not much art that qualifies for the role, in Foster's view. What Foster calls neo-conservative postmodernism is condemned as profoundly ahistorical, even though it assumes historical forms, and accused of commercially exploiting the stylistic openings created by the deconstructionist art of the 1970s. Foster is especially hard on Jencks's and Stern's postmodern architecture, which, although parodic, only 'plays upon responses that are already programmed. In effect, architectural signs become commodities to be consumed' (28). The rapid politicization of Foster (followed by others involved in the deconstructionist attack of the late 1970s and early 1980s) is signaled by the fact that the more radical artists who still lay outside Foster's purview in the 1982 essay 'Subversive signs', have in the revised version of 1985 already lost much of their appeal because they, too, are in the last analysis not radical enough. Discussing the work of Daniel Buren, Michael Asher, Marcel Broodthaers, and Hans Haacke, Foster notes that of these four, once considered radically political in their attacks on the institution, only Haacke, with his emphasis on corporate and private collectors' interests, '*thematizes* the intertextuality of art and power', a practice which enables him 'to use the limits of the gallery/museum as a screen for his political attacks' (103).

Foster has some faith in a younger generation that, like Haacke, focuses on 'the economic manipulation of the art object – its circulation and consumption as a commodity-sign – more than its physical determination by its frame' (104). He is also kindly disposed towards feminist art, even though he still clings to a deconstructionist model (art that allows itself to slip 'into this fallacy of a true or positive image' reduces itself to 'ideology pure and simple, not its critique' (155)). But he puts his real faith in two 'models' of resistance, that of Deleuze and Guattari's 'minor' and that of Fredric Jameson's 'cultural revolution', which both avoid playing into the hands of the ubiquitous, virtually omnipotent late capitalist 'code' (Baudrillard's term). Jameson's 'revolution', which should 'restore the conflictual complexity of productive modes and sign-systems that is written out of the causal history of major culture' and 'decode how our own mode of domination exploits all old and new productive modes and sign-systems for its own purposes' (178), lies largely beyond the realm of culture as I have used the term here. As far as cultural politics is concerned, Jameson is decidedly pessimistic, seeing not much of a realistic possibility for truly oppositional practices within western culture. In his 'Hans Haacke and the cultural logic of postmodernism' (1986) he describes the strategy of Haacke's installations (as he had earlier described E.L. Doctorow's fiction in the same terms) as '*homeopathic*: ever greater doses of the poison – to choose and affirm the logic of the simulacrum to the point at which the very nature of that logic is itself dialectically transformed'. Such a strategy, reminiscent of Roland Barthes's notion that speech must be 'fought, led astray' within speech, is our only hope: 'modest and as frustrating as it sometimes may seem, a homeopathic cultural politics seems to be all we can currently think or imagine' (Jameson 1986b: 43).

By comparison, Deleuze and Guattari's notion of the 'minor' seemed more promising. It would, moreover, gain wide popularity in the second half of the 1980s. A 'minor' is, in Foster's words, 'an intensive, often vernacular use of a language or form which disrupts its official or institutional functions' (1985: 177). It cannot have hegemonic aspirations; it succumbs neither to a 'romance of the marginal' (knowing too much about marginality), nor to a 'romance of the subject' (it is supposed to thematize 'a postindividual experience based less on the dispersal of subjectivity than on the articulation of a collectivity' (177)); and has obvious deconstructionist aspects. Foster gives some examples of such an 'articulation of collectivity': Black gospel, reggae, surrealist Latin American fiction. Such minors, he argues, are resistant to semiotic appropriations, and are thus 'able to expose the very "mishmash" that the code seeks to exorcise' (178). In other words, they highlight difference where the 'code' seeks to establish unity. A minor will thus 'ruin or exceed the code as a system' (178).

Center and margin, elite and popular

Although minors are in themselves important, for Foster they can only achieve true political effectiveness if connections with other minors are established. But for many critics 'minors', especially in the form of subcultures within a hegemonic culture, were politically effective simply because of their marginal status. Not coincidentally, those subcultures were popular rather than elitist in orientation (of the examples that Foster gives, black gospel and reggae are obvious 'popular' forms). Indeed, the popular can itself be said to be marginal within the modernist scheme of things. A reevaluation of the popular will thus have anti-modernist, even implicitly deconstructionist implications. The popular, too, devalues concepts of uniqueness, of authorial genius, of formal purity, and so on, even if such devaluations are by-products rather than a conscious intention.

In the second half of the 1980s we see critics focus on the political potential of popular cultures, even of that totally commodified popular culture that we call mass culture. Against Jameson, Baudrillard, and others who have inherited the Frankfurt School's dim view of mass culture, John Wyver's 'Television and postmodernism' (1986) argues, for instance, that

> We live in a mass culture to which we do not simply submit. We take its images, its narratives, its formulations of desire, and measure them against our real experiences of a real world. At the same time we re-work and re-use them, in our conversation and gossip, in our fantasies, in every aspect of our lives. And this re-use is our individual form of resistance.
>
> (Wyver 1986: 54)

Along the same lines, Angela McRobbie suggests 'that the frenzied expansion of the mass media has political consequences which are not so wholly negative' (McRobbie 1986: 55). Ann Kaplan sees a similar political potential in some rock videos (Kaplan 1988: 39), while Kaja Silverman argues for the deconstructionist impulse implicit in so-called 'retro' fashion, which, 'by putting quotation marks around the garments it revitalizes', signals that 'the past is available to us only in a textual form, and through the mediation of the present' (Silverman 1986: 150). Retro fashions thus enable a critique of what mainstream culture considers 'natural'. What we see here is the same cautious return to the subject – or perhaps it is better to speak of agency – that more generally characterizes the postmodern debate after the mid–1980s. The position taken by Wyver, McRobbie, and a good many others in the second half of the eighties, is clearly influenced by the work of the University of Birmingham's Centre for Contemporary Cultural Studies and by feminist criticism, which had never abandoned agency or subjectivity (although it had, of course, abandoned the subject of patriarchy). McRobbie's 'Postmodernism and popular culture' (1986), for example, does not only put up a defense of mass culture, but also identifies a 'resistant' popular subculture that largely constitutes itself out of the odds and ends of mass culture:

> There is no recognition [in Jameson's 'Postmodernism and consumer society'] that those elements contained within his diagnosis of post-modernism – including pastiche, the ransacking and recycling of culture, the direct invocation to other texts and other images – can create a vibrant critique rather than an inward-looking, second-hand aesthetic. What else has black urban culture in the last few years been, but an assertive re-assembling of bits and pieces, 'whatever comes to hand', noises, debris, technology, tape, image, rapping, scratching, and other hand me downs?
> (57)

Such subcultures that exist 'within the cracks' of the hegemonic culture play a political role: 'Far from being overwhelmed by media saturation, there is evidence to suggest that these social groups and minorities are putting it to work for them' (58).

Jim Collins's *Uncommon Cultures: Popular Culture and Post-Modernism* (1989) offers a similar defense of popular culture. Arguing that 'the Berlozian vision of the artist as revolutionary and the Frankfurt School attacks on mass culture have been appropriated by popular as well as avant-garde texts' (1989: 15), he constructs a form of popular culture that is double coded in Charles Jencks's sense. There are, he tells us, 'numerous mass culture texts that construct fantasy visions of the state reminiscent of those imagined by the Frankfurt School' (14). Such mass cultural texts – one of his examples is Paul Verhoeven's *Robocop* – successfully aim at a mass audience while they simultaneously succeed in expressing the Frankfurt School's critique of mass culture. The sign systems of mass culture can thus be made politically effective (130).

George Lipsitz's 'Cruising around the historical bloc: postmodernism and popular music in East Los Angeles' goes even further and claims that 'minority group culture reflects the decentered and fragmented nature of contemporary human experience.' Lipsitz can then go on and suggest that those belonging to minorities 'often understand that their marginality makes them more appropriate spokespersons for society than mainstream groups unable to fathom or address the causes of their alienation' (Lipsitz 1986–7: 160). Fredric Jameson also privileges authentic margins over the inauthentic center in his 'On magic realism in film' (1986), but for him such authenticity is only to be found outside the late capitalist west, where all authenticity has been destroyed by the inexorable march of capital. Steven Connor points out that in a curious reversal the margin becomes the center, in such arguments, in that it can articulate what the center only vaguely apprehends. In fact, the mainstream is doubly alienated, on this account. It is not simply alienated from itself, it is also worried by its inability to trace the causes of its alienation.

There are some problems with this exaltation of the 'minor'. First of all, no matter where the marginal is located, in the real Third World, in Third World enclaves or in alienated subcultures within the affluent West, to privilege it in this way is a doubtful theoretical maneuver. Clearly western representation has no unmediated access to the real. As a consequence its representations are always representations of earlier representations and are inescapably political. It is not easy to see, however, why marginal cultures would have a more direct access to the real and why their representations and cultural practices would be less coded than those of mainstream western culture. One can agree that from the margins the coded nature of mainstream representation is more visible than from within the mainstream – and that this deconstructionist potential is politically important – but that does in no way privilege marginal representations as authentic. Another problem is that 'minors' do not automatically veer towards the progressive left in their alienation from mainstream politics. They may equally well subscribe to politics that belong to the extreme right. Marginality does not automatically grant political enlightenment, as a good many critics seem to believe.

However, in the course of the 1980s these sharp distinctions between what is politically correct and what isn't begin to dissolve, at least in the debate on cultural politics. A number of critics who started out from a radically oppositional position, such as Abigail Solomon-Godeau, begin to realize that, like critical art, critical writing, 'regardless of the writer's politics, can in no way consider itself as independent of the cultural apparatus it seeks to contest' (Solomon-Godeau 1988: 209). There is, moreover, a growing awareness that dependence and complicity are not necessarily all that bad. As John Tagg and others have pointed out, any cultural politics that wants to be effective will simply have to implicate itself in what it seeks to undo. In 1985, Hal Foster could still condemn the art of Thomas Lawson and David Salle for its strategy of 'sabotage in painting'; in the later 1980s, however, the once so sharp line of demarcation between resistance and complicity begins to fade. The model of a radical, purely resistant postmodern art gives way to a new model that proposes a postmodern cultural politics that both deconstructs and reconstructs simultaneously, in an unending dialectic with no prospect of a Hegelian sublation.

RESISTANCE AND COMPLICITY

In the 1980s, mass and popular culture were increasingly theorized in terms of political resistance, and thus, paradoxically, in terms that up till then had been reserved for high culture. Simultaneously, this upgrading of the political potential of mass culture was matched by a devaluation of that of high culture in yet another postmodern rapprochement between high and low culture. After the heyday of Foster's politically pure deconstructionist postmodernism had passed, high culture increasingly came to be seen in terms of complicity with the capitalist enemy. In the late 1980s and early 1990s such a complicity even gained a new respectability. Or perhaps it is better to say that it regained respectability. After all, Alan Wilde had already in the mid–1970s defended a deeply complicitous postmodern art, a postmodernism that, as he put it in 1982, managed to combine 'the problematic *and* the assentive' (Wilde 1982: 182). Charles Jencks's postmodernism, which took shape a little later, attempted a similar reconciliation of affirmation and critique, even though later it would largely lose its critical edge.

It is Jencks's model that, as we have already seen, was in the later 1980s borrowed by Linda Hutcheon to theorize a double coded postmodern literature (in her *A Poetics of Postmodernism: History, Theory, Fiction* of 1988) and a similarly double coded postmodern photography (which shares the limelight with literature in *The Politics of Postmodernism* of 1989). Postmodernism, Hutcheon argues, is 'unavoidably political' (1989: 1). However, it is also 'unavoidably compromised' (119). For Hutcheon, postmodernism 'ultimately manages to install and reinforce as much as undermine and subvert the conventions and presuppositions it appears to challenge' (1–2). Postmodernism thus both confirms and subverts representation, the subject, liberal humanism, and even capitalism itself. Complicity, she argues, is unavoidable, and perhaps even necessary, because 'you have to signal – and thereby install – that which you want to subvert' (152). This is not to say that Hutcheon's postmodernism has no elements in common with that of Crimp or Foster. She, too, takes care to draw a distinction between a deconstructionist 'postmodern parody' and the 'nostalgic, neoconservative recovery of past meaning going on in a lot of contemporary culture' (98), thus recalling Foster's distinction between a postmodernism of resistance and a neoconservative postmodernism, and her postmodern artists – Kruger, Haacke, Burgin, Levine, Sherman, Kelly – are familiar enough. Her postmodernism owes, in fact, a good deal more to deconstructionism than to Charles Jencks. Hutcheon's postmodernism follows deconstructionist postmodernism in seeing the problematization of representation as a political strategy. Like the deconstructionist avant-garde, Hutcheon situates freedom in process, not in resolution. What is significant is that she readmits representation in order to enable 'the investigation of the social and ideological production of meaning' (7). Also important is her readmission into the postmodern pantheon of a number of artists who, in the course of the 1980s, had been progressively thrown out by such ever more demanding purists as Crimp and Foster. Hutcheon deconstructs the rigid opposition between politically 'contaminated' art and politically 'pure' art that dominated much of the 1980s and her insistence on the inevitability of 'contamination' is an important step towards a less pure, that is, less modernist, and a politically more promising, even if more compromised, postmodernism.

Even more oppositions are deconstructed in Charles Altieri's 'The powers and the limits of oppositional postmodernism' (1990). Discussing the political positions of the British artist/critic Victor Burgin and of Hal Foster and the artistic practices of Sherrie Levine, Barbara Kruger, and Hans Haacke (in order of increasing political involvement), Altieri, who has once again followed the spirit of the times, finds them all wanting. Levine, whose work 'provided the clearest semantic model for what would later become the full politics of oppositional postmodernism' (1990: 448), is accused of 'tak[ing] refuge in processes of reproduction that she can control, without registering the degree to which we ourselves are reproduced within the plethora of images constituting imaginative life in a media-governed society' (449). Her position is thus one of false consciousness. Kruger, who avoids this particular trap in her struggle to control her own image, remains for Altieri 'so tied to bourgeois priorities that they can probably be reconciled with all manner of economic injustice, so long as there is increased sensitivity to questions of individual empowerment' (450). Only Haacke addresses wider issues of economic control and social injustice. Haacke's art, however, 'gives its audience no theater for self-consciousness except one whose primary values involve differentiating the morally righteous from those who commit gross atrocities' (475).

This would seem to suggest that whereas Levine's and Kruger's art is not political enough, Haacke's art is politically acceptable but too reductionist from a moral perspective. Altieri's objections, however, are more fundamental. His ultimate target is oppositional, resistant postmodernism itself, at least as theorized by Burgin and Foster. Altieri has no quarrel with Foster's politics or with those advocated – either implicitly or explicitly – by Foster's protégé(e)s, but in spite of that he has little sympathy with their efforts. First of all, they allow themselves to be guided by 'an abstract morality or an ideal of critical purity that ought to be highly suspicious to any political group', by a politics of 'an existential authenticity most compatible with traditional liberal principles of independence and critical lucidity' (458). As we have just seen, Hutcheon's model tries to break with this. Secondly, the art of resistance is so elitist that it can only be recognized as political within the art world. Thirdly, it 'can succeed only in terms of the very logic of simulacra that it rejects: the success of the artist consists in being recognized by the art world for producing certain effects within the approved information system' (458). Like Hutcheon, Altieri recognizes the inevitably compromised nature of all, and therefore also all political, art. What is even worse, however, is that Foster and Burgin's oppositional art 'cannot actually focus substantial political discussion because its language of resistance allows neither the self-representation nor the respect for the other necessary for significant debate' (461):

> the abstract bleakness emphasized by political artists traps their work into ignoring important differences both in the qualities of particular states and in the resources enabling individuals to find relief from that oppression. In the name of politics, art fails to make distinctions among aspects of bourgeois life, while doing very little to convince us that political action will change what is most disturbing in our culture. Ironically, the emphasis on critique deprives art of those modes of idealization which might build upon those possible individual states to project plausible goals for the political order.
>
> (468)

Again like Hutcheon, Altieri deconstructs the (two) moral categories set up by such oppositional art by mobilizing the eminently postmodern notion of difference against its rigid binarism.

Altieri's criticisms are of course not wholly new. They are sophisticated and radicalized reformulations of objections voiced earlier by feminist and black critics against the undifferentiated character of much postmodern politics. However, taking his recognition of art's compromised nature to its logical consequence, Altieri then makes a surprising plea for the political potential of the openly representational (and accommodating) art so despised by theorists on the left. Such art, although based upon 'a frankly bourgeois aesthetic' (468) is not necessarily wholly subservient to the establishment: 'Accommodation does not require rejecting all critical functions for art, but it does require recognizing one's dependency on the others that one criticizes' (475). Moreover, its playfulness 'allows us to keep in touch with those parts of the psyche's capacities for pleasure and identification which all too easily become subordinated to the realism of the marketplace or to the counterrealism of political opposition' (476). At the very least, Altieri tells us, the 'lyricism' of the two female painters that he discusses (and who Foster and probably even Hutcheon would consider at best neo-conservative)

> reminds us of the personal states that we want our political commitments to make possible for greater numbers of people, while also holding out the promise that art can temper the psychological violence inherent in formulating and pursuing those political goals.
>
> (476–7)

Altieri's travels through the postmodern, that began with a commitment to a Heideggerian postmodernism of immanence, and that put him in the late 1970s on the poststructuralist barricades, have, at least for the time being, ended in a tempered, humane, view of the narrow margins within which the human condition can be effectively addressed. But perhaps he has left the postmodern behind, depending on one's view. Foster would certainly think so, and so would Crimp, Hutcheon, and most other critics involved in the debate. On the other hand, postmodernism has never stayed long in one particular place and the critical tide would now seem to move wholly towards the new forms of representation signaled first in the seventies. For all we know, the very modest postmodern politics that Altieri sees at work in the paintings of Jennifer Bartlett and Elizabeth Murray, and that remind one of the postmodern bourgeois liberalism of Richard Rorty (see Chapter 7), may already be replacing those of Sherman, Levine, Kruger, Haacke and others.

NOTES

1 The generally Althusserian interest in ideology and its 'naturalizing' effects upon reality as experienced by those subjects who have successfully been 'interpellated' or called by ideology and *Screen*'s interest in the political effects of formal properties, of 'signifying practices', are clearly related to the postmodern cultural politics that I'm outlining here. However, the insistence of Althusser and his followers on the scientific nature of their project, their conviction that they themselves stand outside ideology and can thus speak from an external vantage point, is too much at odds with what is central to postmodernism.

2 The extent to which poststructuralism was identified with purely textual approaches is illustrated by the definition that Rosalind Krauss published in the *Soho Art Supplement* of 29 September 1981. Poststructuralism, she argued, 'is grounded in the fundamental perception that nothing cultural escapes writing – that everything is modelled on the structure of language and the process of inscription. Cultural reality is thus linguistic and grammatological' (p. 5).

3 The exhibition was appropriately called 'Image Scavengers' and showed work by what had in the meantime become the old guard (Barbara Kruger, Cindy Sherman, Sherrie Levine, Richard Prince) and by a new generation of appropriators. It was the new generation that incurred Crimp's wrath.

4 This is not to say that purely deconstructionist art lost all credibility overnight. In some disciplines deconstructionism managed to retain its political aura well into the late 1980s. For example, Philip Auslan-

der's 1987 discussion of the Wooster Group's *L.S.D. (. . . Just the High Points . . .*) still clearly identifies a deconstructionist theatrical practice with a 'postmodern political theatre' (Auslander 1987: 21).

5 I will limit myself at this point to summarizing Owens's argument. For an overview of the discussion of the (ambivalent) feminist response, see Chapter 9, note 1.

Part II

. . . AND POSTMODERNITIES

6

THE 1980s

Theorizing the postmodern condition

INTRODUCTION

Up till the early 1980s the debate on postmodernism remained almost exclusively confined to architecture and to the arts, even if some of the critics involved were more than willing to diagnose a new *Zeitgeist*. But all of that would change dramatically in the course of the 1980s when postmodernism began to engage the serious attention of professional philosophers and of leftist critics of a more traditional persuasion than that of Douglas Crimp, Hal Foster, and others. Between 1981 and 1984 postmodernism became an indispensable concept in theories of the contemporary – to borrow from the subtitle of Steven Connor's book on the postmodern.[1] Jürgen Habermas, Jean-François Lyotard, Fredric Jameson, Jean Baudrillard, and Richard Rorty definitively put postmodernism and postmodernity on the theoretical map. The contributions of Habermas and Jameson mark the long overdue participation of the traditional left in the debate, Baudrillard emerges as the champion of the radical left, and Lyotard and Rorty, in spite of their important differences, paradoxically come to represent a domesticated postmodernism, a safe and respectable postmodernism to which even liberal humanists, although they might not share all its premises, cannot very well take exception without giving the appearance of puritanical intolerance.

The first indication of the new direction that the debate would take – and simultaneously a major impulse to that reorientation – was the article that the German philosopher Jürgen Habermas published in *New German Critique* in 1981. Titled 'Modernity versus postmodernity', the article translated the speech Habermas had given the year before in Frankfurt at the occasion of being awarded the City of Frankfurt's Adorno Prize. Habermas's speech was provoked by the attacks on cultural modernism by Daniel Bell and other neo-conservatives and by the even more violent attacks on modernity – and in particular the rationality that was held responsible for the ills of modernity – that were part and parcel of the French poststructuralism that had taken the intellectual world by storm in the course of the 1970s. In his speech Habermas sought to defend the still unrealized potential of the Enlightenment. The most radically anti-rational exponent of the poststructuralism that had caused Habermas's wrath was Jean-François Lyotard, who even if Habermas never mentions him is generally seen as his major target.

At the time, Lyotard was hardly known in the US, although he had published a number of articles in, for instance, *Yale French Studies* and *Semiotext(e)*. But one of his links with the American critical scene would be of great importance for the history of the debate. In November 1976 he had attended 'The International Symposium on Post-Modern Performance' organized by the Center for Twentieth Century Studies of the University of Wisconsin at Milwaukee, surely one of the first-ever conferences to refer to the postmodern in its title. It is tempting to think that the keynote speaker, Ihab Hassan, did actually make him aware of the term's potential right then and there. Lyotard's reference in the printed version of his own paper to what he at that point clearly saw as Hassan postmodernism – 'the theatrical, critical, artistic, and perhaps political inquiries which make up what Ihab Hassan calls "post-modernism" ' (Lyotard 1977: 95) – certainly suggests as much. (Hassan paid back the compliment of quotation in his 'The critic as innovator: the Tutzing statement in x frames' of 1977.)[2] In any case, around the mid-1970s Hassan was one of the very few to use the term consistently in print and Lyotard has openly acknowledged his debt to Hassan (Lyotard 1984c: 85).

It is one of the ironies of the history of the debate that *La Condition postmoderne* was not translated until 1984. The irony is compounded, moreover, by the way that translation was embedded between a rather dismissive introductory foreword by Fredric Jameson, who in the meantime had entered the debate with 'Postmodernism and consumer society' (1983), and an appendix that must have been the source of serious confusion. That appendix, called 'Answering the question: what is postmodernism?' was a translation of Lyotard's 'Réponse à la question: qu'est-ce que le post-moderne' of 1982, which instead of the 'postmodern condition' has aesthetic postmodernism as its subject and at first sight has not all that much in common with the earlier essay. (An earlier translation of 'Réponse' had appeared in Ihab and Sally Hassan's collection *Innovation/Renovation: New Perspectives on the Humanities* of 1983, but Lyotard's impact obviously dates from after the publication of *The Postmodern Condition.*) As the upshot of all this one of the major players of the 1980s made a belated and somewhat unfortunate entry into the game. (As a further complication, the book that had paved the way for *La Condition postmoderne*, a set of dialogues with Jean-Loup Thébaud entitled *Au Juste* (in English, *Just Gaming*) wasn't translated until 1985.)

Similar vicissitudes befell another major force in the debate as it unfolded in the course of the 1980s, the work of Lyotard's one-time associate (in the *Socialisme ou barbarie* group) Jean Baudrillard. Originally a sociologist, Baudrillard had in the course of the 1970s gradually abandoned classical – and leftist – sociology in favor of an apodictic and increasingly apocalyptic theorizing that turned out to have great appeal for the American critical left. Like Lyotard, Baudrillard had made earlier appearances upon the American scene, but it was only when *October* translated one of his articles in 1982 and especially after *In the Shadow of the Silent Majorities* and *Simulations* (which includes the famous 'The precession of simulacra') were published in 1983 that his name was made as an important theorist of the postmodern.

Because of their respective translation histories, a historical account of Lyotard's and Baudrillard's contributions to the debate is by no means a straightforward matter, especially not if one wants to respect the inner logic of their work's development. (In Lyotard's case that logic is almost completely obscured by the way in which his work has become available in English. His *Economie libidinale* of 1974 had to wait until 1992 before it was published integrally.) Habermas presents much less of a problem; he is, moreover, relatively marginal to the debate, given his insistence that modernity is still an 'incomplete project',[3] and his assertion that what Lyotard calls the postmodern is not much more than a throwback to Nietszchean irrationalism, in other words, an anti-modern rather than post-modern phenomenon.

The work of Richard Rorty and Fredric Jameson has for obvious reasons not been dogged by translation problems. Like Habermas, Rorty cannot very well be considered a fully-fledged theorist of the postmodern. At a number of occasions Rorty has advanced the idea that his version of traditional American pluralism is what postmodernism is (or at least should be) all about. Relaxed and affable in an avuncular way, Rorty has undoubtedly struck a responsive chord in large numbers of mainstream critics, but he remains, as we shall see, a theorist of American pluralism as a *Weltanschauung* rather than one of postmodernity.

Fredric Jameson is not avuncular, but he certainly has come to occupy a central position in the debate. After 'Postmodernism and consumer society' of 1983, Jameson produced a steady stream of articles that theorized various aspects of the postmodern, always from a traditional Marxist point of view, although gradually incorporating – or perhaps paying lip-service to – the poststructuralist critique of Marxist totalization in his work of the later 1980s. Jameson's work is, with Hassan's pioneering effort, the most significant American contribution to the debate and the first serious attempt to fully contextualize the postmodern, that is, see it in terms of (global) political economy. Later attempts to come to terms with a postmodernism that manifests itself as much in the socio-economic and political sphere as in the cultural-philosophical sphere, such as David Harvey's *The Condition of Postmodernity: An Enquiry into the Origins of Cultural Change* (1989), invariably take their departure from Jameson.

This and the following chapters will deal with this international cast. I will begin with a brief discussion of Habermas, not so much because of his importance as a theorist of the postmodern, but because his philosophical project, which can only be sketched in the most general terms here, provides a constant and formidable background of which all postmodern theorizing cannot help being aware. The presence of Habermas looms in the background, even if he is not invoked.

JÜRGEN HABERMAS AND POST-RATIONALIST MODERNITY

As I have noted earlier, the left's engagement with the postmodern was initially not a fruitful one. When it finally did enter the discussion, it was the avant-gardist left rather than its more traditional counterpart, which preferred to keep its distance.

This curious vacuum gave Jürgen Habermas's 'intervention' of 1981, the publication of his 1980 Adorno lecture in *New German*

Critique, its special, trail-blazing character. Habermas does not only offer a lucid and provocative account of modernity and modernism, he also articulates clearly what from a left-liberal perspective is ultimately at stake. But before we arrive at a discussion of 'Modernity versus postmodernity' we must look briefly at the intellectual position that had made Habermas the obvious target of Lyotard's *La Condition postmoderne*.

Central to Habermas's thought is that, in spite of admitted disasters, the Enlightenment, the emancipatory project of modernity, must not be abandoned. Unlike most poststructuralists of the 1960s and 1970s, Habermas is not prepared to see a monolithic rationality as the sole cause of the ills of modernity. Like them, he is wary of 'the snares of Western logocentrism' (1985: 196), that is, of a 'foundationalism that conflicts with our consciousness of the fallibility of human knowledge' (193; note, however, Habermas's non-poststructuralist reasons for his wariness), but he insists that for political reasons we cannot dispense with rationality or with a philosophy that seeks to defend (non-foundationalist) rationalism. Defending philosophy against the irreverent attacks of Richard Rorty, he remarks that '[t]he stubbornness with which philosophy clings to the role of the "guardian of reason" can hardly be dismissed as an idiosyncrasy of self-absorbed intellectuals, especially in a period in which basic irrationalist undercurrents are transmuted once again into a dubious form of politics' (195). Habermas's problem, then, is to define and to argue the plausibility of a rationality that distinguishes itself from the rationality denounced by the poststructuralists and that is not transcendent in the sense that it is foundationalist, but yet transcends the limitations of time and place. Such a rationality, although inevitably subject to change over time, must have a 'unifying power' that will enable a workable consensus. Without such a rationality, emancipatory, that is, leftist politics become an illusion.

Now Habermas is of course not unaware of the obstacles in the way to what in his massive *The Theory of Communicative Action* (originally 1981) he calls 'communicative reason'. There is, first of all, the problem of the three 'cultural value spheres' that Max Weber, following Kant, distinguished. Each of these spheres – the theoretical (science), the practical (morality), and the aesthetic (art) – has its own inner logic that cannot be easily reconciled with those of the others. Contrary to the hopes of the Enlightenment, these spheres have become increasingly differentiated, to the point where they are now 'separated from each other institutionally in the form of functionally specified systems of action' (199). We are faced, therefore, with 'three different forms of argumentation: namely, empirical-theoretical discourse, moral discourse, and aesthetic critique', three different 'rationality complexes' (207) that have their own, different, institutional embeddings and have, moreover, become virtual monopolies of coteries of experts. Far from informing and enriching everyday life, as the Enlightenment expected, they have increasingly distanced themselves from the 'life-world'. A further complication is that under the regime of 'capitalist modernization' the empirical-theoretical, or cognitive-instrumental, rationality complex has so clearly come to dominate and marginalize other modes of knowing. It has, moreover, more and more developed into a mercenary means-end rationalism. It is this rationalism, Habermas agrees, that fully deserves the poststructuralist charges, but to equate modernity with such a narrow means-end rationalism is to seriously misread its project.

In order to reconnect these rationality complexes at the level of the life-world and to counter what he calls the 'colonization' of the life-world by instrumental rationality, Habermas develops his concept of 'communicative reason' or 'communicative rationality'. *The Theory of Communicative Action* argues that the structure of language itself, its procedural rationality, offers us the means to arrive at a form of communication that is not strategic, that is, does not serve other interests than those of perfecting itself, of creating absolutely unimpeded communication. In this imagined 'ideal speech situation' communication will 'no longer be distorted', in Christopher Norris's words, 'by effects of power, self-interest or ignorance' (Norris 1985: 149). For Habermas, who like his opponents rejects intuition and metaphysics in defining what is reasonable, a universal rationality that is latently present in the procedures that structure argumentative discourse can be brought to light 'through the analysis of the *already* operative potential for rationality contained in the everyday practices of communication' (196). Following French theory, albeit at a safe distance and with wholly different intentions, Habermas, too, gives language an absolutely central place. As Thomas Docherty has put it, in Habermas 'Marxism has taken "the linguistic turn" ' (Docherty 1993: 3).

The notion that language offers formal procedures for adjudicating differences – that is, competing truth claims – and can thus cure the ills of our one-sided modernity, leads Habermas away from what he sees as a typically modernist, subjectivistic, 'philosophy of consciousness' towards a philosophy of intersubjectivity, that is, of communication and consensus (a 'non-reified everyday communicative practice' is 'a form of life with structures of an undistorted intersubjectivity' (210)). Such a consensus is of course predicated upon a general willingness to accept communicative rationality. It rests, therefore, not only on that rationality's scientific status, but also on individual acts of social solidarity. It 'requires a democratic context in which anyone may question the argumentative claims of anyone else, so long as each party aims at consensus and agrees to concur with positions that he or she cannot refute' (Poster 1989: 23). Habermas's intersubjectivity is thus all-inclusive in that the only ones who are excluded by his procedural approach are those who exclude themselves by rejecting its procedures, that is, communicative reason. The desirability of an intersubjectivistic consensus built upon communicative reason marks Habermas's distance from the deconstructionist avant-gardists (and their supporters, such as Lyotard) of the previous chapter. For Habermas anti-representationalism can indeed have emancipatory aspects in that it may serve to trigger changes that will bring us closer to the ultimate consensus that communicative reason has enabled, but it can never be an end in itself. On the contrary, the permanent representational crisis of the deconstructionists will never lead to the consensus that Habermas envisages and thus effectively blocks the implementation of the left-liberal politics that he advocates, that is, the completion of the project of modernity. Habermas mobilizes an utopian representation that is ultimately enabled by a quasi-transcendental communicative rationality against the attacks on representation by a deconstructionist avant-garde for whom emancipation depends precisely on the anti-representational impulse. Progress comes about by untiring attempts to achieve an ever more enlightened consensus on the basis of reasoned debate, not by way of a permanent crisis that refuses to resolve itself. As Richard Rorty has put it: 'Abandoning a standpoint which is, if not transcendental, at least "universalistic," seems to Habermas to betray the social hopes which have been central to liberal politics' (Rorty 1985: 162).

To be sure, Habermas is not the only contemporary thinker who refuses to give up on the 'unifying, consensus-creating power of reason' (197), but his undisputed stature as a philosopher makes him the most formidable of those who believe in what one might call a post-rationalist modernity. He was, therefore, the natural target for the attack by Jean-François Lyotard that I will discuss later in this chapter.

HABERMAS AND POSTMODERNISM

'Modernity versus postmodernity', the title under which Habermas's Adorno lecture of 1980 appeared in English, is a densely packed piece. It presents an analysis of (aesthetic) modernism, it defends that modernism against 'neo-conservative' detractors (such as Daniel Bell), it gives an explanation for the 'failure' of the surrealist revolt, and it ends with an overview of anti-modernists and their positions, ranging from the 'old conservatives' to the 'neo-conservatives' by way of the 'young conservatives'. Even this short outline should make clear that Habermas brought a new intellectual dimension to the debate. By way of reminder: when Habermas presented 'Modernity versus postmodernity' as a lecture in New York, in March 1981, the American discussion of the postmodern encompassed William Spanos's Heideggerian postmodern, the all-inclusive but elusive postmodernism of Ihab Hassan, the architectural postmodernism of Charles Jencks and Robert Stern, the attack on representation by the deconstructionist avant-garde, and the dismissive and irritable attitude of the traditional left, as exemplified by Gerald Graff's collection *Literature Against Itself* of 1979. Habermas's 'intervention' had the welcome effect of widening the intellectual and historical scope of the debate and of substantially adding to its depth. Even if he himself never took part in it, Habermas cleared the way for the serious engagement of the traditional left with the postmodern that came under way in the course of the 1980s in, for instance, the work of Andreas Huyssen and that of Fredric Jameson.

The importance of 'Modernity versus postmodernity' lies in this historical role, rather than in any theory of the postmodern that it offers. As my outline has made clear, the postmodern is only marginally present in Habermas's qualified defense of modernism. But even that defense, with its focus on the historical avant-garde, is of interest to the debate on the postmodern, as would somewhat later be Peter Bürger's *Theory of the Avant-Garde* (1984), on the 1974 German original of which Habermas partly draws.

'Modernity versus postmodernity' opens with a strategical maneuver that from an Anglo-American point of view must be decidedly surprising: it locates the spirit of modernism exclusively in the avant-garde and its nineteenth-century precursors. 'The spirit and discipline of aesthetic modernity assumed clear contours in the work of Baudelaire. Modernity then unfolded in various avant-garde movements, and finally reached its climax in the Café Voltaire of the Dadaists' (1981: 4). This avant-gardistic modernism (or aesthetic modernity, as Habermas prefers to call it here) 'understands itself as invading unknown territory', a 'yet unoccupied future', and discloses in its very celebration of dynamism a 'longing for an undefiled, an immaculate and stable present' (4–5). After noting the recent revival of this avant-gardist impulse in the art of the 1960s – which he, then, does *not* see in postmodernist terms – Habermas defends it against the accusations of 'hedonistic motives' leveled against it by Daniel Bell in *The Cultural Contradictions of Capitalism.* In Habermas's reading, or perhaps it is better to speak of misreading, Bell makes the mistake of holding the 'adversary culture' responsible for a dissolution of the Protestant ethic that in truth is caused by the very processes of modernization that Bell supports: 'protest and discontent originate exactly when spheres of communicative action, centered on the reproduction and transmissions of values and norms, are penetrated by a form of modernization guided by standards of economic and administrative rationality' (7–8). Habermas sees the split between social modernization and modernist culture as a reactive defense against the increased penetration of the life-world by 'economic and administrative rationality'.

What is more, he sees aesthetic modernity (avant-gardist modernism) as engaged in an attempt to enable a return to the project of modernity as it was originally conceived. That project, as formulated by the philosophers of the Enlightenment,

> consisted in their efforts to develop objective science, universal morality and law, and autonomous art, according to their inner logic. At the same time, this project intended to release the cognitive potentials of each of these domains to set them free from their esoteric forms. The

> Enlightenment philosophers wanted to utilize this accumulation of specialized culture for the enrichment of everyday life, that is to say, for the rational organization of everyday social life.
>
> (9)

In Habermas's analysis of modernity, the project has foundered because of the absolute domination of 'objective science' under capitalism; the empirical-theoretical, or cognitive-instrumental, rationality complex (called 'functional rationality' in his more recent work), has marginalized all other modes of cognition and has thus effectively thwarted the hoped-for 'rational organization of everyday social life'. Following Peter Bürger's lead, Habermas argues that the avant-garde, and in particular the surrealists, in trying to bridge the gulf between art and everyday life sought to bring about a reintegration of that which under the pressure of functional rationality had been differentiated. To do so, the avant-garde saw itself forced to first break out of the self-imposed isolation that had served to protect art against the ever more threatening encroachment of functional rationality and forced too to divest art of the aura (in Walter Benjamin's sense) that had served the same purpose. But the avant-gardist revolt was doomed to fail. As Habermas puts it, 'when the containers of an autonomously developed cultural sphere are shattered, the contents get dispersed. Nothing remains from a desublimated meaning or a destructured form; an emancipatory effect does not follow' (10). When the protective shield is dropped, the futility of artistic intervention is revealed. Apart from that, even if successful, the 'surrealist revolt would have replaced only one abstraction' while true emancipation can only be based on simultaneous revolutionary action in all three domains: 'A reified everyday praxis can be cured only by creating unconstrained interaction of the cognitive with the moral-practical and the aesthetic-expressive elements. Reification cannot be overcome by forcing just one of those highly stylized cultural spheres to open up and become more accessible' (11). Needless to say that such an overall revolution and the ensuing general de-reification do not seem to be on the cards for quite a while and that as a result the deconstructionist avant-garde of the late 1970s and early 1980s is bound to suffer a fate similar to that of its predecessors.

Still, the original project of modernity should not be abandoned. To give up means to hand over modernity to those who will abuse it, that is, to those who will reify one of its spheres and 'aestheticize politics' or, alternatively, 'replace politics by moral rigorism' or 'submit it to the dogmatism of doctrine' (11). Contrary to what Lyotard and other poststructuralists have argued, these phenomena, although all too real, historically, should not be identified with modernity as it was originally conceived, and should not lead us 'into denouncing the intentions of the surviving Enlightenment tradition as intentions rooted in a "terroristic reason" ' (11).

As I have noted above, Habermas distinguishes between three different conservative positions: the 'premodernism' of the 'old conservatives' (F.R. Leavis, although Habermas does not mention him, perfectly fits the bill), the 'anti-modernism' of the 'young conservatives' (Foucault, Derrida, and their followers), and the 'postmodernism' of the 'neo-conservatives', that is, Daniel Bell and others (13–14). To begin with the neo-conservatives, these at first sight rather unlikely postmodernists accept the finality of the separation of the spheres of science, morality, and art from each other and from the life-world, and they accept the ascendancy of functional rationality (at the expense of morality) on the level of social organization (politics). Since, from Habermas's point of view, they have thereby chosen to give up the project of modernity and have effectively moved beyond it, they are the only true postmodernists in sight.

The young conservatives, a category that includes Foucault and Derrida, have, by contrast, not moved beyond modernity at all. Heeding the call of Nietzsche, they 'recapitulate the basic experience of aesthetic modernity', claiming 'as their own the revelations of a decentered subjectivity, emancipated from the imperatives of work and usefulness' (13). In a passage that suggests the early Lyotard and Deleuze/Guattari rather than Derrida – with Foucault hovering in between – Habermas asserts that the young conservatives

> remove into the sphere of the far away and the archaic the spontaneous powers of imagination, of self-experience and of emotionality. To instrumental reason, they juxtapose in manichean fashion a principle only accessible through evocation, be it the will to power or sovereignty, Being or the dionysiac force of the poetical.
>
> (13)

Four years later, in a footnote undoubtedly prompted by the fierce criticism that this characterization of the poststructuralist effort had provoked, Habermas still stood by his original analysis: 'They all take from Nietzsche the radical gesture of a break with modernity and a revolutionary renewal of pre-modern energies, most often reaching back to archaic times' (1985: 229). By then, moreover, his contention that poststructuralism replayed modernist tunes with a somewhat radicalized score had found influential supporters such as Andreas Huyssen.

In 1981, however, Habermas's historical positioning of the poststructuralist enterprise and his reading of poststructuralism as an anti-progressive force did not make much of an impression. Neither did 'Modernity versus postmodernity' have much impact in terms of its analysis of the postmodern; a critical milieu for which postmodernism had in the meantime become equated with radical politics had obviously little use for a redefinition in terms of technocratic conservatism. The essay, however, made very clear in which ways what was left of the project of modernity was endangered and suggested that an engagement with the forces of anti-modernism was a moral duty for those who wished to save that project from oblivion. Moreover, 'Modernity versus postmodernity' provided a kind of solid backdrop, an old-fashioned norm against which other efforts to define the postmodern or to develop a postmodern politics could be measured. As for instance Linda Hutcheon's model has already suggested, in the later 1980s and early 1990s postmodernism developed more and more into a dialogic space intellectually bounded on the one side by Habermasian consensus – that is, representation – and on the other by the radical dissensus – or anti-representationalism – proposed by Lyotard. That anti-representationalism will be discussed in the following section.

MULTIVALENCE AND POLYPHONY: JEAN-FRANÇOIS LYOTARD

Presenting Lyotard's position – or, rather, positions – is no straightforward matter. Doing justice to his trajectory prior to his sudden American fame would at least require a survey of his work of the early 1970s, *Discours, figure* (1971), *Dérive à partir de Marx et Freud* (1973), and *Economie libidinale* (1974). But that would give a false impression of his role in the debate on the postmodern, which has its proper beginning in 1984 when *La Condition postmoderne* of 1979 appeared in English. It is only after 1984 that Lyotard's new Anglophone readership was led to his earlier work, in which they found a substantially different Lyotard, who, according to some, is more postmodern than the later Lyotard of *La Condition.*

Since 1984 Lyotard's authority has been invoked in two separate attempts to come to terms with the postmodern that are substantially different in their intellectual premises. The first bases itself on *The Postmodern Condition,* the second on the earlier work. There is, moreover, the not inconsiderable influence of Lyotard's notion of a 'postmodern sublime', first proposed in 'Answering the question: what is postmodernism?' of 1983. That postmodern sublime deserves separate treatment, even if its theater of operations remains limited to the arts. However, since the impact of Lyotard has its proper beginning with the publication of *The Postmodern Condition* I will leave the chronology of Lyotard's intellectual career for what it is and begin this brief discussion of his work with *The Postmodern Condition.*

THE POSTMODERN CONDITION: A REPORT ON KNOWLEDGE

As its subtitle indicates, *The Postmodern Condition* is not so much a study of postmodernity *tout court,* but rather a study of postmodern knowledge, or, as Lyotard puts it in his preface, 'the condition of knowledge in the most highly developed societies' (Lyotard 1984c: xxiii). Although he has indeed some things to say about the world under postmodernity, there is little, if anything, that is new here. His remarks on late twentieth-century social developments follow mostly the familiar scenario of the postindustrial society as sketched by Alain Touraine, Daniel Bell, and others, the scenario in which information replaces the manufacture of material goods as a central concern in the most advanced economies.[4] This 'computerization of society' (67) will affect the nature of our knowledge. It is not very clear how exactly our knowledge will change, but Lyotard offers the prediction that 'the direction of new research will be dictated by the possibility of its eventual results being translatable into computer language' (4). Knowledge, moreover, has become 'an informational commodity'; science has been forced to abandon its original integrity and has become an instrument in the hands of power (46). As in Habermas's analysis, in Lyotard's account of modernity instrumental rationality has come to dominate other forms of reason. But that is virtually all he has to say about the sociopolitical aspects of knowledge under the regime of postmodernity – a knowledge not to be confused with postmodern knowledge, as will become clear below. The social and the political are seemingly relegated to the background, even if the criticisms leveled at postindustrial capitalism occasionally remind us of Lyotard's former, but since long abandoned, Marxist orientation.

Lyotard's point of departure is the demise of what he terms 'metanarratives': 'Simplifying to the extreme, I define *postmodern* as incredulity towards metanarratives' (xxiv). Those metanarratives or 'grand' narratives are, broadly speaking, the supposedly transcendent and universal truths that underpin western civilization and that function to give that civilization objective legitimation, a term that Lyotard borrows from Habermas and that will turn out to be *The Postmodern Condition*'s key concept. All of this is wholly in keeping with the general, textualizing thrust of French theory of the 1960s and 1970s. Building upon the later Wittgenstein Lyotard suggests that these metanarratives have been replaced by a great number of 'language games'. These language games range from Wittgensteinian 'models of discourse', that is, various forms of utterance – denotative, performative, prescriptive, etc. – that all follow their own specific set of rules, via the discourses that are employed by social institutions and professions, to full-scale narratives (for which he also uses the term *petit récits* or little narratives). Such narrative language games can accommodate elements such as 'deontic statements prescribing what should be done . . . with respect to kinship, the difference between the sexes, children, neighbors, foreigners, etc.' (20). In other words, narrative language games can even underpin whole cultures. However, because of their narrative status such language games can have only limited social and historical validity, or, in Lyotard's terms, legitimation, even if to those who live inside them they seem inevitable and natural ('Narratives . . . define what has the right to be said and done in the culture in question, and since they are themselves a part of that culture, they are legitimated by the simple fact that they do what they do' (23)).

Lyotard is of course aware that practically all metanarratives have since long been unmasked as fictions, even if they have not necessarily lost their popular appeal because of that. One language game, however, still tenaciously clings to its special status. Modern science has successfully managed to safeguard its aura of transcendence. It has done so, Lyotard argues, by privileging the language game of 'denotation' to the exclusion of all others. Scientific knowledge sees itself as standing outside and above all language games, that is, outside and above narration. But that, Lyotard argues, is an untenable position. Science, too, can only find legitimation through narrative: 'Scientific knowledge cannot know and make known that it is the true knowledge without resorting to the other, narrative, kind of knowledge, which from its point of view is no knowledge at all' (29).

Lyotard's real object in *The Postmodern Condition* is to expose the legitimation of science and thus the transcendent status of scientific knowledge as belonging to the realm of narrative. In Lyotard's analysis, the modern pursuit of knowledge is characterized by the way it legitimates itself through a metadiscourse that makes 'an explicit appeal to some grand narrative, such as the dialectics of Spirit, the hermeneutics of meaning, the emancipation of the rational or working subject, or the creation of wealth' (xxiii). There are two major versions of this 'narrative of legitimation': a political one that we have inherited from the French Enlightenment and a philosophical one that we have inherited from German idealism. In the political version the pursuit of knowledge is justified, in Axel Honneth's words, 'by way of a philosophy of history which construes the history of the species as a process of emancipation'. The 'legitimating instance' here is 'the moral principle of universal freedom'. In the philosophical version, legitimation is provided by 'a philosophy of history which construes the process of history as a realisation of Reason in the sciences'; here it is the principle of universal knowledge that functions as the legitimating instance (Honneth 1985: 151).

Lyotard argues that, first of all, such legitimations have lost their power: 'Speculative or humanistic philosophy is forced to relinquish its legitimation duties' (41). He does not explain why that should be the case, except by a vague reference to internal erosion, nor does he convincingly argue why the loss of transcendent legitimation should be so damaging to science (in fact, it is not difficult to see that it isn't). But his real target is not science itself, or its transcendent status, but the principle of transcendent legitimation itself. It goes without saying that the utilitarian, capitalist, legitimation by way of performativity, 'the best input/output equation' – the instrumental reason which for both Habermas and Lyotard has virtually displaced the theoretical reason that sees the discovery of 'truth' as the goal of science (46) – is wholly unacceptable. And so he turns to Wittgenstein for 'a kind of legitimation not based on performativity'. Non-performative, immanent legitimation is what the postmodern world is all about (41). As Nancy Fraser and Linda Nicholson put it in a discussion of Lyotard's relevance for feminist theory, 'in the postmodern era legitimation becomes plural, local, and immanent. . . . Instead of hovering above, legitimation descends to the level of practice and becomes immanent in it' (1988: 87). Narrative is thus for Lyotard the inevitable source of all legitimation, and therefore of all value and truth.

Under the new, postmodern, dispensation a basically modern science that seeks to legitimate itself through appeals to metanarratives still survives, even if it has meanwhile succumbed to the performativity principle, that is, become merely instrumental. Next to it we have now, however, a postmodern science that sees itself as a language game and finds its legitimation in its own avant-gardist strategies:

> Postmodern science – by concerning itself with such things as undecidables, the limits of precise control, conflicts characterized by incomplete information, 'fracta,' catastrophes, and pragmatic paradoxes – is theorizing its own evolution as discontinuous, catastrophic, nonrectifiable, and paradoxical. It is changing the meaning of the word *knowledge,* while expressing how such a change can take place. It is producing not the known, but the unknown. And it suggests a model of legitimation that has nothing to do with maximized performance, but has as its basis difference understood as paralogy.
>
> (60)

It is this postmodern science that more generally stands for the entire 'postmodern condition'. Whereas modern science worked towards stable, timeless representations of the world, postmodern science seeks to be expressly anti-representational. In other words, it seeks to prevent consensus, which is, indeed, exactly what it from Lyotard's point of view must do, unlikely as that may seem. Arguing that Habermas's promotion of consensus – 'an agreement between men, defined as knowing intellects and free wills . . . obtained through dialogue' – is 'based on the validity of the narrative of emancipation' (60), Lyotard suggests that Habermas is wrong in identifying emancipation with an ultimate consensus. For Lyotard, consensus is only 'a particular *state* of discussion, not its end' (65; emphasis added). In the field of science the end is paralogy – 'a move (the importance of which is often not recognized until later) played in the pragmatics of knowledge' (61) – and in other fields the ends are similar moves that seek to contribute to diversity, uncertainty, and undecidability. It is not that Lyotard does not believe in the necessity of political emancipation, it is just that he expects it to be realized through dissensus, not through Habermasian consensus. As he put it in an interview published practically simultaneously with *The Postmodern Condition*: 'the pedagogical task, once stripped of its trappings, that of the great narrative of emancipation, can be designated by one word: an apprenticeship in resistance' (1984b: 18). Four years later he was equally explicit:

> The real political task today, at least in so far as it is also concerned with the cultural . . . is to carry forward the resistance that writing offers to established thought, to what has already been done, to what everyone thinks, to what is well known, to what is widely recognized, to what is 'readable,' to everything which can change its form and make itself acceptable to opinion in general.
>
> (Lyotard 1988b: 302)

For Lyotard, consensus is the end of freedom and of thought; it is dissensus that allows us to experience freedom and to think, that is, to extend our possibilities. Whereas for Habermas emancipation follows a route that leads via temporary consensuses to an ultimate consensus, for Lyotard emancipation depends on the perpetuation of dissensus, that is, on a permanent crisis in representation, on 'an ever greater awareness of the contingent and localized – the unstable – nature of all norms for representing the world' (Herman 1993: 163). Like the deconstructionist avant-garde, Lyotard advocates a radical anti-representationalism.

Postmodern language games

As I have just suggested, Lyotard's anti-representational postmodern science stands for the 'postmodern condition' *tout court.* Let us return to the 'heterogeneity of language games' (xxv) – I have already indicated their diversity – that constitutes the field of the social under postmodernity. These language games are engaged in constant struggle, if not against each other, then against themselves:

> to speak is to fight, in the sense of playing, and speech acts fall within the domain of a general agonistics. This does not necessarily mean that one plays in order to win. A move can be made for the sheer pleasure of invention. . . . Great joy is had in the endless invention of turns of phrases, of words and meanings, the process behind the evolution of language on the level of *parole.* But undoubtedly even this pleasure depends on a feeling of success won at the expense of an adversary – at least one adversary, and a formidable one: the accepted language or connotation. (10)

Communication, instead of establishing rational grounds and working towards perfection in Habermasian fashion, will always be a struggle. This view is wholly incompatible with what Lyotard calls Habermas's 'belief . . . that humanity as a collective (universal) subject seeks its common emancipation through the regularization of the "moves" permitted in all language games and that the legitimacy of any statement resides in its contributing to that emancipation' (66). Contending that '[c]onsensus has become an outmoded and suspect value' (66), and dismissing Habermas's emancipatory legimitation, Lyotard replaces consensus with his 'general agonistics' in which the moves that contribute to the game in question are those that serve to keep it going (while additionally bringing joy and pleasure to the players). In such discursive moves the experimental and the political are identical, as the (scientifically) experimental and the political were identical in the moves of postmodern science. As a consequence, the only moves that are not permitted are those of 'terror': 'By terror I mean the efficiency gained by eliminating, or threatening to eliminate, a player from the language game one shares with him' (63). Terror, which leads to enforced consensus, stops the free flow of the game and thus effectively cuts short its political potential. Since 'invention is always born of dissension' (xxv), there will be no 'invention' under conditions of terror. Such inventions, which are born, in Kenneth Lea's phrase, of 'the anarchic, creative play of desire' (Lea 1987: 90), belong to the realm of postmodern knowledge, whose 'principle is not the expert's homology, but the inventor's paralogy' (xxv).

It will be clear that Lyotard's version of the postmodern condition is not without its problems and those in favor of a more traditional emancipatory politics have been quick to articulate them. Nancy Fraser and Linda Nicholson sum up the debilitating effect of Lyotard's principle of heterogeneity on traditional politics: 'Lyotard insists that the field of the social is heterogeneous and nontotalizable. As a result, he rules out the sort of critical social theory that employs general categories like gender, race, and class' (1988: 89). Moreover, what about the vexing problem of justice in a world of heterogeneous language games? Lyotard is not unaware of it and hastens to tell us that 'justice as a value is neither outmoded nor suspect.' However, since consensus *is* suspect, '[w]e must arrive at an idea and practice of justice that is not linked to that of consensus' (66). It is not only that the heterogeneity of language games leads to what Lyotard elsewhere calls a 'multiplicity of justices', justice, like everything else in his postmodern world, 'consists in working at the limits of what the rules permit, in order to invent new moves, perhaps new rules and therefore new games' (Lyotard 1985: 100). In Lyotard's universe of language games, norms and values are always created and re-created through discursive intervention and are never given.

Lyotard's conception of justice conforms to the general experimental anti-representationalism of the postmodern condition, except, of course, in the absolutist ban on the elimination of rival players from a game. Although this meta-rule involves him in contradiction – it is clearly not subject to experimentation – it is also clearly necessary for the viability of his experimental/political model. As Steven Connor has pointed out, this meta-rule brings him closer to Habermas than he probably would want to be:

> Lyotard seems to be offering a universal discursive norm which is very similar to that offered by Habermas, namely,

> that all subjects and groups of subjects shall be permitted access to discourse, and no subject or group of subjects shall be hindered by compulsion, whether internal or external to discourse, which will constrain or prevent such access.
>
> (Connor 1992: 114)

In the final analysis, both Habermas and Lyotard would seem to pursue a left-liberal politics. What keeps them apart is the respective routes that must lead towards that end.

Language games and liberal pluralism

Let me return to the reception of *The Postmodern Condition.* It was immediately assimilated by 'theory', as the various sorts of avant-garde criticism and (pseudo-)philosophizing that one finds in American Departments of English are nowadays collectively called. However, what went into that process of assimilation as a variety of French poststructuralism came out as an innocuous version of American pluralism. For the large majority of his American readers Lyotard's 'incredulity toward metanarratives' served as welcome additional evidence that such large-scale ideological constructs as, say, patriarchy, capitalism – the metanarrative according to which emancipation will follow from the free operation of the market – or the supposed superiority of the white race, fatally lacked legitimation. More in general, Lyotard's language games served as an effective weapon against all totalizing pretensions, with the advantage of apparently leaving the home base of the attacker (as often as not a pragmatic liberal humanist) safe and intact. Steven Best and Douglas Kellner's reading of Lyotard sums it all up:

> In a sense, Lyotard's celebration of plurality replays the moves of liberal pluralism and empiricism. His 'justice of multiplicities' is similar to traditional liberal pluralism which posits a plurality of political subjects with multiple interests and organizations. He replays tropes of liberal tolerance by valorizing diverse modes of multiplicity, refusing to privilege any subjects or positions, or to offer a standpoint from which one can choose between opposing political positions.
>
> (Best and Kellner 1991: 174–5)

This is indeed how *The Postmodern Condition* was widely read and why it made postmodernism eminently safe for the middle-of-the-road critic who abhors radicalism of any kind. On this reading, postmodernity only means more business as usual. But it is a one-sided reading that is unfair to Lyotard, especially if it goes accompanied with accusations of neo-conservatism. What such readings of *The Postmodern Condition* leave out is its radically anti-representational stance and its emphasis on restless experimentation in every conceivable field. Instead of a comparatively complacent liberal pluralism, Lyotard promotes a radically revolutionary ethos that is that of the modern avant-garde. As Fredric Jameson already pointed out in his foreword to *The Postmodern Condition*, Lyotard's postmodernism has a good deal in common with 'modernism as its first ideologues projected it – a constant and ever more dynamic revolution in the languages, forms, and tastes of art' (Jameson 1984c: xvi). There is, moreover, Lyotard's dismissal of the subject, which is unthinkable in the liberal pluralism that Best and Kellner describe. For Lyotard, 'moves' in a language game are not the intentional actions of autonomous subjects, but come about as agents act upon the prompting of desire. Indeed, in his next book he would drop the term 'language game' because of its subjectivistic overtones:

> it seemed to me that 'language games' implied players that made use of language like a toolbox, thus repeating the constant arrogance of Western anthropocentrism. 'Phrases' came to say that the so-called players were on the contrary situated by phrases in the universes those phrases present, 'before' any intention.
>
> (Lyotard 1984b: 17)

THE POSTMODERN SUBLIME

'Answering the question: what is postmodernism?', originally published in 1982, was included by Ihab and Sally Hassan in their *Innovation/Renovation* collection of 1983, but it only began to attract wide attention after its inclusion as an appendix in *The Postmodern Condition*. In the essay Lyotard resolutely marks his distance from much of what passes for postmodern art. Achille Bonito Oliva's 'transavantgarde', for instance, is accused of a 'cynical eclecticism' in its attempts to go beyond – and simultaneously to suppress – the historical avant-garde while plundering and recycling that same avant-garde's achievements. Such eclectic postmodernism (which also includes Jencks's postmodern architecture) has accommodated itself to the 'power . . . of capital' and is

> the degree zero of contemporary general culture: one listens to reggae, watches a western, eats McDonald's food for lunch and local cuisine for dinner, wears Paris perfume in Tokyo and 'retro' clothes in Hong Kong; knowledge is a matter for TV games. It is easy to find a public for eclectic works. By becoming kitsch, art panders to the confusion which reigns in the 'taste' of the patrons. Artists, gallery owners, critics, and public wallow together in the 'anything goes,' and the epoch is one of slackening.
>
> (334–5)

But if postmodern eclecticism is a debased and false form of art, so is postmodern representation, the return to the figurative. Representational art is impossible since modernity has already revealed the ' "lack of reality" of reality' (336). It has already confronted us with the impossibility of representation, with the unpresentable: modern art 'present[s] the fact that the unpresentable exists' (337).

In trying to find an answer to the question how painting can make visible what is unpresentable, Lyotard turns to Kant: 'Kant himself shows the way when he names *formlessness, the absence of form*, as a possible index to the unpresentable' (337). This is the strategy of the historical avant-garde in its attempts to present the unpresentable. In that strategy Lyotard distinguishes two modes that shade into each other: a nostalgic one (German Expressionism, Malevitch, de Chirico) and one that emphasizes 'the increase of being and the jubilation which results from the invention of new rules of the game, be it pictorial, artistic, or any other' (339). The latter mode, which includes Braque, Picasso, Lissitsky, and Duchamp is close to – and indeed sometimes overlaps with – the postmodern. Although 'Answering the question' sees the postmodern as part of the modern, it also makes a crucial distinction. Both modern and postmodern aesthetics are aesthetics of the sublime, equally concerned with the unpresentable. The modern sublime, however, is a nostalgic sublime, and its form 'continues to offer to the reader or viewer matter for solace or pleasure' (340). It cannot shake its longing for the merely beautiful. The postmodern, avant-gardistic sublime

> puts forward the unpresentable in presentation itself; that which denies itself the solace of good forms, the consensus of a taste which would make it possible to share collectively the nostalgia for the unattainable; that which searches for new presentations, not in order to enjoy them but in order to impart a stronger sense of the unpresentable.
>
> (340)

The postmodern sublime is Lyotard's radical anti-representationalism in the aesthetic field. The enemy is once again consensus, because consensus can never lead beyond the beautiful (to speak of beauty is to invoke norms) and because it actively prevents the experience of the sublime. As Lyotard put it a few years later, '[w]ith the sublime, there is no criterion for assessing the role of taste, and so everybody is alone when it comes to judging' (1986: 11). The sublime evokes a 'contradictory' feeling that is 'deep and unexchangeable'. Lyotard's art of the sublime is thus an art of negation, a perpetual negation, since the rules that sublime works of art will in spite of themselves establish must always again be broken. Like postmodern science, and like his discursive moves, Lyotard's postmodern aesthetic is based on a never-ending critique of representation that should contribute to the preservation of heterogeneity, of optimal dissensus. The sublime does not lead towards a resolution; the confrontation with the unrepresentable leads to radical openness.

This turn towards Kant, and especially towards the Kantian sublime, generally characterizes Lyotard's work of the 1980s, although it is a Kant who, in Lyotard's reading, takes on a curiously proto-postmodern shape. This is a Kant of 'language games (which, under the name of faculties, [he] knew to be separated by a chasm)' and a Kant who 'knew that the price to pay for [transcendental] illusion is terror' (1983: 341). There is, however, no major new departure in that more recent work. *Le Différend* of 1983, translated in 1988, drops the 'language games' and replaces them with 'regimes of phrases', as we have seen, because Lyotard feels that such terms as 'game' and 'player' might suggest intentionality and a liberal humanist concept of the subject. Apart from this, Lyotard introduces the notion of 'the differend' (*différend*) , which he defines as 'a case of conflict between (at least) two parties that cannot be equitably resolved for lack of a rule of judgment applicable to both arguments' (1988a: xi). Such differends are of course the lifeblood of Lyotard's postmodern universe and should under no condition be forced to resolve themselves into consensus. Proper respect for the differend guarantees that all potential players (to use the discarded terminology for another moment), no matter how marginal in a given language game, are allowed to make their moves, that is, participate in the agonistics of the game, and are not prematurely silenced.

DESIRE

Let me now look briefly at Lyotard's work of the early 1970s. As I have pointed out above, with the exception of a number of essays from *Dérive à partir de Marx et Freud* of 1973 that work has only become available in the later 1980s, and a complete publication of *Economie libidinale* had to wait until 1992. The early Lyotard, although in no way as influential in the debate as the Lyotard of *The Postmodern Condition*, is, however, a major presence in some recent theories of the postmodern. The sociologist Scott Lash tells us that his

> conception of postmodern de-differentiation via an aesthetics of desire was . . . in large part dependent on Lyotard's work. Little of this draws on Lyotard's *The Postmodern Condition*. . . . The work in which Lyotard is the most valuable about postmodernism is, I think, his earlier work, in which he does not directly address the topic at all.
>
> (Lash 1990: 174)

If we follow Lash in globally distinguishing between two major camps in French post-fifties theory, a Saussurean one that emphasizes language and structure (the early Barthes, Lacan, Derrida) and a Nietzschean one that emphasizes power and desire (Foucault, Deleuze and Guattari), then Lyotard is unique in his reorientation from the latter to the former. The general drift in the late 1960s and early 1970s was from the linguistic position to a position that highlighted power and desire. Lyotard, however, went against the grain, although never the whole way. One of the most ardent champions of desire in the early 1970s, he began to frame desire in language games in his dialogues with Thébaud of 1977–8, arriving at the position outlined in *The Postmodern Condition* in 1979.

But the Lyotard of the early 1970s was, in Lash's phrase, 'unchallenged as "the metaphysician of desire" ' (90) and thus as one of the most radical enemies of reason: 'Reason and power are one and the same thing. You may disguise the one with dialectics or prospectiveness, but you will still have the other in all its crudeness: jails, taboos, public weal, selection, genocide' (Lyotard 1984b: 11). This is the Lyotard for whom instrumental reason, under the regime of capital, has succeeded in gaining control over language and over representation. It has succeeded in doing so by privileging 'discourse' at the expense of 'figure' – in other words, through the repression of desire and its manifold manifestations. Drawing on Freud's concept of libidinal economy, Lyotard argues that under capitalism the flow of libidinal energy, the primary process, is continually thwarted by the secondary process which involves 'transformation and verbalization' and bows to a reality principle and to the demands of an ego that are ultimately constructed by capital. Let me quote Albrecht Wellmer's lucid summary of Lyotard's position:

> for Lyotard, subject, representation, meaning, sign, and truth are links in a chain which must be broken as a whole: 'The subject is a product of the representation machine, it disappears with it.'
>
> Neither art nor philosophy have to do with 'meaning' or 'truth,' but solely with 'transformations of energy,' which cannot be derived from 'a memory, a subject, an identity.' Political economy is transformed into lidibinal economy, liberated from the terror of representations.
>
> (Wellmer 1985: 340)

It is the free flow of desire, especially as it manifested itself in art (in the widest sense of the term), that once guaranteed an authentic communication that the capitalist regime, under which desire is structured and controlled by language, has made impossible.

Lyotard first fully outlines his philosophy of desire in *Discours, figure* of 1971, but presents its most radical version – Best and Kellner speak of 'a highly aggressive Nietzschean philosophy of affirmation' (1991: 148) – in *Economie libidinale* of 1974. In *Economie libidinale* Lyotard embraces desire in all its possible manifestations. Unlike Deleuze and Guattari, who offered a similarly Nietzschean philosophy in their *L'Anti-Oedipe* of 1972 (trans. 1983), Lyotard celebrates desire even in its negative manifestations. Deleuze and Guattari see desire as an essentially positive force, but are not unaware that positive forces can be appropriated for negative ends. *Economie libidinale*, however, throws all caution to the wind in its tireless promotion of unconstrained and undirected libidinal energy. In this period Lyotard is very close to the celebration of vitalism that Gerald Graff saw in the American counterculture of the 1960s, witness this passage from an essay originally published in 1973:

> Here are the 'men of profusion', the '*masters*' of today: marginals, experimental painters, pop, hippies and yippies, parasites, madmen, binned loonies. One hour of their lives offers more intensity and less intention than three hundred thousand words of a professional philosopher. More Nietzschean than Nietzsche's readers.
>
> (1979: 53)

This sums it all up: raw experience and amoral energy are privileged at the expense of reflection and intention.

It is perhaps somewhat unfair to highlight a position that Lyotard has in the meantime publicly repudiated, although there are clearly important continuities between the work of the early 1970s and *The Postmodern Condition.* However, as I have just pointed out, Lyotard's early work has given rise to one of the most interesting sociological accounts of the postmodern, that of Scott Lash, which I will discuss later, with other sociologies of the postmodern. But let me first turn from Lyotard's avant-gardistic postmodern condition to other accounts of a fully-fledged postmodernity.

NOTES

1 Steven Connor, *Postmodernist Culture: An Introduction to Theories of the Contemporary* (1989).

2 [t]he main point is this: art . . . is becoming, like the personality of the artist himself, an occurrence without clear boundaries: at worst a kind of social hallucination, at best an opening or inauguration. That is why Jean-François Lyotard enjoins readers to abandon the safe harbour offered to the mind by the category of 'works of art' or of signs in general, and to recognize as truly artistic

nothing but *initiatives* or events, in whatever domain they may occur.

Ihab Hassan, 'The critic as innovator: the Tutzing statement in x frames,' *Amerikastudien* 22, 1: 55.

3 The Adorno lecture of 1980 was reprinted in Hal Foster's *Anti-Aesthetic* (Foster 1983a) under the title 'Modernity – an incomplete project'.

4 In a note Lyotard mentions Touraine's *La Société postindustrielle* of 1969 and Bell's *The Coming of Post-Industrial Society* of 1973.

7

ANTITHETICAL RADICALISMS

Richard Rorty and Jean Baudrillard

RORTY AND POSTMODERN PRAGMATISM

In his response to Richard Rorty's 1985 'Habermas and Lyotard on postmodernity' Habermas remarks that Rorty 'wants to destroy the tradition of the philosophy of consciousness, from its Cartesian beginnings, with the aim of showing the pointlessness of the entire discussion of the foundations and limits of knowledge' (1985: 193). This is a not unreasonable assessment, as we will see; it was, however, no surprise to anyone familiar with Rorty's career. *Philosophy and the Mirror of Nature* (1980) and the essays collected in *Consequences of Pragmatism (Essays: 1972–1980)* (1982) had left little doubt as to his philosophical orientation – that is, for those who were aware of Rorty's work. Although one comes across the occasional reference to *Philosophy and the Mirror of Nature* in the early 1980s, it is only with his provocatively titled 'Postmodernist bourgeois liberalism' of 1983 that Rorty begins to attract real attention in postmodernist circles and it is not until 1985 that his 'Habermas and Lyotard on postmodernity' would definitely seem to confirm his postmodernism. Yet Rorty has never played the major role that for a moment seemed in the offing for him and for the American pragmatism that he stands for. From the perspective of practically all theorists involved in the debate Rorty's position is decidedly conservative and thus implicitly anti-emancipatory, even though Rorty would certainly deny this. This view, that gradually gained ground in the wake of Christopher Norris's *The Contest of Faculties: Philosophy and Theory after Deconstruction* of 1985 and similar attacks, effectively prevented the incorporation of pragmatism into the postmodern complex, aided, in all probability, by Rorty's openly anti-theoretical stance.[1] Indeed, since postmodernism is, if anything, relentlessly theoretical in its continuation and intensification of modern self-reflexiveness, Rorty could paradoxically be said to be the most postmodern theorist of them all in his desire to go beyond the sort of theorization that characterized modernity and has been further developed by the theorists that are generally called postmodern.

I will discuss here only the two articles that directly engage the postmodernist debate. Taken together, they offer a fairly complete survey of Rorty's position. Let me begin with the article on Habermas and Lyotard, which offers more detail and background than the earlier one.

Rorty on Habermas and Lyotard

In one of his characteristic colloquialisms, Rorty summarizes Lyotard's objections against Habermas in the remark that for Lyotard Habermas scratches where it doesn't itch:

> This . . . suggests that we read Lyotard as saying: the trouble with Habermas is not so much that he provides a metanarrative of emancipation as that he feels the need to legitimize, that he is not content to let the narratives which hold our culture together do their stuff. He is scratching where it does not itch.
>
> (1985: 164)

For Rorty, Habermas's urge to scratch, that is, his felt need to operate on the basis of a universal legitimation, can be traced back to Descartes's reinforcement of ultimately Platonic ideas:

> By taking the ability to do [theoretical-analytical] science as a mark of something deep and essential to human nature, as the place where we got closest to our true selves, Descartes preserved just those themes in ancient thought which Bacon had tried to obliterate. The preservation of the Platonic idea that our most distinctively human faculty was our ability to manipulate 'clear and distinct ideas,' rather than to accomplish feats of social engineering, was Descartes' most important and most unfortunate contribution to what we now think of as 'modern philosophy.'
>
> (1985: 170)

What is wrong with 'modern philosophy' is that it has abandoned modest Baconian 'self-assertion' for 'self-grounding', and that its self-consciousness has ever since driven it relentlessly in a futile search for essence. From Rorty's perspective, 'the canonical sequence of philosophers from Descartes to Nietzsche' is nothing but 'a distraction from the history of concrete social engineering which made the contemporary North Atlantic culture what it is now, with all its glories and all its dangers' (173). Rorty is of course aware of the crucial role that modern philosophy claims for itself in the constitution of modernity. If one could however, for a moment, forget about those claims, one would see that it is not so much Habermasian 'elements of reason' that have dominated the development of modernity, but rather 'those untheoretical sorts of narrative discourse which make up the political speech of the Western democracies' (165–6).

Now if Habermas's defense of modern philosophy is rather irrelevant because it never played the major part it claims, so is the poststructuralist attack on its terrorist intentions. If I may allow myself another lengthy quotation:

> What links Habermas to the French thinkers he criticizes is the conviction that the story of modern philosophy (as successive reactions to Kant's diremptions) is an important part of the story of the democratic societies' attempts at self-assurance. But it may be that most of the latter story could be told as the history of reformist politics, without much reference to the kinds of theoretical backup which philosophers have provided for such politics. It is, after all, things like the formation of trade unions, the meritocratization of education, the expansion of the franchise, and cheap newspapers, which have figured most largely in the willingness of the citizens of the democracies to see themselves as part of a 'communicative community'.
>
> (1985: 169)

We need neither a ponderous defense, nor an overheated assault, if the modern philosophy of self-consciousness – and thus, implicitly, legitimation – that began with Descartes and was so formidably reinforced by Kant 'was just a side-show, something which an isolated order of priests devoted themselves to for a few hundred years, something which did not make much difference to the successes and failures of the European countries in realizing the hopes formulated by the Enlightenment' (171).[2]

His dismissal of philosophical theory leads Rorty to a middle course between Lyotard and Habermas. Lyotard is right in his rejection of metanarratives and of Habermas's 'universalistic philosophy' (his search for communicative rationality); Habermas is right in his insistence on 'liberal politics', which the poststructuralists are 'ready to abandon . . . in order to avoid universalistic philosophy' (162). Rorty splits the difference – his phrase – between them in his suggestion that what is needed is a 'detheoreticized sense of community'. From such an untheoretical perspective 'one could accept the claim that valuing "undistorted communication" was of the essence of liberal politics without needing a theory of communicative competence as backup' (173). The project of concrete social engineering in a situation of unconstrained discourse that would result from such an approach would welcome all the moves in Lyotard's language games. Needless to say that such a vision, which privileges communication and a succession of consensuses, has little patience with Lyotard's 'assumption that the intellectual has a mission to be avant-garde', to find a place outside the obtaining 'rules and practices and institutions' that will enable ' "authentic criticism" ' (174), or, for that matter, with the anti-representational sublime:

> Social purposes are served, just as Habermas says, by finding beautiful ways of harmonizing interests, rather than sublime ways of detaching oneself from others' interests. The attempt of leftist intellectuals to pretend that the avant-garde is serving the wretched of the earth by fighting free of the merely beautiful is a hopeless attempt to make the special needs of the intellectual and the social needs of the community coincide.
>
> (174–5)

Postmodern sublimity as championed by Lyotard has its *frissons*, but serves no political interest: 'Those who want sublimity are aiming at a postmodernist form of intellectual life. Those who want beautiful social harmonies want a postmodern form of social life, in which society as a whole asserts itself without bothering to ground itself' (175)

The sensitivities of the intellectual avant-garde do not constitute one of Rorty's main concerns, as he had already made clear in entitling his earlier article 'Postmodernist bourgeois liberalism'. That earlier article goes over much the same ground as 'Habermas and Lyotard on postmodernity', but is somewhat sketchier. Rorty here sets up a distinction between 'Kantians' and 'Hegelians'. The Kantians believe in 'intrinsic human dignity', and 'intrinsic human rights', whereas the Hegelians see issues of dignity and rights in terms of specific communities, that is, as subject to history. Kantian criticism of this position predicts that the practices and institutions which safeguard morality and rights 'will not survive the removal of the traditional Kantian buttresses, buttresses which include an account of "rationality" and "morality" as transcultural and ahistorical' (1983: 584).

It is at this point that Rorty introduces the term postmodern, which he uses 'in a sense given to this term by Jean-François Lyotard' (Rorty is one of the very few Americans to refer to *La Condition postmoderne* before it appeared in translation). 'Postmodernist bourgeois liberalism' is for Rorty 'the Hegelian attempt to defend the institutions and practices of the rich North Atlantic democracies without using [the traditional Kantian] buttresses' (584–5), that is, without appeal to universalist metanarratives.

For postmodernist bourgeois liberals (among whom Rorty includes himself), morality is thus stripped of its transcendent wrapping and may, for any given society, be equated with 'loyalty to itself', a loyalty to its own institutions and practices that 'no longer needs an ahistorical backup' (585). What this implies is the necessity of an ungrounded communitarian solidarity. This in turn depends on a very modest view of the subject's capacity for self-determination. The 'crucial move', Rorty tells us is

> to think of the moral self, the embodiment of rationality, not as one of Rawls's original choosers, somebody who can distinguish her *self* from her talents and interests and views about the good, but as a network of beliefs, desires, and emotions with nothing behind it – no substrate behind the attributes. For purposes of moral and political deliberation and conversation, a person just *is* that network.
>
> (585–6)

Such 'moral selves' constantly reweave themselves 'in the hit-and-miss way in which cells readjust themselves to meet the pressure of the environment' (586). From the postmodernist liberal perspective, 'rational behavior is just adaptive behavior of a sort which roughly parallels the behavior, in similar circumstances, of the other members of some relevant community' (586). Moral dilemmas are thus usually 'reflections of the fact that most of us identify with a number of different communities and are equally reluctant to marginalize ourselves in relation to any of them' (587). We always find ourselves inside other-determined discourses, which inevitably provide us with our moral and political horizons – 'we always have to work out from the networks we are, from the communities with which we presently identify' (589) – and conflicting loyalties appear at the intersections of such discourses.

Both temperamentally and politically, Rorty has far more in common with Habermas than with Lyotard. He is not interested in permanent crisis and has no use for anti-representational crusades. For Rorty representation is a positive social act rather than a form of logocentric terrorism. He has, furthermore, no real quarrel with the content of Habermas's metanarrative – that of communicative rationality – and willingly grants that 'valuing "undistorted communication" [is] of the essence of liberal politics' (1985: 173); he just thinks that Habermas should know better than to waste his energy on futile projects. Rorty's dismissal of the tradition of radical self-consciousness that is at the root of both the Lyotardian and the Habermasian position, leads him to a rather optimistic assessment of the world as he has found it. For Rorty the sort of free and easy communicative interaction that guarantees that the ball of social and moral progress will keep rolling has at least *de jure* been realized in the democracies of the west. Political freedom is the *sine qua non*; once it has been realized, 'truth and goodness will take care of themselves' (1989: 84). That this is perhaps a too rosy view of things is emphasized by for instance Joseph Natoli and Linda Hutcheon who point out that Rorty's optimism is based upon a consensus that may well be imaginary, even in western democracies:

> Despite his emphasis on the historically specific and pragmatic basis of all thought, he fails to acknowledge that in one culture the experiences of some persons or groups may be radically different from those of another. In such situations a problem is how to develop a capacity to engage in emphatic translation rather than 'conversation.' It is mis-

> leading and dangerous to assume that everyone is engaged in more or less the same 'language game.' It is not evident how either systematic biases or constraints within a culture may be acknowledged within, much less resolved by, conversation.
>
> (Natoli and Hutcheon 1993: 420)

Rorty does indeed have a tendency to forget that not everyone is a member of the potentially postmodern liberal bourgeoisie that benefits most from the conditions for free communication that he sketches elsewhere (a free press, high social mobility, universal literacy, easily accessible higher education, enough leisure time to listen and think, et cetera). In other words, he overrates the consensus-creating capacities of the west's democracies and their political willingness to spend the money (on education and more generally on issues relating to equality) that might broaden the consensus. With the politicization of those who were, for all practical purposes, disenfranchised, consensus now quite rightly has its price and it is by no means sure that the bourgeoisie will want to pay it.

JEAN BAUDRILLARD AND THE POSTMODERN HYPERREAL

To discuss the postmodernisms of Rorty and Baudrillard in one and the same chapter is to go from one extreme to the other. While Rorty adopts a homely and commonsensical stance and is the most optimistic of all postmodern theorists – and thus, perhaps unintentionally, situates himself in a tradition of hard-headed Yankee optimism that goes back as far as Benjamin Franklin – Baudrillard increasingly turns away from common sense and skepticism. In his later writings he sketches a surreal apocalypse in terms that leave no room for argument. Far from Yankee hard-headedness, his later work exhibits all the worst traits of poststructuralism: a contempt for facts and definitions, a style that is equally reluctant to give concessions to the demands of the concrete, and a grand vision that develops distinctly metaphysical overtones. But these very contrasts make it worthwhile to discuss them back-to-back, so that Rorty's somewhat myopic optimism will be tempered by Baudrillard's grim analysis of the postmodern condition while Baudrillard's soaring claims will be seen in the perspective of Rorty's down-home insistence on the actual. Just like Rorty split the difference between Habermas and Lyotard, we should, unlikely as that may seem, split the difference between him and Baudrillard.

Jean Baudrillard's first appearance on the American scene dates from 1975 when his *Le Miroir de la production* of 1973 was published as *The Mirror of Production.* After that first appearance there was a period of silence which ended when Kathleen Woodward included 'The implosion of meaning in the media and the implosion of the social in the masses' in her *The Myths of Information: Technology and Post-Industrial Culture* (1980) and when *Pour une Critique de l'économie politique du signe* (1972) appeared as *For a Critique of the Political Economy of the Sign* in 1981. From then on, Baudrillard would stay in the news. In 1982, *October* published his 'L'Effet Beaubourg: implosion et dissuasion' (originally from 1977) and in 1983 Semiotext(e) published two Baudrillard titles: *In the Shadow of the Silent Majorities,* which collects his *A l'Ombre des majorités silencieuses* of 1978 together with some other articles, and *Simulations,* which collects the famous 'The precession of simulacra' (originally published in *Simulacres et simulation* of 1981) and the earlier 'The orders of simulacra', which had originally appeared in *L'Echange symbolique et la mort* of 1976. Baudrillard had suddenly become a major voice: 'The precession of simulacra' also appeared in *Art & Text* in 1983 (and was reprinted in Brian Wallis's *Art After Modernism: Rethinking Representation* of 1984). Moreover, still in 1983 Hal Foster's *The Anti-Aesthetic: Essays in Postmodern Culture* included 'The ecstasy of communication' and suggested, by way of that inclusion, that Baudrillard was definitely a theorist of the postmodern. Indeed, the following year, 1984, Baudrillard seemed to present himself in such terms in a brief article, 'On nihilism' (1984b; originally a 1980 lecture), and an interview, 'Game with vestiges' (1984a). Since then, more of his work, both early and late, has been translated. His growing status was confirmed by the fairly speedy translations of recent work that is arguably of much lesser interest than his earlier books and by the appearance of both a *Selected Writings* and a *Baudrillard Reader.*

It seems useful to provide a short overview of Baudrillard's intellectual trajectory prior to what one could call his conversion to postmodernism, since even some of the positions that he has meanwhile abandoned have retroactively come to play a role in the debate on the postmodern.[3] I will concentrate, however, on those texts that most clearly have contributed to the debate, even if they are not necessarily the intellectual high water marks of his career: *In the Shadow of the Silent Majorities* and *Simulations* and the articles that appeared in 1983 and 1984.

The ills of modernity: capital and Marx

With *Le Système des objets* (1968) Baudrillard made an important contribution to the semiologically inspired analysis of consumer society that was in the air in the late 1960s. More thoroughly than other theorists of the period Baudrillard explores, in Mark Poster's words, 'the possibility that consumption has become the chief basis of the social order and of its internal classifications' (Poster 1988: 2). The system of objects of his title functions as a 'system of classification' which is constituted by 'categories of objects' that 'undertake the policing of meanings' (Baudrillard 1988: 16–17). For Baudrillard, the primary function of consumer objects is their sign function which is promoted by so-called life style advertisements, television commercials, and so on, and which persuades us to invest in them. (In this phase of his career Baudrillard's neo-Marxism still allows other 'systems of recognition', although they 'are progressively withdrawing' (19).) What we buy is not so much the product as its sign value, which then differentiates us from others. Consumer products or objects thus have come to 'constitute a classification system that codes behavior and groups' (Poster 1988: 2) and Baudrillard argues that such a system can more usefully be analysed in terms of the sort of differential perspective developed by Saussurean linguistics than in terms of political economy, although he is careful not to exaggerate his claims: 'The object/advertising system constitutes a system of signification but not a language, for it lacks an active syntax: it has the simplicity and effectiveness of a code' (19). On the other hand, it is on its way to becoming ubiquitous. This 'code of "social standing" ' (19) 'establishes, for the first time in history, a *universal* system of signs and interpretation' (20). Since the essence of this fabulously successful 'system' is simply difference for the sake of difference, its possibilities are clearly endless – 'Object-signs are equivalent to each other in their ideality and can proliferate indefinitely' (25) – and so is its money-making potential.

In *La Société de consommation* (1970) Baudrillard further develops his thesis that consumer products function within a differential sign system that programs individual consumption and through that consumption structures the social, and moves further towards the position that consumption has become 'a fundamental mutation in the ecology of the human species' (29). Rejecting analyses of consumption – by Galbraith and others – in terms of 'the naive anthropology of *homo economicus*, or at best *homo psychoeconomicus*' (44), he suggests that 'the system of consumption is based on a code of signs (objects/signs) and differences, and not on need and pleasure' (47). This is not to deny needs, but to argue that consumption, as 'a system of meaning' (46), is not organized along lines of needs, pleasure, etc.:

> What is sociologically significant for us, and what marks our era under the sign of consumption, is precisely the generalized reorganization of this primary level in a system of signs which appears to be a particular mode of transition from nature to culture, perhaps *the* specific mode of our era.
>
> (47–8)

I quote this passage to illustrate that Baudrillard, in spite of the reservation implied by his 'perhaps', is here already on his way to the relentlessly totalizing vision that will mark his later work. 'We don't realize', he suggests, 'how much of the current indoctrination into systematic and organized consumption is *the equivalent and the extension, in the twentieth century, of the great indoctrination of rural populations into industrial labor, which occurred throughout the nineteenth century*' (50).

Pour une Critique de l'économie politique du signe (1972) adds another element to the Baudrillardian world that Anglophone readers came to know in the early 1980s. *Pour une Critique* is a sweeping deconstruction of the Marxist distinction between use value – 'the hypothesis of a concrete value' (99) – and exchange value and the Saussurean distinction between the signified and the referent and brings political economy and semiology together in an attempt to 'show how the logic, free play and circulation of signifiers is organized like the logic of the exchange value system' (63). Arguing that 'use value is very much a social relation' (66), and that we now, 'at the present stage of consummative mobilization', can see that needs, 'far from being articulated around the desire or demand of the subject, find their coherence elsewhere: in a generalized system' (68), Baudrillard can go on to conclude that use value and needs 'are only an effect of exchange value' (70) and thus strip them of their residual essentialist, that is, metaphysical elements. Likewise, the Saussurean referent 'does not constitute an autonomous concrete reality at all'. The world is 'seen and interpreted through the sign' so that 'there is no fundamental difference between the referent and the signified' (87). In fact, the world is an effect of the sign, just like use value is an effect of exchange value. As a result, '[t]he process of signification is, at bottom, nothing but a gigantic *simulation model of meaning*' (91). There would seem to be no way out of this 'simulation model' which is totally dominated by a general political economy of the sign in which 'the commodity is immediately produced as a sign, as sign value, and where signs (culture) are produced as commodities' (80), that is, in which one can no longer make a distinction between the cultural (representations in the broadest sense) and the economic. In a world in which commodity and sign have become virtually interchangeable – '*the logic of the commodity and of political economy is at the very heart of the sign*' while '*the structure of the sign is at the very heart of the commodity form*' (78–9) – only that which cannot be named, the symbolic, that which is outside the sign, can escape its political economy. But this Baudrillardian sublime does not stand much chance against the forces of the sign: 'All the repressive and reductive strategies of power systems are already present in the internal logic of the sign, as well as those of exchange value and political economy.' Our only hope if we want to 'restore the symbolic', that is, meaning, is 'total revolution' (92).

This, however, is not the revolution of the proletariat. Not surprisingly, Baudrillard's radical anti-representationalism and his increasing subordination of political economy (with its privileging of production) to a general political economy of the sign (based on consumption) led him to abandon his earlier Marxism in *Le Miroir de la production: ou, l'illusion critique du matérialisme historique* of the following year. Anthropologically, in its conception of man, Marxism has never broken with 'Western rationalism'; its conceptual apparatus must therefore be considered as implicated in metaphysics and even in 'repressive simulation'. Marxism is caught up in the very structures that it seeks to criticize. Baudrillard now prefers a Nietzschean aesthetics of aristocratic disdain and excess, as mediated by Bataille, to the suffocating politics of rationalism and utilitarianism that Marxism has in common with its arch-enemy:

> Marxism is therefore only a limited petit bourgeois critique, one more step in the banalization of life toward the 'good use' of the social! Bataille, to the contrary, sweeps away all this slave dialectic from an aristocratic point of view, that of the master struggling with his death. One can accuse this perspective of being pre- or post-Marxist. At any rate, Marxism is only the disenchanted horizon of capital.
>
> (1975: 60)

The notion of the mode of production has become irrelevant in a world dominated by a 'mode of signification' that in turn is controlled by the 'code'. This 'code', much more hazily defined, but immensely more powerful, than the 'code of "social standing" ' of his first book, apparently operates, in Mark Poster's words, 'by extracting signifieds from the social, redeploying them in the media as "floating signifiers" ' (Poster 1988: 4). Baudrillard here completes the turn towards an independent regime of the sign that was launched a year earlier in *Pour une Critique.* As Douglas Kellner puts it:

> The entirety of Baudrillard's subsequent work to the present . . . rests henceforth on the proposition that we have entered a new stage in history, in which sign control is almost complete and totalitarian. Signs, simulations and codes have become the primary social determinants, and supposedly follow their own logic and order of signification.
>
> (Kellner 1989: 50)

It is this shift in his position that enables Baudrillard to historicize the sign, to trace it back to its origins (the Renaissance) and sketch a development in which, as further evidence of his break with Marxism, capitalism grows out of a new mode of signification.

Simulacra and simulations

With the essays collected in *L'Echange symbolique et la mort* (1976), Baudrillard entered the phase of his career that in the early 1980s would almost instantaneously make him a major voice in the debate on the postmodern, leading to a somewhat belated discovery of his earlier work in the years that followed. The essays of the second half of the 1970s and the early 1980s that appeared in English in 1983 and 1984 immediately proved immensely influential and were seminal in drawing attention to the role of the media, and especially television, in the formation of postmodern culture. I will leave the chronology of Baudrillard's career for what it is now and concentrate on the main themes of this first post-Marxist phase.

In 'The orders of simulacra', which was originally published in *L'Echange*, Baudrillard more urgently than before links the 'neo-capitalist cybernetic order that aims now at total control' (1983c: 111) with contemporary structures of communication, that is, the media. Building upon his earlier 'Requiem for the media' (1972) (in Baudrillard 1981: 164–84), which had argued that the mass media actually prevent communication because of their very form, Baudrillard now sees that form as actively contributing to the 'hyperreal' that has replaced the real. After the first order of simulacra, the period from the Renaissance to the industrial revolution, in which value was still 'natural', that is, grounded; and after the second order, that of the industrial era, in which value was 'commercial', that is, based upon exchange; we have now entered the third order of simulacra, which is that of the differential value of the sign. This third order, which is an order of 'simulation' and is 'controlled by the code' (83), is also the order of the media, which form and embody the code. It is especially, but by no means exclusively, the electronic media through which the hyperreal has managed to replace the real: 'we must think of the media as if they were, in outer orbit, a sort of genetic code which controls the mutation of the real into the hyperreal' (55). In 'The ecstasy of communication' Baudrillard argues that advertising and television have destroyed both public space – 'advertising in its new dimension invades everything, as public space (the street, monument, market, scene) disappears' (1983a: 129) – and private space: 'the most intimate processes of our life become the virtual feeding ground of the media' (130). The distinction between the two thus disappears and what is left is the 'obscenity' of 'transparence and immediate visibility, when everything is exposed to the harsh and inexorable light of information and communication' (130), leading to 'a state of terror proper to the schizophrenic: too great a proximity of everything'

(132), and to 'a loss of the real' (133). All depth, authenticity, and even alienation have disappeared from this information-saturated world. Such a surplus of information paradoxically leads to the 'loss of the real' because, as Baudrillard argues in 'The implosion of meaning in the media', 'where we think that information is producing meaning, it is doing the exact opposite' (1983b: 97).

Information turns into non-information because of the media's binary structure of question and answer which preprograms all responses. This programming works through polls, tests, and similar exercises – 'test and referenda are, we know, perfect forms of simulation: the answer is called forth by the question, it is designated in advance' (1983c: 117) – it works through so-called democratic elections and it works in 'TV and the electronic media, which we have seen are also only a perpetual game of question/answer, an instrument of perpetual polling' (126). Although the media would thus always seem to evoke response, such responses are invariably simulations and real exchange has become impossible. In Baudrillard's terminology, 'the media' increasingly comes to stand for what Michael Clark has very usefully called 'an organizational practice that governs all forms of exchange' (Clark 1989: 248). Baudrillard can thus even accommodate his earlier consumer society within this 'universe of structures and binary oppositions', this 'new *operational* configuration' that is characterized by '[c]ybernetic control, generation by models, differential modulation, feedback, questionnaires' (1988: 139). From the perspective sketched here, consumer objects, and even the electoral system – which both 'poll' the masses – arguably function as mass media.

In 1981, in 'The precession of simulacra' (translated in 1983), Baudrillard refined his historicist approach of the sign, now distinguishing four 'phases of the image', beginning with the image as a reflection of basic reality and ending with the image as 'its own pure simulacrum', as bearing 'no relation to any reality whatever' (1983c: 11). We have entered the hyperreal, as I have already indicated. Whereas the real was *produced*, the hyperreal is *reproduced*. The hyperreal is a reproduced real, the real as 'the generation by models of a real without origin or reality' (2), constructed 'from miniaturised units, from matrices, memory banks and command models' (3), a 'meticulous reduplication of the real, preferably through another, reproductive medium' (1988: 144). In the hyperreal, the idea of representation has become irrelevant. Labor, production, the political, everything persists, but lacks all referentiality and is reduced to the status of meaningless sign: 'Labor power is no longer violently bought and sold; it is designed, it is marketed, it is merchandised. Production thus joins the consumerist system of signs' (quoted in Smart 1992: 126). Even power dissolves into simulacra (in the polemical *Oublier Foucault* of 1977): 'it undergoes a metamorphosis into signs and is invented on the basis of signs' (1987: 59) so that Foucault's strategies in charting power and its effects have already become obsolete in a situation in which power has become abstract and dematerialized. To make things worse, if anything could be worse, in our inarticulate awareness of this predicament we have taken to 'a panic-stricken production of the real and the referential' (1983c: 13) that only adds to the hyperreal while we foolishly take it for the real. (We do of course experience the hyperreal as real; it is therefore equally painful, euphoric, or, as the case may be, just dull.) The only thing that is real is the omnipotent code, that paradoxically thrives on our attempts to break its hold on us.

Let us have a look at some concrete examples. A simulation, Baudrillard tells us,

> is characterized by a *precession of the model*, of all models around the merest fact – the models come first. . . . Facts no longer have any trajectory of their own, they arise at the intersection of the models; a single fact may even be engendered by all the models at once.
>
> (1983c: 32)

These simulations or simulacra are variously defined. One category results from the act of duplication. Baudrillard suggests that the replica of the caves of Lascaux (built near the original which had to be closed to preserve the famous paintings) has destroyed the authenticity of its original: 'from now on there is no longer any difference: the duplication is sufficient to render both artificial' (18). This is a claim with major implications. Every duplication forces both replica and original into the realm of simulation. Moreover, from here it is only a minor step – but again one with major implications – to claim that anything that *can* be duplicated is already under the spell of the artificial, already a potential simulacrum and hence at least on the threshold of the hyperreal.

But there are other categories of simulacra. In another example offered in 'The precession of simulacra' Baudrillard presents Richard Nixon's bombing of Hanoi, towards the end of America's military involvement in Vietnam, as a simulacrum: 'The intolerable nature of this bombing should not conceal the fact that it was only a simulacrum to allow the Vietnamese to seem to countenance a compromise and Nixon to make the Americans swallow the retreat of their forces' (1983c: 69). One might simply see this as the sort of cynical, face-saving deal that is of all ages. If this qualifies as a simulacrum it is not surprising that Baudrillard should see them everywhere. A similar objection can be raised to the example of the executions at Burgos, during the last phase of the Franco regime, which Baudrillard sees as 'a gift from Franco to Western democracy, which finds in them the occasion to regenerate its own flagging humanism, and whose indignant protestation consolidates in return Franco's regime by uniting the Spanish masses against foreign intervention' (34). The 'simulation' is, again, nothing that seems particularly striking. However, what these simulacra have in common, and what they, in their turn, have in common with the global simulacrum of nuclear deterrence, Baudrillard's favorite example, is that always two seemingly antagonistic agents have a hidden agenda to maintain a status quo. Both cash in on a perhaps unintentional collusion and in so doing neutralize themselves and reaffirm the code. In the Baudrillardian universe every oppositional act (such as the exposure of the Watergate scandal) ultimately consolidates the 'neo-capitalist cybernetic' code. In 'a field *unhinged by simulation* . . . every act terminates at the end of the cycle having benefited everyone' (31).

Although such efforts would seem rather superfluous, as if to ensnare those who are still not taken in by the hyperreal, there are places like Disneyland with their implicit confirmation of the hyperreal as the real. As Baudrillard puts it in one of his characteristic inversions:

> Disneyland is there to conceal the fact that it is the 'real' country, all of 'real' America, which *is* Disneyland (just as prisons are there to conceal the fact that it is the social, in its entirety, in its banal omnipresence, which is carceral). Disneyland is presented as imaginary in order to make us believe that the rest is real, when in fact all of Los Angeles

> and the America surrounding it are no longer real, but of the order of the hyperreal and of simulation.
>
> (25)

After the mid–1970s, Baudrillard sees everything exclusively in terms of cybernetic control. Disneyland's role within a traditional capitalist ideology is here ignored and replaced by its function as a purposefully unsuccessful simulation of another, perfect, simulation: the hyperreal.

The force that, next to the media, plays a major role in Baudrillard's cybernetic universe is that of the mass, or masses. In *In the Shadow of the Silent Majorities* (1978; translation 1983) Baudrillard rejects the familiar fear that the incessant 'bombardment of signs' to which the masses are exposed can be made instrumental in their manipulation:

> It is thought that the masses may be structured by injecting them with information, their captive social energy is believed to be released by means of information and messages. . . . Quite the contrary. Instead of transforming the mass into energy, information produces even more mass. Instead of informing as it claims, instead of giving form and structure, information neutralises even further the 'social field'; more and more it creates an inert mass impermeable to the classical institutions of the social, and to the very contents of information.
>
> (1983b: 25)

For all practical purposes, the social has disappeared since 'there is no longer even any social referent of the classical kind (a people, a class, a proletariat, objective conditions)' (19). The only 'referent' which still functions is the 'silent majority', but it is a referent that cannot be represented because it 'no longer belong[s] to the order of representation' (19–20). Functioning like a 'gigantic black hole' (9), the masses allow of no representation. All that are left are simulations, created through surveys, polls, and referenda. And with the disappearance of the social, politics disappears as well and turns into its own simulation.

Curiously, this 'absorption and implosion' on the part of the masses is presented as a tactical maneuver; the 'indifference' which is 'their true, their only practice' (14) is for Baudrillard 'an explicit and positive counter-strategy' (11), a 'collective retaliation and . . . a refusal to participate in the recommended ideals, however enlightened' (14). Refusing all recommendations and directives, the masses hide in their silence.

In *L'Echange symbolique* Baudrillard had still advocated 'symbolic exchange' – the exchange of that which still has no place in the system of consumer object/signs: looks, presents, acts of wastefulness, etcetera – as a way to beat the system; now he begins to seek refuge in silence. In *Les Stratégies fatales* (1983) this notion is developed further into a not too plausible strategy. What Baudrillard recommends is that since thinking, let alone effective action, from the perspective of the subject has become impossible under the regime of the code, we might as well join the objects: try to think and act from the perspective of the object, that is, the simulated object, since there is nothing else in sight. In the history of the philosophy of subjectivity ('banal theory'), the subject has 'always believe[d] itself to be more clever than the object'. In a 'fatal' theory, however, 'the object is always taken to be more clever, more cynical, more ingenious than the subject, which it awaits at every turn' (1988: 198). Since its devastating victory over us, subjects, has amply demonstrated the object's 'cunning genius' (185), the perspective of the object will offer whatever insight into our predicament is to be had. It is not clear what exactly Baudrillard has in mind, although the idea of a paradoxical cooperation with the code in order to subvert it had already occurred to him a few years earlier: 'a system is abolished only by pushing it into hyperlogic, by forcing it into an excessive practice which is equivalent to a brutal amortization. "You want us to consume – O.K., let's consume always more, and anything whatsoever; for any useless and absurd purpose" ' (1983b: 46). What is clear, in any case, is that these are desperate strategies.

We are left with a hyperreal that has escaped our control and that is beyond conceptualization in spite of the 'obscene' visibility of every single detail. Baudrillard's relentlessly dystopic vision of late modernity, as he saw it in the seventies, or postmodernity, as he has since then come to see it, leaves no exits. 'Postmodernity . . . is a game with the vestiges of what has been destroyed. This is why we are "post" – history has stopped, one is in a kind of post-history which is without meaning,' as he said in an interview that, appropriately, was published in 1984 (1984a: 25).

Baudrillard's theoretization of the contemporary world as one that is completely controlled by the binary structure of a system of electronic communication that has absorbed consumer goods, electoral procedures, and so on, has clear affinities with a wider attempt to theorize postwar developments in terms of a transition from an older, industrial capitalism to a new form of capitalism – variously called late, disorganized, or postindustrial capitalism – that is centrally concerned with information technology and high-tech electronics and thus with reproduction rather than production. Baudrillard acknowledges his debts to earlier theorists of this development, especially Marshall McLuhan, from whom he borrows the notion that the central aspect of the new electronic media is their form – McLuhan's 'the medium is the message' – whereas their content can for all practical purposes be ignored, and such key concepts as 'implosion', the absorption of one element by another. Baudrillard, however, leaves all other theorists far behind in the nightmarish character of his conclusions. Whereas for McLuhan the electronic revolution had definitely utopian aspects, for Baudrillard that revolution has effectively made us the helpless victims of a technological determinism that through its unassailable code serves the interests of a hyperreal, meaningless capitalist order.

Fortunately, Baudrillard's own position is by no means unassailable. The standard objection is of course: how can he know? In a world in which everything has imploded into the hyperreal there is apparently still room for the critical distance that enables Baudrillard to come up with an analysis that strongly smacks of the metaphysics he himself has so radically rejected. But what he thinks he knows is also open to pertinent criticism. Let me quote Mark Poster, who by no means underestimates his importance, on Baudrillard's various shortcomings:

> He fails to define his major terms, such as the code; his writing style is hyperbolic and declarative, often lacking sustained, systematic analysis when it is appropriate; he totalizes his insights, refusing to qualify or delimit his claims. He writes about particular experiences, television images, as if nothing else in society mattered, extrapolating a bleak view of the world from that limited base. He ignores contradictory evidence such as the many benefits afforded by the new media, for example, by providing vital information to

> the populace (the Vietnam War) and counteracting parochialism with humanizing images of foreigners. The instant, worldwide availability of information has changed the human society forever, probably for the good.
>
> (1988: 7–8)

Other commentators are equally critical. Connor remarks that '[w]hen Baudrillard breezily dismisses concepts like state, class and power as empty mystifications, it is in the service of the well-nigh official mystification of our time, the nullification of collective life in any form, and its ruthless processing into fiction' (1989: 60). Norris sees in Baudrillard's work 'an ultimate stage of disenchantment with the concepts and categories of enlightenment thought' (1990: 172) and Best and Kellner accuse him of blindness to 'the continuing importance of the economy, state, race and gender domination' (1991: 125) and of taking 'contemporary trends as finalities' (143). Craig Calhoun quite rightly asks the question 'whether there is not a great deal of internal differentiation among "the masses" which might be addressed by an empirical theory more focused on cultural variation' (Calhoun 1992: 273).

There is no doubt that Baudrillard deserves all this. And there is more. At the concrete level of actual examples, the evidence that he adduces is often far less convincing than its theoretization has suggested. In fact, as Poster also indicates, the reader is as often as not surprised that such mice can be made to bring forth such mountains. And yet Baudrillard has undeniably become a major influence. Although the terms do not necessarily originate with him, it is through Baudrillard's work that the simulacrum, simulations, the hyperreal, implosion, and so on, have become part of our critical vocabulary. Undoubtedly the political climate of the American 1980s substantially contributed to Baudrillard's sudden importance. Under a seemingly simulated presidency and administration and with the help of such perfect simulations as the Iran–Contras affair and its protagonists, Baudrillard's writings seemed prophetic of a new order that had already come to pass.

But there are better reasons to take Baudrillard seriously, in spite of all the hyperbole and totalization and the unorthodox, to say the least, ways of arguing his positions. Baudrillard's analysis of the formative influence of the electronic media has given important new impulses to critical theory and his contention that the discursive organization that the media impose on the social field is inimical to any response that is not prestructured has contributed to our awareness of their repressive potential. Likewise, his earlier analysis of a general political economy of the sign (or, rather, the consumer object/sign), has become the starting-point for other important theorizations of the postmodern in which the economical and the cultural have collapsed ('imploded') into each other. Fredric Jameson's analysis of postmodernism as the 'cultural logic' of late capitalism, which I will discuss in the following chapter, is a case in point. (As we will see, Jameson's account is more generally indebted to Baudrillard.) Moreover, to return to the later Baudrillard, discussions of postmodern culture, if not of postmodernity *tout court*, must come to terms with the claim that the electronic media's reproductive powers turn or have already turned the real into the hyperreal. It is, after all, not all that difficult to find convincing simulations, even if Baudrillard's own examples are not always to the point. (One might of course dispute Baudrillard's somewhat nostalgic claim that the real once has indeed been the real and argue that it must always already have been a simulation.) Even if we refuse to follow him into the dystopia of his later work – and there are excellent reasons to do so – Baudrillard leads us to a vantage point from where we have a better view of the contemporary scene.

NOTES

1 Norris unhesitatingly places Rorty on the political right: 'It will be evident by now that Rorty's "liberal" assumptions have a great deal in common with "conservative" thinking on issues of culture and politics' (1985: 152). Thomas Docherty sees a Rortyan pragmatism 'at the root of many of the neo-conservative political stances which claim to derive from a postmodern attitude' (1993: 320). Rorty has indeed declared that he does not see an alternative to capitalism but his lack of a revolutionary ethos does not automatically condemn him to conservatism.

2 Rorty is of course not the only one to have reservations concerning the claims of philosophy. Anthony Giddens, for instance, has voiced similar doubts: 'evolutionism, in one version or another, has been far more influential in social thought than the teleological philosophies of history which Lyotard and others take as their prime objects of attack' (1990: 5).

3 For an excellent study of Baudrillard's intellectual career see Douglas

Kellner, *Jean Baudrillard: From Marxism to Postmodernism and Beyond*, 1989.

8

FREDRIC JAMESON

Fear and loathing in Los Angeles

'Postmodernism and consumer society' of 1983 was, strictly speaking, not Jameson's first engagement with the postmodern.[1] It was, however, his first concentrated effort at theorizing postmodernism and would, with the much expanded version that was published the following year in the *New Left Review* as 'Postmodernism, or the cultural logic of late capitalism', become one of the most influential 'interventions' of the 1980s. Although many commentators see Lyotard as the most influential theorist of the postmodern, 'Postmodernism' is, in Douglas Kellner's words, 'probably the most quoted, discussed, and debated article of the past decade' (1989: 2). Jameson's macro-analysis of the postmodern has indeed been immensely productive and was seminal in getting the more traditional, that is non-poststructuralist, left involved in the discussion. I will concentrate here on those two bombshells that Jameson threw into the debate in 1983 and 1984. They remain the most quoted of Jameson's contributions, even if he has worked out some of their themes in greater detail in later articles. Of the later essays, 'Reading without interpretation: postmodernism and the video-text' (1987) seems to me the most pertinent and I will treat it accordingly. Other essays, such as 'Baudelaire as modernist and postmodernist: the dissolution of the referent and the artificial "sublime" ' (1985), 'On magic realism in film' (1986), 'Hans Haacke and the cultural logic of postmodernism' (1986), 'Cognitive mapping' (1988), and 'Marxism and postmodernism' (1989), will be brought in to clarify points or further illustrate certain arguments but will not be treated in their own right. Finally, the new material in the voluminous *Postmodernism, or, the Cultural Logic of Late Capitalism* of 1991, which collects some of Jameson's major statements on the postmodern, will likewise be used sparingly, since it does not substantially affect his position.

PASTICHE AND SCHIZOPHRENIA

'Postmodernism and consumer society' opens with a survey of postmodern art that reminds one of the inclusive listings that Ihab Hassan had published a decade earlier:

> the poetry of John Ashbery, for instance, but also the much simpler talk poetry that came out of the reaction against complex, ironic, academic modernist poetry in the '60s; the reaction against modern architecture and in particular against the monumental buildings of the International Style, the pop buildings and decorated sheds celebrated by Robert Venturi in his manifesto, *Learning from Las Vegas*; Andy Warhol and Pop art, but also the more recent Photorealism; in music, the moment of John Cage but also the later synthesis of classical and 'popular' styles found in composers like Philip Glass and Terry Riley, and also punk and new-wave rock with such groups as the Clash, the Talking Heads and the Gang of Four; in film, everything that comes out of Godard – contemporary vanguard film and video – but also a whole new style of commercial or fiction films, which has its equivalent in contemporary novels as well, where the works of William Burroughs, Thomas Pynchon and Ishmael Reed on the one hand, and the French new novel on the other, are also to be numbered among the varieties of what can be called postmodernism.
>
> (1983: 111)

Jameson's first conclusion is that these postmodernisms 'emerge as specific reactions against the established forms of high modernism' (111); his second one concerns the 'effacement', in this list, 'of some key boundaries or separations, most notably the erosion of the older distinction between high culture and so-called mass or popular culture' (112). A similar process of erosion has created 'a kind of writing simply called "theory" ' out of formerly distinct academic disciplines – philosophy, political science, sociology, literary criticism – and this, too, must 'be numbered among the manifestations of postmodernism' (112). Given the cultural range of these manifestations, it is not surprising that Jameson, like Hassan, Lyotard and Baudrillard before him, sees his postmodernism in terms of periodization. Like Baudrillard, he sees a causal relationship between new developments in western capitalism and the rise of the postmodern. Consequently, his postmodernism is

> a periodizing concept whose function is to correlate the emergence of new formal features in culture with the emergence of a new type of social life and economic order – what is often euphemistically called modernization, post-industrial or consumer society, the society of the media or the spectacle, or multinational capitalism. This new moment of capitalism can be dated from the postwar boom in the United States in the late 1940s and early '50s or, in France, from the establishment of the Fifth Republic in 1958.
> (113)

This multinational, consumer, or late capitalism is characterized by new consumption patterns, by an ever faster turnover in the areas of fashion and styling, by planned obsolescence, by the ubiquitous presence of advertising and the media (especially television), by the explosion of suburbia (at the expense of both city and country), by the demands of standardization, by the arrival of automobile culture, and so on. It is this moment in the postwar development of capitalism that has spawned postmodern culture, the formal features of which 'in many ways express the deeper logic of that particular social system' (125).

That deeper logic, with its key element of perpetual change, has led to 'the disappearance of a sense of history' in the culture, to a pervasive depthlessness, to a 'perpetual present' (125) from which all memory of tradition has disappeared. In postmodern art, that deeper logic surfaces in two basic features: that of pastiche and that of schizophrenic discontinuity. Pastiche, in Jameson's use of the term, arrives at the scene when as a result of radical fragmentation we have 'nothing but stylistic diversity and heterogeneity' (114). Pastiche is 'blank parody', parody without parody's 'ulterior motive, without the satirical impulse, without laughter, without that still latent feeling that there exists something *normal* compared to which what is being imitated is rather comic' (114). In the age of total eclecticism pastiche is all that remains of a parody that has lost its former function. Moreover

– and this is a late and rather curious echo of John Barth's 'The literature of exhaustion' (1967) that Jameson will later drop –

> [t]here is another sense in which the writers and artists of the present day will no longer be able to invent new styles and worlds – they've already been invented; only a limited number of combinations are possible; the most unique ones have been thought of already.
>
> (115)

For all practical purposes, the artist is condemned to lifeless imitations and permutations, that is, to produce art that is essentially about art itself and, more specifically, about its own failure. This artistic dilemma is not limited to high art, it also pervades mass culture, and is instantiated, for example, in what Jameson calls the 'nostalgia film' (116), historical films that paradoxically are utterly ahistorical. Jameson sees

> the very style of nostalgia films invading and colonizing even those movies today which have contemporary settings: as though, for some reason, we were unable today to focus on our own present, as though we have become incapable of achieving aesthetic representations of our own current experience.
>
> (117)[2]

Such movies present the real in terms of simulations.

The second basic feature of postmodernism is what Jameson calls 'its peculiar way with time', which he discusses in terms of Lacan's view of schizophrenia as a language disorder resulting from the subject's failure 'to accede fully into the realm of speech and language' (118). Since it is language that gives us our 'experience of temporality, human time, past, present, memory, the persistence of personal identity' (119), such a failure leads to an absence of the experience of temporal continuity in the patient who therefore is condemned to live in a perpetual, always discontinuous, present: 'schizophrenic experience is an experience of isolated, disconnected, discontinuous material signifiers which fail to link up into a coherent sequence' (119).

This, then, is Jameson's postmodernism: 'the transformation of reality into images, the fragmentation of time into a series of perpetual presents' (125). He is of course aware that pastiche and radical discontinuity were elements within 'modernism proper', but argues that they were only marginal and never enjoyed the central position they have come to occupy in contemporary cultural production. Moreover, postmodernism's position within the culture at large is radically different from that of modernism. Where a less radically discontinuous modernism had subversive potential, in its day and age, even the 'most offensive' forms of postmodern art are 'taken in stride by society' and picked up by the market – which, by the way, should not surprise us if they indeed express the underlying logic of late capitalism.

It will be clear that Jameson, too, sees the postmodern as a profound crisis in representation. History has disappeared and the present has dissolved in images. The anti-representationalism that for the modernists had political value because it could be mobilized against a still largely representational culture, has for us become a trap from which there is no escape. Parody, which satirized a representational practice and could therefore have the emancipatory potential that for instance Linda Hutcheon claims for it, turns in the absence of such practices ('something *normal*') into the empty gesture of pastiche. Far from seeing anti-representation in the manner of Lyotard as a necessary defensive maneuver against the terror of representational consensus, Jameson, like Irving Howe twenty-odd years before him, sees what from their perspective is the impossibility of representation as the end of an emancipatory politics, a position that he would clarify in the follow-up to 'Postmodernism and consumer society'.

TOWARDS A GRAND UNIFIED THEORY OF THE POSTMODERN

The year after the publication of the first article, its partially revised and much expanded version, 'Postmodernism, or the cultural logic of late capitalism', appeared in the British *New Left Review*, to become a major factor in creating the sustained and productive British interest in the postmodern of the later 1980s.

'Postmodernism, or the cultural logic of late capitalism' offers a number of wholly new theoretical insights, next to expanding most of the themes of 'Postmodernism and consumer society', in particular the impossibility of representation. Most striking, perhaps, is its forceful presentation of the Hegelian–Lukácsian Marxism that one is familiar with from Jameson's earlier work. Much clearer than in 'consumer society', Jameson offers a totalizing perspective of the postmodern and then seeks to approach postmodernism 'dialectically, as catastrophe and progress all together' (1984a: 86), even if he is often betrayed by his own rhetoric into a dystopian vision. A major theme is now also the newly developed concept of 'cognitive mapping', a new representational practice, which he later will define as 'nothing but a code word for "class consciousness" ' (1991: 418). Jameson remains faithful to the Marxist representation of history as the story of class struggle. As a consequence, issues of race, gender, and ethnicity do not play roles of any prominence in Jameson's theorizing. Such a classically Marxist position is decidedly unpopular with the contemporary left and one can understand why during a Marxist conference in the later 1980s Jameson 'frequently had the feeling that [he was] one of the few Marxists left' (1988: 347). On the other hand, for all the orthodoxy of its Marxism, 'Postmodernism, or the cultural logic of late capitalism' also draws on Althusser's notion of semi-autonomy and it liberally borrows from the poststructuralist, anti-Marxist camp: the notion of 'schizophrenia' from Lacan and from Deleuze and Guattari, 'intensities' and the 'sublime' from Lyotard, the 'simulacrum' from Deleuze and from Baudrillard, and the idea of a 'homeopathic' strategy from Baudrillard (as a version of the latter's 'fatal' strategies).

Although it dates from 1984, 'Postmodernism, or the cultural logic of late capitalism' has been reprinted 'without significant modifications' in *Postmodernism, or, the Cultural Logic of Late Capitalism* and can thus still be considered representative of Jameson's views. The essay, in Jameson's words,

> take[s] up in turn the following constitutive features of the postmodern: a new depthlessness, which finds its prolongation both in contemporary 'theory' and in a whole new culture of the image or the simulacrum; a consequent weakening of historicity, both in our relationship to public History and in the new forms of our private temporality, whose 'schizophrenic' structure (following Lacan) will determine new types of syntax or syntagmatic relationships in the more temporal arts; a whole new type of emotional ground tone – what I will call 'intensities' – which can best be grasped by a return to older theories of the sublime; the deep constitutive relationships of all this to a whole new

> technology, which is itself a figure for a whole new economic world system; and, after a brief account of postmodernist mutations in the lived experience of built space itself, some reflections on the mission of political art in the bewildering new world space of late multinational capital.
>
> (1984a: 54)

Postmodernism, then, is depthless; it offers 'a new kind of superficiality in the most literal sense' (60). This lack of depth is 'perhaps' postmodernism's 'supreme formal feature' (60) and is intimately connected with the 'waning of affect' in postmodern culture. That disappearance of affect must, in its turn, be seen in terms of the so-called death of the individual subject, a death that does not mean the end of all feeling, but of the modernist feelings of alienation and *Angst* embodied in a painting like Edvard Munch's *The Scream.* Under postmodernism, feelings become, in Lyotard's term, 'intensities', in the sense that they 'are now free-floating and impersonal and tend to be dominated by a peculiar kind of euphoria' (64). In a later interview Jameson usefully clarifies his juxtaposition of modernist anxiety and postmodern intensities: 'Anxiety is a hermeneutic emotion, expressing an underlying nightmare state of the world; whereas highs and lows really don't imply anything about the world, because you can feel them on whatever occasion. They are no longer *cognitive*' (Stephanson 1988: 4–5). Cognitive alienation has given way to a non-cognitive 'fragmentation' of the subject (63). Finally, postmodern depthlessness manifests itself in contemporary theory, which repudiates 'at least four other fundamental depth models':

> the dialectical one of essence and appearance (along with a whole range of concepts of ideology or false consciousness which tend to accompany it); the Freudian model of latent and manifest, or of repression (which is of course the target of Michel Foucault's programmatic and symptomatic pamphlet *La Volonté de savoir*); the existential model of authenticity and inauthenticity, whose heroic or tragic thematics are closely related to that other great opposition between alienation and disalienation, itself equally a casualty of the poststructural or postmodern period; and finally, latest in time, the great semiotic opposition between signifier and

> signified, which was itself rapidly unravelled and deconstructed during its brief heyday in the 1960s and 1970s.
>
> (62)

The impossibility of representation under postmodernity (even anxiety is no longer 'cognitive'), is underscored by contemporary theory's suicidal repudiation of representation, a strategy which for all practical purposes condemns it to the realm of simulations.

As in 'Postmodernism and consumer society', the weakening of historicity is illustrated through the nostalgia mode in contemporary film and through the fiction of E.L. Doctorow, whom Jameson in the earlier article had called 'one of the few genuinely Left or radical novelists at work today' (1983: 118). Jameson's remarks on Doctorow's fiction are worth our attention since they illustrate the impossibility of a genuine cultural politics under conditions that do not allow of representation. Submitting that Doctorow's 'great theme' is 'the waning of the content' – representation – under the postmodern dispensation, he argues that even in the work of a novelist of impeccable political credentials postmodern ahistoricity outweighs the writer's genuinely historicist impulse, as a result of which the historical referent must remain elusive:

> If there is any realism left [in *Ragtime*] . . . it is a 'realism' which is meant to derive from the shock of grasping [our] confinement, and of slowly becoming aware of a new and original historical situation in which we are condemned to seek History by way of our own pop images and simulacra of that history, which itself remains forever out of reach.
>
> (71)

All that Doctorow can do is signal the impossibility of representation. Later, Jameson will change his mind and argue (again with reference to Doctorow's work) that it is possible 'to work at dissolving the pastiche by using all the instruments of pastiche itself, to reconquer some genuine historical sense by using the instruments of what I have called substitutes for history'. This is the strategy of 'undo[ing] postmodernism homeopathically by the methods of postmodernism' (Stephanson 1988: 17). Like Baudrillard's 'fatal strategies', this is a truly desperate bid and might, if thought through, even lead to the rehabilitation of theory, now seen in a homeopathic light. It is not at all clear how small doses of non-representation, mobilized against a massive non-representational system, could lead to a revival of representation under conditions that have not changed.

LATE CAPITALISM

Although Jameson had used the term 'late capitalism' in 'Postmodernism and consumer society', he had used it as seemingly interchangeable with other terms. In the revised version, however, Ernst Mandel's definition of late capitalism occupies a privileged position. Mandel's *Late Capitalism* (1978) distinguishes three periods within the history of capitalism, a tripartite division that for Jameson has its correspondences in the culture: there is a first period dominated by market capitalism and by its aesthetic corollary, realism; a second period of monopoly or imperialist capitalism, which gives rise to modernism; and a third period, the current one, of late capitalism, which then corresponds to the postmodernist aesthetic. This third period is characterized by an unprecedented 'expansion of capital into hitherto uncommodified areas' which

> eliminates the enclaves of precapitalist organization it had hitherto tolerated and exploited in a tributary way: one is tempted to speak in this connection of a new and historically original penetration and colonization of Nature and the Unconscious: that is, the destruction of precapitalist third world agriculture by the Green Revolution, and the rise of the media and the advertising industry.
>
> (1984a: 78)

Particularly in the west, late capitalism has succeeded in penetrating and commodifying representation ('the media') itself.

Some commentators, familiar with Mandel's book, have pointed out that Mandel sees late capitalism emerging as early as 1945, while Jameson's cultural postmodernism only dates from the 1960s, and have faulted Jameson for not explaining this considerable time lag. Jameson has reacted ambiguously to such criticisms. Mike Davis's 'Urban renaissance and the spirit of postmodernism' (1985), which must have been the first article to draw attention to the time lag, is accused of 'bad faith' in the notes to the reprinted version of 'Postmodernism, or the cultural logic of late capitalism' – not, however, because of this particular criticism, to which Jameson does not respond, but because of his criticisms of Jameson's analysis of the Westin Bonaventure hotel, which I will discuss in a moment. Davis's attack is perhaps not offered in the friendliest of spirits, but it is certainly damaging. Pointing out that Mandel's book was originally published in 1972 and therefore could only cover the 'the long postwar wave of rapid growth' (Mandel's phrase), he argues that in his subsequent writings Mandel – much like the other theorists that I will discuss in Chapter 10, give or take a couple of years – 'regards the real break, the definitive ending of the long wave, to be the "second slump" of 1974–75' (1985: 107). To support the implicit thesis that the beginnings of postmodernity as a new socio-economic matrix should be looked for in the early 1970s, Davis adduces impressive architectural evidence:

> the corporate 'workers' housing' of the High Modern (or International) Style totally dominated postwar urban renewal, reaching an apotheosis of sorts during the late 1960s in the construction of such surreal super-skyscrapers like the World Trade Center, the John Hancock and Sears buildings. 'Modernism', at least in architecture, remained the functional aesthetic of Late Capitalism, and the sixties must be seen as a predominantly *fin-de-siècle* decade, more a culmination than a beginning.
>
> (108)

This is obviously a very strong argument against Jameson's periodization of postmodernism.[3] It is hard to deny that Mandel's break of 1974–5, or David Harvey's division of postwar capitalism into two periods, with 1973 as the dividing moment, seems more productive with respect to a periodization of the postmodern than a post–1945 late capitalism. Most theorists see two periods in postwar capitalism, the first of which is a continuation of the prewar, Fordist, capitalism of modernity, which is then followed by the post-Fordist and postmodern capitalism of the last two decades.[4]

But let us turn to a second major proposition. According to Mandel, his capitalist triad has produced three separate and fundamental technological revolutions, the third of which has led to 'machine production of . . . electronic and nuclear-powered apparatuses since the 40s of the 20th century' (quoted by Jameson: 1984a: 78). This suggests to Jameson another area from which representation has disappeared and simultaneously another twist of the Kantian sublime, the so-called 'hysterical sublime' (76). According to Jameson, 'the technology of our own moment' – the computer, the television set, and other 'machines of reproduction rather than of production' – no longer possesses the 'capacity for representation' (79) that characterized the technologies of capitalism's earlier stages. Whereas the 'older machinery of the futurist moment', the 'older speed-and-energy sculpture' still represented its historical moment, television 'articulates nothing' (79). Our reproductive technology cannot represent the real, even though it fascinates us precisely because it would seem to allow representational access to 'some immense communicational and computer network' that in its turn would lead us to the 'whole new decentred global network of the third stage of capital itself' (79–80). It is our awareness of that 'enormous and threatening, yet only dimly perceivable, other reality of economic and social institutions' (80) that gives rise to the postmodern sublime.

The postmodern hysterical sublime is a vague intimation of the real world of late capitalism, a world in which 'our bodies are bereft of spatial coordinates' (87) and that is beyond representation. In the sublime this unrepresentable 'new global space' becomes 'most explicit, has moved the closest to the surface of our consciousness, as a coherent new type of space in its own right' (88). It is this sublime that gives rise to 'intensities' that are both exhilarating and fearful. Whereas for Lyotard the experience of the sublime, which is equally ambivalent, is politically enabling, for Jameson it is nothing of the sort, the more so since the experience remains inarticulated and is therefore ultimately unsettling. In the interview with Stephanson, Jameson tells us that 'in the conscious sublime, it is the self that touches the limit', whereas in the postmodern sublime 'it is the body that is touching its limits, "volatized," in this experience of images, to the point of being outside itself, or losing itself' (Stephanson 1988: 5). In a reversal of Lyotard's (modernist) sublime, which shocks us out of our representational schemes through a confrontation with the unrepresentable, Jameson's postmodern sublime unsettles us by lifting us out of a non-representational state of affairs, which we falsely mistake for the real, and bringing us closer to representation. In the postmodern sublime we almost become aware of what amounts to false consciousness.

The physical disorientation that Jameson's discussion of the sublime suggests, is more generally brought on by postmodern space, a notion which is central in his analysis of a 'full-blown postmodern building' (80), the Westin Bonaventure hotel in Los Angeles which Jencks and virtually everybody else, by the way, sees as late modernist rather than postmodern. The 'postmodern hyperspace' that Jameson sees in the Bonaventure and in the postmodern world at large 'has finally succeeded in transcending the capacities of the individual human body to locate itself, to organize its immediate surroundings perceptually, and cognitively to map its position in a mappable external world'. This

> alarming disjunction point between the body and its built environment . . . can itself stand as the symbol and analogue of that even sharper dilemma which is the incapacity of our minds, at least at present, to map the great global multinational and decentred communicational network in which we find ourselves caught as individual subjects.
>
> (83–4)

This suggests that the Westin Bonaventure is exactly the sort of representation of the postmodern that Jameson thought impossible – so perfect that it reproduces the disorientation that postmodernism produces more generally. It is, in fact, so perfect that we cannot assimilate it, cannot arrive at a representation, so to speak, of this representation. This is a major problem, not simply with reference to the Bonaventure. With the 'prodigious expansion of culture throughout the social realm' – the implosion of culture and the social – the 'minimal aesthetic distance' required by cultural politics, that is, 'the possibility of the positioning of the cultural act outside the massive Being of capital' (87), may have gone. If so, then the 'Archimedean point' from which capital could be critiqued has disappeared. This would indeed appear to be the case:

> What the burden of our preceding demonstration suggests . . . is that distance in general (including 'critical distance' in particular) has very precisely been abolished in the new space of postmodernism. We are submerged in its henceforth filled and suffused volumes to the point where our now postmodern bodies are bereft of spatial coordinates and practically (let alone theoretically) incapable of distanti-

> ation; meanwhile, it has already been observed how the prodigious expansion of multinational capital ends up penetrating and colonizing those very pre-capitalist enclaves (Nature and the Unconscious) which offered extraterritorial and Archimedean footholds for critical effectivity.
>
> (87)

Under such circumstances 'even overtly political interventions . . . are all somehow secretly disarmed and reabsorbed by the system of which they themselves might well be considered a part, since they can achieve no distance from it' (87).

What is desperately needed therefore, if we do not want our critical faculties to disappear in a postmodern black hole, is a representational effort that will create that distance and will allow us to get a handle on that elusive postmodern reality, a 'political form of postmodernism' that 'will have as its vocation the invention and projection of a global cognitive mapping' (92). It is not that we do not know that reality 'in some abstract or "scientific" way' – after all, Jameson fully accepts Mandel's analysis of late capitalism – but it is 'unrepresentable, which is a very different matter' (91). A cultural politics, however, depends on representation and its reorientational function. It is this gap between abstract knowledge and concrete representation that the aesthetic of cognitive mapping will have to bridge:

> the new political art – if it is indeed possible at all – will have to hold to the truth of postmodernism . . . the world space of multinational capital – at the same time at which it achieves a breakthrough to some as yet unimaginable new mode of representing this last.
>
> (92)

Should that breakthrough come about, 'we may again begin to grasp our positioning as individual and collective subjects and regain a capacity to act and struggle which is at present neutralized by our spatial as well as our social confusion' (92).

It is clear that Jameson, although engulfed by late capitalism's non-representational logic and (presumably) just like the rest of us prey to disorientation, still clings to the representational capacities of the Marxist model. Far less clear is why cultural representations of the postmodern are impossible when representation at the level of political economy is apparently not ruled out. As Best and Kellner point out, Jameson 'does not consider the possibility that postmodern space is no more difficult to map than an earlier modern space' (1991: 189). Elsewhere Jameson has argued that under 'the multinational or "world" system of late capitalism . . . the principle of structural intelligibility is for the first time completely invisible to the individual subject whose lives it organizes' (1984b: 116), but surely such invisibility is not so spectacularly new and not so daunting as Jameson thinks. In spite of Jameson's promise of a dialectical approach, the picture of postmodernism that emerges from his two accounts is one of practically unrelieved gloom. In his equation of cognitive mapping with 'class consciousness', even if it is one 'of a new and hitherto undreamed of kind' (1991: 418), Jameson allows a dubious Marxist position – has the proletariat ever been a unified subject or was there ever a chance that it would develop into one? – to blind him to the very real politics of the last twenty years. Because he focuses so exclusively on 'class' as the center of political struggle, that is, on the working class as the agent *par excellence* of progressive change, Jameson must assume that in the contemporary absence of a class struggle – of a center – we are simply lost. Consequently, he cannot see the value of the multiform feminist, ethnic, and ecological politics that have developed in the recent past. Indeed, from his perspective, such non-class politics are not only marginal, they presumably play into the enemy's hands as well.

Yet, 'Postmodernism, or the cultural logic of late capitalism' is an impressive, even a grand, performance, no matter if it is indebted to Baudrillard and – in the more distant background – Henri Lefebvre's *La Production de l'espace* (1974), from which it borrows its emphasis on space. The essay reminds one of some baroque turn-of-the-century palace on the Riviera: vast and yet elegant, full of unexpected corners containing intellectual surprises – such as Jameson's mobilization of Althusser and Lacan, which I have omitted here – yet the obvious result of an architectural master plan. But on closer inspection one sees the cracks in the façade, has one's doubts about the plumbing, and more than suspects that the landslide that will sweep the whole edifice down towards the sea is already in the making. As a matter of fact, the essay's not-so-hidden agenda *is* that landslide. Jameson's real topic is the crisis in contemporary Marxism, a crisis that he chooses to discuss in terms of postmodernism, hence the Cold

War rhetoric that he employs against the postmodern while simultaneously asserting that to the true dialectician moral judgments are irrelevant. The unspoken theme of Jameson's article is that in the contemporary world the credibility of Marxism is in various ways – politically, philosophically – at stake, and 'Postmodernism' must be read as an attempt to recoup lost territory. What is clear is that Jameson is not sure how to effectuate a Marxist counterattack – the postmodern bodies that wander bereft of coordinates through postmodern space are of course those of Jameson and other traditional Marxists rather than anybody else's.[5]

Jameson's strategy here is to slay – or at least dialectically tame – the monster of postmodernism by pulling it within the paradigm of Marxist 'science'. One can sympathize with his plight: Marxism, dressed up or not, has not many places to go these days. It is in this light, finally, that we must see the widespread interest among Marxist intellectuals in Jameson's cognitive mapping. The term has almost become a rallying cry, an appeal to close the ranks and to once more put the shoulder to the wheel in the service of the Marxist project, which, after the general onslaught of the early 1980s (only outdone by the political developments of the late 1980s), could indeed do with a new élan.

POSTMODERN VIDEO

The most interesting of the essays that Jameson published between 'Postmodernism, or the cultural logic of late capitalism' and his definitive book of 1991 seems to me his 1987 'Reading without interpretation: postmodernism and the video-text', a densely argued approach to a cultural form that more and more has suggested itself to Jameson as a superior index to the *Zeitgeist*, as the most promising hermeneutic vehicle 'for some new description of the system itself' (1987: 201).

'Video-text' (as I will call the essay here) proposes that video – which in Jameson's somewhat misleading use of the term includes both experimental video or video art *and* commercial television (which of course antedates the invention of video proper) – gives us privileged access to the postmodern. But it does so in a very circumspect way, for Jameson has become very cautious indeed: 'This is not a proposition one proves; rather, one seeks, as I will in the remainder of this essay, to demonstrate the interest of presupposing it, and in particular the variety of new consequences that flow from assigning some new and more central priority to video processes' (201). This is as close as one can get to declaring that one's intellectual exercises are perhaps not gratuitous, but cannot claim more status than that of a contribution to Rorty's cultural conversation or a move in an intellectual language game.

Because he wants to theorize both television – which I, following Jameson, will call commercial video here – and experimental video within one single framework, Jameson, in a sort of Derridean inversion, starts his analysis with video art, and not with its older sibling. Video time, Jameson tells us, is real, non-fictive, time and must be distinguished from the time presented in film. In film, reality is always foreshortened, by means of various narrative techniques. Fictionality in film (and more in general) thus would seem to substitute 'fictive and foreshortened temporalities' for 'a real time we are thereby enabled momentarily to forget'. Experimental video, however, is '*not* fictive in this sense' and 'does not project fictive time', even if it works with narrative structures (205). What Jameson finds in the 'video process' is 'the ticking away of real time, minute by minute, the dread underlying irrevocable reality of the meter running' (206). Real time is 'objective time', it is measurable time, a product of rationalization and reification. Experimental video is unique, then, in that 'it is the only art or medium in which this ultimate seam between space and time is the locus of the form' and 'because its machinery uniquely dominates and depersonalizes subject and object alike, transforming the former into a quasi-material registering apparatus for the machine time of the latter and of the video image or "total flow" ' (206). In its unique mechanical depersonalization, experimental video forces us to confront time in a materialist way and the video machine tells us that this is not a materialism of matter but of machinery. Hence experimental video, 'so closely related to the dominant computer and information technology of the late or third stage of capitalism – has a powerful claim for being the art form of late capitalism *par excellence*' (207).

It is by now clear that this bottom line of materalism was where Jameson was heading in the first place. Although quite willing to admit that 'there are many, many diverting and captivating videotexts of all kinds' (204), Jameson ignores them because it is only by way of his twenty-one minute stretch of video-boredom (the example that he uses) that he can get where he wants to be. Just like the atrium of the Westin Bonaventure embodied the essence of all postmodern space, so experimental video-boredom leads us to the essence of the medium itself, an essence that presumably remains hidden in those diverting and captivating videos precisely because they are diverting and captivating and thus successfully conceal the underlying nature of their relation with the audience. Moreover, it becomes clear how strategic Jameson's move of discussing commercial television in terms of experimental video really is. Now that video art has been reduced, for all theoretical purposes, to non-fictive video in which video-time equates real, that is, machine time (leading to a sort of panicky *ennui*), commercial television, theorized then – no matter how implausibly – in terms of non-fictive video, can be submitted to the same fate and be exposed in all its materiality.

To arrive at that conclusion, Jameson first projects Raymond Williams's 'total flow' upon commercial television to suggest that in a situation in which 'the contents of the screen stream[] before us all day long without interruption' notions such as critical distance and memory have become obsolete (202). He then argues that this total flow is punctuated by material or machine time 'by way of the cycles of hour and half-hour programming, shadowed as by a ghostly afterimage, by the shorter rhythms of the commercials themselves'. Such 'regular and periodic breaks' allow the 'simulation' of the sort of closure one finds in the other arts and in film and thereby also allow 'the production of a kind of imaginary fictive time' (207). In other words, commercial television's non-fictive essence as far as time is concerned (which has nothing to do with the fictionality of its series and dramas), is concealed by the false closures that are programmed into its flow.

Still, the center of attention in 'Video-text' is experimental, anti-representational, video, which here comes to embody the postmodern:

> what characterises this particular video process (or 'experimental' total flow) is a ceaseless rotation of elements such that they change place at every moment, with the result that no single element can occupy the position of 'interpretant' (or that of primary sign) for any length of time; but must

> be dislodged in turn in the following instant (the filmic terminology of 'frames' and 'shots' does not seem appropriate for this kind of succession), falling to the subordinate position in its turn, where it will then be 'interpreted' or narrativised by a radically different kind of logo or image-content altogether.
>
> (218)

From this perspective, 'anything which arrests or interrupts [the process] will be sensed as an aesthetic flaw' (218). Representation is thus simply out of bounds:

> If interpretation is understood, in the thematic way, as the disengagement of a fundamental theme or 'meaning', then it seems to me clear that the postmodernist text – of which we have taken the videotape in question to be a privileged exemplar – is from that perspective defined as a structure or sign-flow which resists meaning, whose fundamental inner logic is the exclusion of the emergence of themes as such in that sense, and which therefore systematically sets out to shortcircuit traditional interpretive temptations (something Susan Sontag prophetically intuited at the very dawn of what was not yet called the postmodern age.) New criteria of aesthetic value then unexpectedly emerge from this proposition: whatever a good, let alone a great, video-text might be, it will be bad or flawed whenever such interpretation proves possible, whenever the text slackly opens up just such places and areas of thematisation itself.
>
> (219)

With all of this established, Jameson can round off his argument and tell us that 'one would want to defend the proposition that the deepest "subject" of all video art, and even of all postmodernism, is very precisely reproductive technology itself' (222). Intentionally (as in experimental video art) or unintentionally (as in commercial television), Jameson's postmodern video is all about an ultimately self-reflexive anti-representationalism.

Even more clearly than 'Postmodernism, or the cultural logic of late capitalism', 'Video-text' shows us that Jameson gets where he wants to be by ignoring or discarding *en route* what does not suit his purposes. Video art comes in various forms and so does television, which need not be commercial in the first place, and which, if it is, is not necessarily programmed in the American way. As in the earlier articles, Jameson's axiomatic point of departure is a radically non-representational postmodernism. Finding a video that fits the bill then allows him to extrapolate a non-representational 'code' – partly overlapping with Baudrillard's simulational one – that governs 'video' *tout court.* As in Baudrillard, in the face of such a master paradigm all differences then become irrelevant.

JAMESON, 1991

However, in the course of the later 1980s, Jameson finds himself increasingly caught between an essentialist Marxism and the powerful pull of strongly anti-essentialist contemporary 'theory', to the point that in the introduction to his 1991 book he feels that it is impossible to tell which is which: 'I would not want to have to decide whether the following chapters are inquiries into the nature of such "postmodernist theory" or mere examples of it' (1991: x). One might argue that this uncertainty is itself a sure sign that 'theory' has won out, but that is not the case. Jameson's horizon remains Marxist, complete with base and superstructure – no matter if it accommodates notions of uneven development, semi-autonomy, and the like – and with class consciousness, even if his view of postmodernist culture is hard to distinguish from some of the deconstructionist approaches that we have encountered earlier. His holding on to a Hegelian–Marxist tradition may in fact well be his most important contribution to the debate.[6] Jameson's theorizations, although indebted to non-Marxists, always adopt a Marxist perspective, even when it is understood by both author and reader (although the author often prefers to forget this understanding) that that perspective has lost its privileged status.

Postmodernism, or, the Cultural Logic of Late Capitalism continues Jameson's theorizations of the postmodern with essays on postmodernist architecture, the utopian potential of postmodern art, postmodernist theoretical discourse, the market under the regime of the postmodern (with a surprising excursion into the work of Gary Becker, who has in the meantime been awarded the 1992 Nobel prize for economics), and on film, before it ends with a conclusion that runs to well over a hundred pages and is almost a book by itself. These essays mostly address the postmodern only indirectly, or do not substantially add to the arguments that we have already examined, at least not substantially enough to warrant discussion in what is, after all, a short overview of Jameson's contributions. The most interesting are the essays that deal with a postmodernist art and architecture that transcends a complicity with late capitalism and engages in the 'cognitive mapping' that must restore our sense of orientation in the bewildering spaces of the postmodern. There is, for instance, the architect Frank Gehry's house, in Santa Monica, California, that tries 'to think' the problem of

> the relationship between that abstract knowledge and conviction or belief about the superstate and the existential daily life of people in their traditional rooms and tract houses. There must be a relationship between these two realms or dimensions of reality, or else we are altogether within science fiction without realizing it. But the nature of that relationship eludes the mind. The building then tries to think through this spatial problem in spatial terms.
> (1991: 128)

And there is the work of Hans Haacke (discussed first in 'Hans Haacke and the cultural logic of postmodernism' of 1986) which draws the museum space itself into its parameters and via that space reaches out to the postmodern world outside: 'the museum itself, as an institution, opens up into its network of trustees, their affiliations with multinational corporations, and finally the global system of late capitalism proper.' Haacke's work thus 'expands into the very ambition of cognitive mapping itself' (1991: 158). This is interesting indeed, not because Jameson does not envisage a place for political art within postmodernism, but because it is unmistakably *postmodern* art that is political here, which is a different matter. In the earlier version of the Haacke essay, Haacke's installations even seem 'to emerge . . . as a solution to certain crucial dilemmas of a left cultural politics based on this heightened awareness of the role of institutions' (1986b: 47).

For Jameson, postmodernism 'is what you get when the modernization process is complete and nature is gone for good' (1991: ix) and when the modernist critique of the commodity, no matter how minimal, has been replaced by 'the consumption of sheer commodification as a process' (x). However, because of the uneven development of late capitalism, postmodernism is not so homogeneous as to preclude 'various forms of oppositional culture: those of marginal groups, those of radically distinct residual or emergent cultural languages' (159). Thus, in spite of the obviously hegemonic position of late capitalism, there is no such thing as cultural or social homogeneity.[7] The presence of political art or architecture within the postmodern should therefore not surprise us. But a political art that speaks the language of postmodernism is a surprise indeed – at least from Jameson's point of view:

> The case of Haacke poses, however, a . . . problem, for his is a kind of cultural production which is clearly postmodern and equally clearly political and oppositional – something that does not compute within the paradigm and does not seem to have been theoretically foreseen by it.
>
> (159)

Disappointingly, Jameson does not take up the challenge that Haacke's political, and thus representational, work presents to, for instance, the theorization of the postmodern in terms of a rigorously non- or anti-representational total flow that we have just examined, or to his all-stops-out description of postmodernism, much later in *Postmodernism*, as

> absolute and absolutely random pluralism . . . a coexistence not even of multiple and alternate worlds so much as of unrelated fuzzy sets and semiautonomous subsystems whose overlap is perceptually maintained like hallucinogenic depth planes in a space of many dimensions.
>
> (372)

It is only later that he very briefly addresses the problem of a genuinely postmodernist cultural politics and makes a distinction between Haacke's strategy of 'undermining the image by way of the image itself' – which he at that point no longer sees in terms of cognitive mapping, but rather as homeopathy, much as he did in the 1986 essay – and cognitive mapping proper, which is then not so much a postmodernist but a 'more modernist' strategy (409), a reassessment with which one can fully agree, given Jameson's equation of cognitive mapping and class consciousness.[8] It is difficult to see what a postmodern class consciousness could be like when postmodernism is defined in radically anti-representational terms. It has, moreover, been clear all along that Jameson mobilizes a modern conceptual system against the intangibility of the postmodern.

The issue of a genuinely political postmodern art leads me, finally, to *Postmodernism*'s 'Conclusion' which develops some new themes. These themes are invariably governed by fragmentation, spatialization, the loss of memory and history, and other characteristics of the Jamesonian postmodern. For Jameson another casualty of the advent of the postmodern is the possibility of genuine politics (as distinguished from cultural politics), a 'totalizing' politics that would include 'the dimension of economics itself, or of the system, of private enterprise and the profit motive, which cannot be challenged on a local level' (330). Such 'older' politics which still 'sought to coordinate local and global struggles' (330) have been replaced by the 'profoundly postmodern phenomenon' (318) of micropolitics, that is, the politics of exclusively local or group interest. That shift, too, must be seen as ultimately determined by late capitalism: 'the transitional nature of the new global economy has not yet allowed its classes to form in any stable way, let alone to acquire genuine class consciousness, so that the very lively social struggles of the current period are largely dispersed and anarchic' (348–9). Since from Jameson's perspective non-class politics, because of their refusal to recognize the class struggle as central to history, cannot effectively address our political condition, they must be seen as fragmented, dispersed and lost in space.

For the time being, spatialization reigns supreme. In a brilliant move, Jameson analyzes historiographical metafiction (Linda Hutcheon's term) in terms of 'spatial historiography' (370) and interprets MTV as the spatialization of music. Even religious fundamentalism, which he also sees as a postmodern phenomenon, is subjected to a spatializing maneuver not unlike those of spatial historiography and thus brought within the postmodern orbit: in a situation in which fundamentalism is not 'residual', but reappears in a 'postmodern environment of completed modernization and rationalization', it may rightfully be considered 'to have a simulated relationship to the past rather than a commemorative one, and to share characteristics of other such postmodern historical simulations' (390). True to his radical view of the postmodern, Jameson does not consider the far more plausible possibility that fundamentalism reacts against the impact of a modernization which is not yet 'completed' and will not be so in the foreseeable future. As a matter of fact, since modernization is an open-ended process, it is difficult to imagine how modernity could ever be completed or what a completed modernity would be like. Finally, in a section that reminds one strongly of Lyotard's language games, Jameson spatializes language into a plurality of languages, of 'codes', although here, too, he does not want to let go of the older dispensation, even while realizing that such a reluctance is 'retrospective and even potentially traditionalist or nostalgic':

> I can *transcode*, that is to say, I can set about measuring what is sayable and 'thinkable' in each of these codes or idiolects and compare that to the conceptual possibilities of its competitors: this is, in my opinion, the most productive and responsible activity for students and theoretical or philosophical critics to pursue today.
>
> (394)

This would seem to mobilize Habermas against Lyotard. However, 'the proliferation of new codes is an endless process that at best cannibalizes the preceding ones and at worst consigns them to the historical dustheap' (394). And thus we ask ourselves once again where Jameson stands on that nowadays sliding, and slippery, scale between Marxism and poststructuralism. Let me end this discussion of his work with the last paragraph of *Postmodernism* – a strategic move that has the double advantage of allowing Jameson to speak for himself and of allowing the reader to decide what he is saying:

> The rhetorical strategy of the preceding pages has involved an experiment, namely, the attempt to see whether by systematizing something that is resolutely unsystematic, and historicizing something that is resolutely ahistorical, one couldn't outflank it and force a historical way at least of thinking about that. 'We have to name the system': this high point of the sixties finds an unexpected revival in the postmodernism debate.
>
> (418)

NOTES

1 See Douglas Kellner's useful discussion of the various 'anticipations' of Jameson's 1980s analyses of the postmodern that one finds in his work of the later 1970s (Kellner 1989: 19–23).

2 See Callinicos (1990: 107–8) for a rather incisive critique of the examples of nostalgia films that Jameson offers.

3 Not all of Davis's arguments are equally convincing. Like some other theorists on the left, he appears to believe that capitalism totters around on its last legs and accuses Jameson of 'miss[ing] the crucial point about contemporary capitalist structures of accumulation: that they are symptoms of global crisis, not signs of the triumph of capitalism's irresistible drive to expand' (109). Here Jameson's view is obviously much nearer the mark. One reason why Davis refuses to accept Jameson's claim that postmodern capitalism has eliminated 'the last enclaves of pre-capitalist production' is that it has 'brazenly recalled the most primitive forms of urban exploitation' (110). One would not want to deny that exploitation, but Davis is wrong in calling it pre-capitalist. The theorists that I will discuss in Chapter 10 (postmodernism in the social sciences) see it, quite rightly I think, as a strategic revival of certain aspects of early capitalism.

4 In his 'Introduction' to *Postmodernism, or, the Cultural Logic of Late Capitalism* Jameson has it both ways, hanging onto Mandel's post-1945 late capitalism while also admitting that postmodernism proper dates from the later 1960s. He there tries to reconcile these positions with each other by arguing that 'the economic preparation of postmodernism or late capitalism began in the 1950s, after the wartime shortages of consumer goods and spare parts had been made up, and new products and new technologies (not least those of the media) could be pioneered' (1991: xx). This is so vague that it is hard to quarrel with but it does not address what to practically every sociologist, social geographer, and political economist is the main issue: the early 1970s transition from a Fordist regime of accumulation to a post-Fordist regime of accumulation and the accompanying reorganizations of capital, labor, production, the market, et cetera.

5 When curiosity propelled me into the Bonaventure I rather disappointingly found nothing of the total disorientation that Jameson had promised. Still, Jameson is clearly not the only one upon whom the Bonaventure has disconcerting effects. Edward Soja's account of the hotel echoes Jameson's – 'Once inside . . . it becomes daunting to get out again without bureaucratic assistance' (1989: 244) – and this is testimony from a man who is thoroughly familiar with the Los Angeles cityscape.

6 That hold is sometimes very tenuous indeed. In 'Marxism and postmodernism' Jameson suggests that we understand 'base and superstructure' not really as a model, but as 'a starting point and a problem, something as undogmatic as an imperative simultaneously to grasp culture in and for itself, but also in relationship to its

outside, its content, its context, and its space of intervention and of effectivity' (1989: 41–2). No intellectual in his or her right mind could object to such a minimal program.

7 Elsewhere, though, Jameson is less inclined to see a certain heterogeneity within late capitalist hegemony:

> Everything is now organized and planned; nature has been triumphantly blotted out, along with peasants, petit-bourgeois commerce, handicraft, feudal aristocracies and imperial bureaucracies. Ours is a more homogeneously modernized condition; we no longer are encumbered with the embarrassment of non-simultaneities and non-synchronicities. Everything has reached the same hour on the great clock of development or rationalization.
>
> (1991: 309–10)

8 Jameson cannot seem to make up his mind about Haacke, or about the difference between homeopathy and cognitive mapping. In 'Hans Haacke and the cultural logic of postmodernism' he somewhat despondently remarks that 'as modest and as frustrating as it may sometimes seem, a homeopathic cultural politics seems to be all we can currently think or imagine' (1986: 43). Haacke's installations are here situated within the same 'homeopathic' framework as Doctorow's *Ragtime*. However, Haacke's art is much more controversial than Doctorow's novels have ever been – we are told that Haacke's *Manet-PROJEKT '74* was excluded by the Guggenheim Museum and by the Cologne Museum that had solicited it in the first place – and Jameson suggests that it is also actively engaged in cognitive mapping: since in Haacke's works – in contrast to that of Doctorow – 'no preexisting aesthetic "pleasure" is present to be demystified, the focus shifts . . . to the attempt to grasp and "map" the social system that subtends them' (1986b: 45).

9

POSTMODERN POLITICS

The 1983–4 contributions to the debate on the postmodern by Lyotard, Rorty, Jameson, and Baudrillard led many to the conclusion that postmodernism and postmodernity had indeed arrived. As a result, we find in the second half of the 1980s a whole range of articles and books that seek to assess the political potential of the postmodern. Some titles clearly announce that political interest: *Postmodernism and Politics* (Arac 1986), 'Postmodernity and politics' (Brodsky 1987), 'Postmodernism and politics' (Aronowitz 1987), *Universal Abandon? The Politics of Postmodernism* (Ross 1988), 'Postmodern politics' (Ryan 1988), *The Postmodern Political Condition* (Heller and Feher, 1988), 'Postmodernism: roots and politics' (Gitlin 1989), 'Periodization and politics in the postmodern' (Turner 1990b). Other titles, such as Steven Best and Douglas Kellner's *Postmodern Theory: Critical Interrogations* or John McGowan's *Postmodernism and its Critics* (both of 1991), are less self-evident but not less pertinent.

It is not coincidental that, with the exception of Agnes Heller, all these critics are male, or that, for that matter, the debate on the postmodern has to a disproportionate extent been conducted by men. Since the mid–1960s, politically oriented female critics had had an agenda of their own, one in which the avant-gardist and seemingly elitist concerns of postmodernism played an at best marginal role. It was only after the publication of Craig Owens's 'The discourse of others: feminists and postmodernism' in 1983, that feminists began to take serious notice of the debate on postmodernism, even if they were not undividedly happy with the way Owens had claimed them for the postmodern.[1] There is, then, parallel to the as often as not highly abstract (and male) discussion on the politics of postmodernism that I have just introduced, a second, at least sometimes politically more concrete, discussion that focuses on the question to what extent postmodernism can facilitate or, as the case may be, stand in the way of a specifically feminist politics. To phrase the question somewhat differently: to what extent are postmodern politics and feminist politics compatible? This is a major issue in such articles and books as Jane Flax's 'Postmodernism and gender relations in feminist theory' (1987) and her *Thinking Fragments* of 1990, in Elspeth Probyn's 'Bodies and anti-bodies: feminism and the postmodern' (1987), Toril Moi's 'Feminism, postmodernism and style: recent feminist criticism in the United States' (1988), Nancy Fraser and Linda Nicholson's 'Social criticism without philosophy: an encounter between feminism and postmodernism' (1988), the articles collected in Linda Nicholson's *Feminism/Postmodernism* (1990), Susan J. Hekman's *Gender and Knowledge: Elements of a Postmodern Feminism* (1990), Anne Friedberg's 'Mutual indifference: feminism and postmodernism' (1991), and so on.

Although the more general discussion of postmodern politics and the feminist one have important elements in common, I will treat them separately in order to highlight the differences between them and, more in particular, to emphasize the feminist critique of the 'postmodern project'. But I will first, by way of backdrop, present some sociological observations on the current political scene.

THE END OF MACROPOLITICS

In their *The Postmodern Political Condition* Agnes Heller and Férenc Feher straightforwardly tell us that their agenda, after 'ascertain[-ing] how much universalism remains even in the postmodern political condition' (1988: 12), is 'the reconstitution of the unity of modernity to whatever degree possible within [that] condition' (14). Such an agenda does not spell much good for their view of the postmodern and indeed, like Zygmunt Bauman, whose work I will discuss in more detail in the next chapter, or, for that matter, like Jameson, they see the arena of contemporary politics as a free-for-all no longer controlled by the (relative) order that used to be imposed on political debates by the great, overarching political visions of modernity, embodied in traditional party politics and trade unions. For Heller and Feher – but one might quote any of a dozen theorists on this point – the postmodern political condition 'is premissed on the acceptance of the plurality of cultures and discourses' (5). As a consequence, postmodern politics are the politics of single-issue movements and of single-issue actions 'aiming at the strengthening or elimination respectively of a single function of modernity' (3), and are wholly incompatible with '[r]edemptive politics of any kind' (4). Although Bauman would deny that the politics of the 'imagined communities' which in his analysis have replaced party politics cannot have redemptive aspects, he, too, agrees that postmodern politics are no longer based on the inclusive emancipatory political platforms of modernity and are thus functional rather than structural. Macropolitics give way to a multiplicity of short-term micropolitics. In an arresting argument, Heller and Feher see these single-issue politics even at work in traditional party politics and interpret Thatcherism ('Thatcher's project of a "popular capitalism" ') in such postmodernist–functionalist terms. This argument has the obvious merit that it extends the sphere of influence of the *Zeitgeist* and in doing so gives that *Geist* more body, so to speak, but one would like to see more supporting evidence than the monomania of one prime minister.

This, in any case, is the background: a widely perceived loss of faith in party politics and thus in the workings of western democracy, that is in traditional macropolitics; the ensuing rise of single-issue movements and single-issue coalitions; a reappearance of the ' "ethnicity component" of politics' (8; since Heller and Feher wrote this the disasters in Bosnia and elsewhere have further confirmed the rise of sometimes fanatical ethnic 'identity' politics); and, as a consequence of these developments, a political field that Heller and Feher assess, rather extremely, as 'almost totally irrational and unpredictable' (8), but that other (modernist) theorists too see as dangerously unstable.

THE PROBLEM OF LEGITIMATION

The postmodern attack on representation, and thus on legitimation, has paradoxical consequences. If our representations – epistemological, moral, political – are ultimately without ground, then they must be the effect of power structures and are unconsciously political. This is at first sight not necessarily a bad thing, as we have seen in the discussion of cultural politics. Many commentators have suggested that this proliferation of the political in all directions (which simultaneously implies the dispersal of power) is positively enabling. After telling us that '[a] postmodern politics must complete the Gramscian move to extend the political into all spheres, domains and practices of our culture', Andrew Ross suggests that there are 'only social gains' in a postmodern

> politics of difference, wherein many of the voices of color, gender and sexual orientation, newly liberated from the margins, have found representation under conditions that are not exclusively tailored to the hitherto heroicized needs and interests of white, male intellectuals and/or white, male workers.
>
> (Ross 1988: xv–xvi)

Best and Kellner likewise suggest that

> [t]he postmodern emphasis on disintegration and change in the present situation points to new openings and possibilities for social transformation and struggle. The postmodern celebration of plurality and multiplicity facilitates a more diverse, open, and contextual politics that refuses to privilege any general recipe for social change or any particular group. The postmodern theory of decentred power also allows for the multiplication of possibilities for political struggle, no longer confined simply to the realm of production or the state.
>
> (1991: 286–7)

If everything is political, then everything can at least theoretically be transformed and given a more desirable shape. Let me quote Michael Ryan, who sees almost utopian possibilities, on this point: 'To embrace politics in a postmodern sense is to place a stake on contingency, on the insight that power, no matter how grounded in "reality", how seemingly bound to "material" necessity, is up for grabs, movable and therefore removable' (1988: 576). Postmodern politics, a 'radically contingent arena of imagination, strategy and creative manoeuvre' (575), offers hitherto unthought-of new possibilities.

However, what postmodern politics does not offer is a legitimation of the interventions that the advent of the postmodern has thus enabled. For postmodernism simultaneously undermines all traditional macropolitics, in that it rejects the metanarratives in which all macropolitics, those of the left as well as those of the right, classically ground themselves. If all is politics, even the legitimations derived from metanarratives, then there is no extra-political, Archimedean point, from which the world can legitimately be moved through political intervention. It does not come as a surprise to find Bauman saying that '[t]here is no conceivable way a realistic Left program could be patched together out of postmodernist theory' (Bauman 1986–7: 86).[2]

Still, this is what the most interesting attempts to formulate a postmodern politics try to do. Seeking to skirt the relativist trap of a politics wholly based on emotivist ethics – moral positions as the expression of personal tastes or individual acts of will – the critics involved in such attempts usually try to reconcile a form of Marxism with postmodern pluralism to create what some of them call a post-Marxist politics that they sharply distinguish from ex-Marxism. Post-Marxist politics can be broadly classified in two categories: those that reject universalism – and are more explicitly postmodern – and those that try to salvage universalism while admitting that universalism cannot have an essentialist basis. The classic texts of the first category, invoked by virtually everyone writing on postmodern politics, are Ernesto Laclau and Chantal Mouffe's *Hegemony and Socialist Strategy: Towards a Radical Democratic Politics* of 1985 ('a book widely discussed as a prospectus for a postmodern politics' (Ross 1988: xiv)), their 'Post-marxism without apologies' (1987), and the various articles they published separately in the later 1980s, for instance in Andrew Ross's *Universal Abandon?* of 1988, on which I will mainly draw here, both for brevity's sake and because in these later articles they try to meet some of the objections raised against their position, especially on the thorny issue of legitimation. The most valorous attempt to defend an ungrounded, anti-essentialist universalism seems to me that formulated in Steven Best and Douglas Kellner's *Postmodern Theory: Critical Interrogations* (1991), with a brief discussion of which I will conclude this section.

Laclau and Mouffe

Hegemony and Socialist Strategy may be described as an attempt to revitalize democracy on the basis of a poststructuralist/postmodern social analysis. Chantal Mouffe tells us that the project outlined in the book

> proposes a reformulation of the socialist project that avoids the twin pitfalls of marxist socialism and social democracy, while providing the left with a new imaginary, an imaginary that speaks to the tradition of the great emancipatory struggles but that also takes into account recent theoretical contributions by psychoanalysis and philosophy. In effect, such a project could be defined as being both modern and postmodern. It pursues the 'unfulfilled project of modernity', but, unlike Habermas, we believe that there is no longer a role to be played in this project by the epistemological perspective of the Enlightenment.
>
> (1988: 32–3)

Yet the political project of the Enlightenment, defined here as equality and freedom for all, does not have to be abandoned because what postmodernism challenges is not modernity *per se*, but its essentialist, rationalistic and humanistic underpinnings, what Mouffe calls 'the Enlightenment project of self-foundation' (34). Laclau argues that

> it is precisely the *ontological status* of the central categories of the discourses of modernity, and not their *content*, that is at stake; that the erosion of this status is expressed through the 'postmodern' sensibility; and that this erosion, far from being a negative phenomenon, represents an enormous amplification of the content and operability of the values of modernity, making it possible to ground them on foundations much more solid than those of the Enlightenment project (and its various positivist or Hegelian–Marxist reformulations).
>
> (1988: 66)

Thus, for Laclau and Mouffe, '[a]bandonment of the myth of foundations does not lead to nihilism' (79). On the contrary, with the 'concomitant dissolution of the category "subject" ' it 'further radicalizes the emancipatory possibilities offered by the Enlightenment and marxism' (80).

Laclau and Mouffe's 'radical democracy' is an emancipatory politics of difference that rejects 'the abstract Enlightenment universalism of an undifferentiated human nature' (36). Abandoning classical Marxism, which they see as severely reductionist, they replace the issues of production and the class struggle with an emphasis on discourse and on multiple, pluriform struggles. Drawing on the poststructuralist apparatus, and more in particular on Derrida's and Foucault's contributions, they argue that identity does not derive from class positions and is never definitive but always relational and that social reality is a differential system constituted by a multiplicity of discourses which in turn produce a multiplicity of subject-positions. Radical democracy acknowledges and privileges difference – the heterogeneous, the plural, 'the existence of different forms of rationality' (38) – and openness, the never finalized, processual character of identity, discourses, and the social field at large. Not surprisingly, the second part of Laclau's claim that he and Mouffe had situated themselves 'squarely within the discussion around postmodernity from the point of view of marxism' (1988: 78) has raised eyebrows among more orthodox Marxists. If this position is not actually closer to Lyotard than to Marx – 'Abandonment of the myth of foundations . . . leads . . . to a proliferation of discursive interventions and arguments that are necessary (Laclau 1988: 79) – it is certainly closer to a liberal pluralist position than a traditional Marxist one. It is not that Laclau and Mouffe are not aware of this: 'The task of the left . . . cannot be to renounce liberal-democratic ideology, but on the contrary, to deepen and expand it' (1985: 176). In fact, their program is all the more attractive because it offers new impulses to social democracy (in the north-west European understanding of the term).

Less satisfactory, however, is their treatment of the problem of legitimation which takes the form of an attempt to undo the binary opposition of objectivism and relativism. Invoking Aristotle's concept of *phronèsis*, 'ethical knowledge' as distinct from scientific knowledge,[3] Laclau and Mouffe argue that the demise of objectivism need not have serious theoretical consequences. 'It is always possible', Mouffe claims with astonishing optimism

> to distinguish between the just and the unjust, the legitimate and the unlegitimate, but this can only be done from within a given tradition, with the help of standards that this tradition provides; in fact, there is no point of view external to all tradition from which one can offer a universal judgment. (1988: 37)

To distinguish between the legitimate and the unlegitimate is perhaps easy enough if the issue is apartheid (at least since the

1960s), but how about, say, abortion, gun control, euthanasia or other issues where the standards of tradition are of not much help – except to those who take the conservative view of things? Mouffe's optimism completely ignores that what we have reason to consider improvements in our sense of what is just or unjust and legitimate or illegitimate have always been established in the face of an oppositional traditionalism. Laclau offers an argument similar to that of Mouffe, suggesting that a given 'ensemble of arguments constitutes the texture of a group's *common sense.* And this common sense, extended in time, is what constitutes a *tradition*' (79). Such a tradition in turn constitutes the 'horizon' of a group and such (inevitably contingent) horizons have taken the place of Enlightenment foundations:

> It is the contraposition between foundation and horizon that I think enables us to understand the change in the ontological status of emancipatory discourses and, in general, of metanarratives, in the transition from modernity to postmodernity. A formation that is unified or totalized in relation to a horizon is a formation without foundation; it constitutes itself as a unity only as it delimits itself from that which it negates.
>
> (81)

Since a horizon is 'an empty locus . . . in which concrete argumentative practices operate over a backdrop of radical freedom, of radical contingency' (81), a tradition 'is responsive to the diverse argumentative practices that take place in society' (79). But why should we have such Lyotardian expectations of radical freedom, or of a tradition's responsiveness to oppositional argumentative practices? The point about, say, fundamentalist traditions, is that they take pride in an aggressive unresponsiveness. The bottom line of Laclau and Mouffe's radical democracy is a set of familiar ethical a prioris that are presented within a postmodern, that is, discursive, context and that apparently are graced with an extraordinary persuasive power.

On closer inspection, the politics of difference always turn out to be a new version of what might somewhat paradoxically be called the politics of (western) uniformity. In order to function – or even to survive – the politics of difference must exclude those who are *really* different, such as Iranian fundamentalists or staunch defenders of apartheid, that is, those who don't include themselves in their idea of difference, for whom it is only the others who are always different. Like Lyotard's language games, difference can only thrive in the absence of non-difference, of terror. Its ultimate enabling condition is freedom, in other words, the metanarrative of universal political emancipation. One can understand why Lyotard, Laclau and Mouffe, and others are reluctant to confront the fundamental otherness of refusing to participate in difference, in the universal agreement to be free. Such a refusal, which effectively puts an end to the politics of difference, can only be confronted through the exercise of power, if not the use of force. Such refusals force difference into an at least temporary unity, into consensus. Still, for obvious reasons one does not want to quarrel with Laclau and Mouffe's program, apart from its well-intentioned naiveté in assuming that (after the necessary exclusions) difference can be simply negotiated within a democratic pluralist framework ('In order that the defense of the worker's interest is not pursued at the cost of the rights of women, immigrants, or consumers,' Mouffe tells us, 'it is necessary to establish an equivalence between these different struggles' (1988: 42)). This sounds suspiciously like the transparent, conflict-free society promised by communism, but there is no guarantee that difference can be negotiated so easily. Against what apparently universal norm should such equivalence be measured? Sympathy for Laclau and Mouffe's program should not blind us to the fact that it is built upon utopian expectations and that it invokes a metanarrative that is foreign to a good many 'traditions' and 'horizons'.

How difficult it is to accept this is illustrated by Best and Kellner. Equally eager as Laclau and Mouffe to reject foundationalist thought – and, with it, what they call 'Habermas' universalistic quasi-foundationalism' – they yet feel that universality is necessary: 'a just society requires establishing certain universal rights like equality, rule by law, freedom, and democratic participation' (1991: 243). That universality, however, is 'not . . . transcendental and essentialist,' but 'a product of historical struggle':

> we would argue that these (historically constructed) universal rights and freedoms are themselves provisional, constructed, contextual, and the product of social struggle in a specific historical context. Although human rights and democratic values are to be defended and extended, they

> should not be mystified. Consequently, we would provide a historicist rather than an [sic] philosophical foundation for these values, interpreting them as the product of struggle and as the progressive constructs of a specific social-historical situation rather than as essential features of human beings or quasi-transcendental postulates of a specific sort, deriving from language or communication.
>
> (1991: 242)

This would seem straightforward enough, its anti-essentialism underscored by the swipe at Habermas. However, Best and Kellner indulge in some mystifications of their own. Their (historicist) legitimation of human rights is deeply romanticized. What is presented glowingly as 'the product of struggle and as the progressive constructs of a specific-historical situation' – the language itself is supposed to win us over – owes its current visibility on the global scene to the enormous military and economic power that the North Atlantic bourgeoisie (Richard Rorty's term) has generated in the past and still continues to generate. The 'historical struggle' has, on the whole, and seen from the perspective of a colonized Third World, taken place between privileged citizens and even more privileged citizens, after which its results were forcefully exported, much like Christianity and, in fact, mostly in its wake. Best and Kellner's historicist legitimation is a rosy view of a series of developments that fortunately have taken place but that legitimate nothing except with reference to the familiar metanarrative of universal emancipation. There is, for those who don't want any part of it, no difference between an essentialist and a historicist universal paradigm if it is forced upon them.

Apart from this, Best and Kellner have much to say about postmodern politics that is quite pertinent. While acknowledging the positive potential of the 'postmodern celebration of plurality and multiplicity,' they find in the various theories of the postmodern that they examine a crippling lack of interest in – or even hostility against – subjectivity, intersubjectivity, agency, structural causation, and systemic relations, not to mention the economy or the state. In other words, a good deal of what is crucial for political theory remains largely or even wholly untheorized.[4] To them, postmodern theory 'is too subjectivist and aestheticized to develop a politics of alliances which requires theories of needs, interests, consensus, and mediation. Indeed, politics is mediation between competing groups, interests and demands' (292). Only Laclau and Mouffe partly escape this malaise. However, while they approve of Laclau and Mouffe's position 'that liberal-democratic discourse is necessary for radical politics insofar as it provides a language which can articulate and defend the needs and political demands of individuals and groups' (198), they have strong doubts about their rejection of universals: 'Where Laclau and Mouffe hold that no democracy is possible "without renouncing the discourse of the universal" . . . it is arguable that democracy is impossible without the universally binding character of law, rights, and freedoms' (204). Indeed, one can only agree that the right to differ must be both universal and binding if difference wants to avoid being forced into unity.

Best and Kellner opt for a politics that should base itself upon theories of society suggested by 'the best of postmodern theory' in combination with 'the best of modern theory' (272). That postmodern 'best' is its determination to respect and honor difference in all its possible manifestations. It is

> one of the lessons of postmodern theory that we are all constituted in a broad range of subject positions and that we should be aware of the constraints involved in living out class, race, ethnic, regional, generational, sexual, and gender positions.
>
> (213)

They seek to mobilize this radically democratic perspective within a framework that draws heavily on critical theory, which for them theorizes what postmodernism has left untheorized. On the basis of this proposed alliance between critical theory and the postmodern, they argue for a combination of micropolitics and macropolitics, of 'detailed and concrete uniperspectival analysis' (270) and multiperspectival theorizing, for an alternation – or, where more appropriate, an 'intersection' – of Marxist, Weberian, and feminist perspectives, while avoiding the 'extreme relativism' of some postmodern theory.

Best and Kellner's proposals which, although sensitive to difference, are not averse to consensus, will be more attractive to (post-) Marxists than to anti-representational postmodern theorists, but they contain substantial postmodern elements. In the work of Laclau and Mouffe and that of Best and Kellner (or, for that matter, Michael Ryan), all of whom work within the Marxist tradition, the influence of postmodern theory – and in particular its emphasis on the pluralist character and the discursive constitution of the social field – is prominently illustrated. Leftist political thought has imaginatively confronted the postmodern.

POSITIVE AND NEGATIVE FREEDOM

In his review article on Lyotard's *The Postmodern Condition*, John Keane argues that Lyotard's postmodernism implies 'the need for democracy, for institutional arrangements which guarantee that protagonists of similar or different forms of language games can openly and continuously articulate their respective forms of life' (1987: 13). Lyotard, however, had already dismissed such an unproblematic translation into politics of the position articulated in his book and thrown his towel in the ring:

> the idea that I think we need today in order to make decisions in political matters cannot be the idea of the totality, or of the unity, of a body. It can only be the idea of a multiplicity or of a diversity. Then the question arises: How can a regulatory use of this idea of the political take place? How can it be pragmatically efficacious (to the point where, for example, it would make one decision just and another unjust)? Is a politics regulated by such an idea of multiplicity possible? Is it possible to decide in a just way in, and according to, this multiplicity? And here I must say that I don't know.
>
> (1985: 94)

Lyotard's reflections bring us to the heart of much postmodern theory and practice: its abhorrence of totality, of unity, and the almost exclusive focus on micropolitics at the expense of the macropolitical that is the consequence of that position.

In the preceding section I have discussed attempts to formulate a postmodern politics that should ideally attend to both the micro and the macro level. Characteristic of such attempts is that although they reject metaphysical legitimations they still seek to legitimate themselves. Legitimations such as those offered by Laclau and Mouffe or Best and Kellner signal a *willingness* to enter the field of the macropolitical; they suggest a positive attitude towards the new directions suggested by postmodern theory.

Such legitimations are, in fact, inevitable, because the politics that they seek to legitimize involve not merely the subversion of existing power, but the attempt to gain and consequently exercise power. They point at a determination to engage the prevailing macrostructures and confront them with alternatives, in other words, at a determination to participate in the macropolitical debate. That determination is based upon a positive interpretation of the freedom from modernity's totalizing impulses that postmodernism has created. Most postmodern theory, however, and hence much of postmodern politics, allows itself to be imprisoned in what John McGowan, following Hegel, Kierkegaard and others, calls negative freedom.[5]

McGowan sees a debilitating paradox in much postmodern thought. 'Phrased positively', he argues, 'postmodernism is the attempt to legitimate knowledge claims and the moral/political bases for action, not on the basis of undubitable truths, but on the basis of human practices within established communities' (McGowan 1991: 24). This is indeed what we have seen in the efforts of Laclau and Mouffe and Best and Kellner. The postmodern attacks on a modernism which 'proclaim[ed] a heady freedom from traditions, from social environments, from reality itself', should be seen against this background: 'Postmodern art and thought have been particularly hard on the characteristic modernist strategy of retreat, arguing that this move ensured the very impotence that modernism wanted to avoid' (8). Modernism stands accused of having created an entirely negative, unproductive, freedom.

Postmodernism, however, repeats the defeatist gestures of modernism, although admittedly on another level. Like Keane, McGowan sees a deeply democratic impulse at work in postmodern thought: 'we should recognize how fully the ideal of an egalitarian, pluralistic democratic order informs most postmodern work' (28). But it is caught in the dilemma created by its deep-rooted suspicion of power: 'postmodernism finds itself between a rock and a hard place, unable to ground democracy by appeal to external, nonhuman principles, but unwilling to accept humanly generated principles as legitimate norms rather than further instances of arrangements imposed by power' (28). Laclau and Mouffe and Best and Kellner belong to that small group of theorists that seek legitimation in the intersubjectivity of their historicist models, to the extent even that they downplay the role that power plays, or has played, in the near background. One way out of the dilemma that McGowan sketches would seem to be offered by the attempt to subvert the existing order by way of play, *jouissance*, but the impotence of such an aestheticist strategy is obvious. Anti-representation has its effects in the field of cultural politics, although even there the longevity of those effects should not be overestimated, but it has little to contribute in the field of social politics. It offers the postmodernist a semblance of freedom, but it is, as McGowan remarks, 'unprofitably close to the modernist goal of autonomy' (2). Significantly, autonomy is the term that Rorty uses to describe the objective of his postmodern 'ironist', who

> is not in the business of supplying himself and his fellow ironists with a method, a platform, or a rationale. He is just doing the same thing that all ironists do – attempting autonomy. He is trying to get out from under inherited contingencies and make his own contingencies, get out from under an old final vocabulary and fashion one which will be all his own. The generic trait of ironists is that they do not hope to have their doubts about their final vocabularies settled by something larger than themselves. This means that their criterion for resolving doubts, their criterion of private perfection, is autonomy rather than affiliation to a power other than themselves.
>
> (Rorty 1989: 97)

Rorty's ironist attempts to retreat to a separate space, far from the political crowd.

This postmodern emulation of negative modernist strategies is the consequence either of the fear of representation and power expressed by Lyotard and by Foucault or of the fear – expressed most clearly by Jameson, Baudrillard, and other theorists who draw on the *Frankfurter Schule* – that the capitalist monolith, so much more powerful now than under modernity, immediately will render all resistance ineffective. (We remember that for Baudrillard resisting simulation is itself a simulation.) If the monolith has indeed become virtually all-powerful, then autonomy, whether on the personal or on the group level, automatically is an important political category, even if ineffective. McGowan's conclusion that postmodern theorists on the whole 'remain wedded to modernist notions of distance and disengagement as enabling radical critique' is fully warranted. In fact, Jameson had already said as much of Lyotard in his foreword to *The Postmodern Condition.* The radical anti-representationalism that is a favorite postmodern strategy in the creation of distance is at the same time politically crippling. On the level of the group, or community, the postmodern insistence on distance and difference hides a similar danger, because on this level difference can exist only in the interstices of hegemony. The centrifugal forces of the postmodern may easily cause a rupture between the margins and the hegemonic center, and thus hurl the margins into what is in effect a political void, even if that void is experienced as a new freedom.

The upshot of all this is that much postmodern theory, because of its fierce opposition to the politics of modernity, is wholly apolitical in the macropolitical sense. The fears of representation, of power, and of a social reality wholly dominated by capitalism, have steered most postmodern theorists towards the tactics of micropolitics while leaving the field of macropolitics to the enemy. Mark Poster has remarked that the problem for theory 'is to generate discourses whose power effects are limited as much as possible to the subversion of power' (Poster 1989: 30). Poster's formulation, no matter how cautious, recognizes that power must not only be subverted but also exercised. It is the refusal to claim power, that is, to move from a negative to a positive conception of postmodern politics that has kept feminists on their guard *vis-à-vis* most postmodern theory.

FEMINISM AND THE POSTMODERN

Craig Owens's 'The discourse of others: feminists and postmodernism' of 1983 evoked a thoroughly ambivalent response in many of its feminist readers because of what was perceived as its patronizing attitude. Owens's suggestion that 'women's insistence on difference and incommensurability may not only be compatible with, but also an instance of postmodern thought' (Owens 1983: 61–2) seemed to relegate feminism to the position of a subsidiary to a (male) main current. Whatever the merit of that suggestion, Owens's article certainly effected a breakthrough. In Susan Suleiman's words,

> [i]n his 1983 essay . . . Owens made one of those conceptual leaps that later turn out to have initiated a whole new train

> of thought. Simply, what Owens did was to theorize the political implications of the intersection between 'the feminist critique of patriarchy and the postmodern critique of representation'.
>
> (Suleiman 1991: 115)

Owens's essay marked the beginning of serious feminist interest in the postmodern. This is not to say that before 1983 Anglo-American feminism was out of touch with the times. French-oriented American feminists such as Alice Jardine (whose 'Gynesis' was published in 1982) were fully aware of the contemporary scene. However, apart from the fact that for them, as for the French themselves, poststructuralism was modernist rather than postmodernist (see, for instance, Jardine's *Gynesis: Configurations of Woman and Modernity* of 1985), their poststructuralist feminism had not all that much in common with the postmodern politics that developed in the course of the 1980s. The same holds for British poststructuralist feminism. The British feminist scene, with its mixture of Lacanian and Althusserian themes, was politically far more alive than American poststructuralist feminism, but one does not want to offend its Marxist orientation by including it in a book on the postmodern. I will therefore restrict myself here to those feminists who actually addressed the postmodernism of the 1980s rather than the poststructuralism of the 1970s.

By and large those feminists were modernist – in the Anglo-American sense of the term – or even pre-modernist in orientation. They had for a fairly long time felt comfortable with a realist epistemology, relying, as Laura Kipnis has noted, 'on a theory of language as transparency' (1988: 159), and had equated the feminine with the biological body, leading them to a politics that had actual women as its subject. For Jardine, by contrast, the feminine signified 'the unknown, the terrifying, the monstrous – everything which is not held in place by concepts such as Man, Truth, Meaning' (Creed 1987: 56). The feminine here signifies a position of otherness, leading to a wholly different and, as for instance Toril Moi has argued, perhaps even impossible politics: 'But simply to equate women with otherness deprives the feminist struggle of any kind of specificity. What is repressed is not *otherness*, but specific, historically constructed agents' (Moi 1988: 12). Finally, American feminism had developed a range of unmistakably essentialist positions, from Shulamith Firestone's targeting of biological differences as the source of sexism in 1970 (in *The Dialectic of Sex*) to Nancy Chodorow's enormously influential theory of mothering published in 1978 (*The Reproduction of Mothering: Psychoanalysis and the Sociology of Gender*).

But such essentialist theorizing has more or less had its day. In 1988 Nancy Fraser and Linda Nicholson could note (not without satisfaction) that '[s]ince around 1980, many feminist scholars have come to abandon the project of grand social theory' (1988: 98). There is no doubt that the gradual demise of that project is related to the feminist response to postmodernism.[6] That response has, not surprisingly, focused primarily on the partly identical problems of essentialism, universalism, and legitimation on the one hand, and on the 'intersection' between the critique of patriarchy and the critique of representation on the other. To be more precise, feminism generally separates the postmodern philosophical critique from the cultural critique. In doing so, it tends to reject the first while welcoming the second.

Let me first qualify this rejection of postmodern philosophy, however. As I have just noted, the loss of interest in grand theories on the part of contemporary feminists is surely related to the impact of postmodernism. The position taken up by Fraser and Nicholson leaves little room for doubt:

> if postmodern-feminist critique must remain 'theoretical', not just any kind of theory will do. Rather, theory here would be explicitly historical, attuned to the cultural specificity of different societies and periods and to that of different groups within societies and periods. Thus, the categories of postmodern-feminist theory would be inflected by temporality, with historically specific institutional categories like 'the modern, restricted, male-headed, nuclear family' taking precedence over ahistorical, functionalist categories like reproduction and mothering.... Moreover, post-modern feminist theory would be nonuniversalist. When its focus became cross-cultural or transepochal its mode of attention would be comparativist rather than universalist, attuned to changes and contrasts instead of to 'covering laws.' Finally, postmodern-feminist theory would dispense with the idea of a subject of history. It would replace unitary notions of 'woman' and 'feminine gender identity' with plural and complexly constructed conceptions of social identity, treat-

> ing gender as one relevant strand among others, attending also to class, race, ethnicity, age, and sexual orientation.
> (1988: 101)

Fraser and Nicholson's privileging of difference and pluralism over essentialist unity needs no further commentary. But this is not the whole story. Even though they are a good deal more receptive to postmodern thought than the average feminist critic, Fraser and Nicholson are still wary of postmodern philosophy, arguing for a 'postmodern-feminist paradigm of social criticism without philosophy' (100). Their position is, not coincidentally, very close to that of Laclau and Mouffe (who are mysteriously absent here; Linda Nicholson's 340-page collection of essays on feminism and postmodernism has the most unlikely characters in its index – such as Robert Frost, Ronald Reagan, and Albert Speer – but not Laclau and/or Mouffe). Like Laclau and Mouffe, Fraser and Nicholson seek to reconcile postmodern difference with Enlightenment emancipation, which, as Toril Moi has pointed out, is essential to (Anglo-American) feminism: 'Present-day feminism is a historically specific movement, rooted in French Enlightenment thought (Mary Wollstonecraft) and in British liberalism (John Stuart Mill), and consequently wedded, in deeply critical style, to notions of truth, justice, freedom, and equality' (Moi 1988: 17).

The feminist rejection of postmodern philosophy is based on what is perceived as postmodernism's rejection of the Enlightenment project. Its rejection is thus based on an equation of postmodernism and the radical anti-representationalism promoted by deconstructionist postmodernism and by Lyotard's *Postmodern Condition.*[7] Sabina Lovibond's reaction is exemplary:

> What, then, are we to make of suggestions that the [Enlightenment] project has run out of steam and that the moment has passed for remaking society on rational, egalitarian lines? It would be only natural for anyone placed at the sharp end of one or more of the existing power structures (gender, race, capitalist class . . .) to feel a pang of disappointment at this news. But wouldn't it also be in order to feel *suspicion*? How can anyone ask me to say goodbye to 'emancipatory metanarratives' when my own emancipation is still such a patchy, hit-and-miss affair?
> (Lovibond 1990: 161)

Nancy Hartsock voices similar suspicions:

> Just when we are talking about the changes we want, ideas of progress and the possibility of systematically and rationally organizing human society become dubious and suspect. Why is it only now that critiques are made of the will to power inherent in the effort to create theory.
>
> (Hartsock 1990: 164)

Her conclusion is that 'postmodernism represents a dangerous approach for any marginalized group to adopt' (160). Susan Bordo argues that it is too soon to let social institutions that have barely begun to respond to modernist social criticism 'off the hook via postmodern heterogeneity and instability' (Bordo 1990: 153). Sandra Harding, who supports the attack on the Enlightenment subject – the naturalized, essentialized subject of liberal humanism – still cannot see how feminism 'could completely take leave of Enlightenment assumptions and still remain feminist' (Harding 1990: 99). Outside the radical poststructuralist camp no feminist wants to break with Enlightenment ideals – rather than Enlightenment *assumptions*, as Harding has it.[8]

The distinction between the political project of the Enlightenment and the essentialist assumptions that have traditionally accompanied it is crucial here, as it was for Laclau and Mouffe. It explains, for instance, why Jane Flax can say that 'despite an understandable attraction to the (apparently) logical, orderly world of the Enlightenment, feminist theory more properly belongs in the terrain of postmodern philosophy' (Flax 1987: 625). What Flax objects to is a set of unacceptable Enlightenment assumptions concerning the subject and representation:

> Feminist notions of the self, knowledge, and truth are too contradictory to those of the Enlightenment to be contained within its categories. The way(s) to feminist future(s) cannot lie in reviving or appropriating Enlightenment concepts of the person or knowledge.
>
> (625)

For Flax, as for Fraser and Nicholson and a good many other feminist critics, postmodernism has had a wholesome influence on the feminist debate. Hegemonic, patriarchal culture had already been exposed as constructed, not given, but postmodernism brought deconstruction into areas that (non-poststructuralist) feminism had left unexamined. Its insistence on difference has for instance deconstructed gender as a natural, essentialist category and has shown up its relational, that is, constructed nature. As Susan Hekman puts it in her discussion of Derrida:

> his inscription of difference, an inscription that, while not denying difference, rejects polarities, opens up a new discourse on women and sexuality. This discourse speaks in a multiplicity of sexual voices; it is a discourse which has no center, neither masculine nor feminine, yet does not erase either the masculine or the feminine.
>
> (Hekman 1990: 175)

Foucault's emphasis on the relation between knowledge and power and on the dispersal of power throughout the social field have similarly been enabling.[9] Moreover, the attack on representation, with its implication that the oppressed have no more direct, unmediated access to the real than their oppressors, has alerted feminism to its own propensity to construct essentialist assumptions. Barbara Creed speaks of the 'paradox' that 'we feminists', while regarding patriarchal discourse as fiction, 'nevertheless proceed as if our position, based on a belief in the oppression of women, were somewhat closer to the truth' (1987: 67). Jane Flax is equally straightforward:

> It is on the metatheoretical level that postmodern philosophies of knowledge can contribute to a more accurate self-understanding of the nature of our theorizing. We cannot simultaneously claim (1) that the mind, the self, and knowledge are socially constituted and that what we can know depends upon our social practices and contexts *and* (2) that feminist theory can uncover the Truth of the whole once and for all.
>
> (1987: 633)

In exposing such essentialist strains, postmodernism has made significant contributions to the current state of the feminist debate.

Both the postmodern critique of philosophy, and the postmodern critique of culture – which is seen to have an important democratizing effect – have made a real difference, as many feminists readily acknowledge. But the anti-representationalism of the Lyotardian philosophical critique is seen as ultimately disabling. Fraser and Nicholson conclude that Lyotard 'rules out the sort of critical social theory that employs general categories like gender, race and class' (1988: 89). To many feminist critics such an abandoning of cross-cultural categories can only lead to an individualist politics that would be disastrous for the feminist effort. And thus, to keep at bay the specter of a wholly discursive postmodernism, in which politics is reduced to individualist rhetorical moves, Fraser and Nicholson plead for a 'carefully constructed postmodernism' that should negotiate the problem of radical anti-representationalism versus (a form of) consensus.

Like the post-Marxists, postmodern feminists find themselves in the position of wishing to preserve Enlightenment ideals, such as freedom and equality, while simultaneously rejecting the universalist assumptions that gave these ideas their original legitimation. As with the post-Marxists, the paradox is giving them a rough ride. But the postmodern feminist position may be even more difficult. The feminist political identity, which from the beginning was tied up with gender, was in its earlier stages essentialist and, paradoxically, hegemonic (in the sense that it expressed the identity of white, middle-class, and often highly educated women). In its deconstruction of gender, postmodern feminism has fragmented that political identity in a top-down process that was met halfway by a bottom-up process that had its grounds in actual political practice (in which women of color, of various ethnic backgrounds, discovered their 'difference' from the white, middle-class norm; see note 6). Postmodernism has offered this fragmentation, and with it the fragmentation of the feminist political agenda, full legitimation (if it was ever in need of that). But it is not necessary to see this in negative terms. Apart from the fact that the new feminisms still have important goals in common, there is also the undeniably democratizing influence of postmodern fragmentation. The fragmentation of postmodern feminist politics may not have made things any easier, but conflict is the price one should be glad to pay for difference.

NOTES

1 Witness, for example, Elspeth Probyn's reaction: 'For all of Craig Owens's magnanimity in negotiating "the treacherous course between postmodernism and feminism" (Owens, 1983: 59), feminism is merely

displayed as a "soft" political spot for postmodernism' (1987: 350). Teresa de Lauretis is more direct in her disapproval of those contemporary discourses, such as that of 'postmodern antiaesthetics' – a clear reference to the Foster collection in which Owens's essay was published – which 'with amazing facility... lump women together with children and slaves, madmen and poets, and go so far as to include in such chaotic typology the entire "Third World" ' (1986: 11). Barbara Creed voices similar reservations: 'writers such as Owens, in his attempt to "introduce" feminism into the postmodern debate, do so on terms which situate feminism as if it were a "guest," the other brought in from the cold to join the "host" ' (1987: 66). Creed hits back with the suggestion that 'it may be possible that postmodern theory is more in debt to feminism than it is prepared to acknowledge' (67). As a matter of fact, Creed is by no means the only critic to suggest that feminism crucially anticipated postmodernism. Probyn thinks that 'it could be argued that what has been labeled as the postmodern dilemma was precipitated not by the supposed passing of modernism but by the questions feminists brought to diverse modernist disciplines' (1990: 178). Patricia Waugh tells us that 'long before poststructuralists and postmodernists began to assemble their cultural manifestos' cultural marginalization had given women 'a sense of identity as constructed through impersonal and social relations of power' (1989: 3), and for Martin Jay '[t]he postmodernist sensibility has also borrowed a great deal from that dimension of feminist thought which rejects the abstract universalism underlying any homogenizing humanist discourse' (1991: 100). I'm not so sure that feminism has contributed all that much to postmodernism. There is not much awareness of feminism in the early stages of the postmodern debate and the indifference to gender of major theorists of the postmodern such as Lyotard, Jameson, and Baudrillard is on a par with modernity's indifference (and has not escaped feminist notice). When Susan Suleiman argues that feminism 'provided for postmodernism a concrete political edge' and 'brings to postmodernism the political guarantee postmodernism needs in order to feel respectable as an avant-garde practice' (1991: 116), she must be thinking of the relatively small group of critics that promoted a postmodern cultural politics. Linda Hutcheon must have the same critical milieu in mind when she claims that feminism 'radicalized the postmodern sense of difference and de-naturalized the traditional historiographic separation of the private and the public – and the personal and the political' (1989: 142). It is more realistic to suppose that in the 1980s postmodernism and feminism – both appreciably different from their earlier incarnations of the 1960s and 1970s – have come to share a good many intellectual sources. The mutual understanding to which this has led obviously does not warrant Owens's claims or Best and Kellner's argument that 'in a sense, certain versions of feminism are inherently postmodern, since they, like postmodern theory, valorize differences, otherness and heterogeneity' (1991: 208). I should, finally, point out that some feminists are not bothered by the prospect of a postmodern take-over. Jane Flax, for instance, speaks of feminist theory as a 'type of postmodern philosophy' (Flax 1987: 624). There is, clearly, an interesting problem to sort out for a future cultural historian.

2 Todd Gitlin offers an interesting (and illuminating) anecdote:

> As Foucault said to a group of us in Berkeley in November 1983, 'There is no universal criteri[on] which permits [us] to say, "This category of power relations are [sic] bad and those are good" ' – although Foucault the person had no trouble taking political positions. Why support some resistances and not others? He could or would not say. As we pressed him to articulate the ground of his positions, he took refuge in exasperated modesty – there was no general principle at stake, and no substantial problem for his system (which was not, after all, intended to be 'a system').
>
> (1989: 358)

When Gitlin goes on to offer his own version of postmodern politics – a 'politics of limits' which 'respects horizontal social relations – multiplicity over hierarchy, juxtaposition over usurpation, difference over deference' – he is very much aware that 'this way of putting it leaves many questions unsettled' (359).

3 Laclau and Mouffe are of course aware that one cannot equate *phronèsis* with postmodern ethics. For one thing, as they point out, Aristotle maintains the distinction between logic and rhetoric that is attacked by 'the postmodern critique'.

4 Many commentators have noted the hostility towards the subject and the absence of a theory of agency in much postmodern theory (it is, indeed, hard to miss in Lyotard, Rorty, Jameson, and Baudrillard). And a fair number of them have signaled the problems involved in constructing a viable political theory on such a basis. McGowan, for instance, remarks that, on the whole, postmodern theorists 'remain wedded to modernist notions of distance and disengagement as enabling radical critique, notions that their own attack on autonomous models of selfhood render inoperable' (McGowan 1991: 211). Linda Hutcheon likewise claims that 'the postmodern has no effective theory of agency that enables a move into political *action*' (1989: 3).

5 This section is indebted to McGowan's *Postmodernism and its Critics.*

6 This does not exclude other causes. Fraser and Nicholson make the fascinating point that

> the practice of feminist politics in the 1980s has generated a new set of pressures which have worked against metanarratives. In recent years, poor and working-class women, women of color, and lesbians have finally won a wider hearing for their objections to feminist theories which fail to illuminate their lives and address their problems. They have exposed the earlier quasi-metanarratives . . . as false extrapolations from the experience of the white, middle-class, heterosexual women who dominated the beginnings of the second wave.
>
> (1988: 99)

7 There is, for exactly the same reason, strong opposition to the post-structuralist feminist position I have mentioned above. Here is, for instance, Toril Moi on Alice Jardine:

> Alice Jardine's radical rejection of Enlightenment thought makes her look for a feminism which will allow us to 'give up the quest for truth' . . . For the truth that women are oppressed? Or is truth here merely the old metaphysical bugbear, which all of us now, happily, agree to disclaim?
>
> (Moi 1988: 18)

8 For obvious reasons, black critics have voiced similar reservations. 'Should we not be suspicious of postmodern critiques of the "subject",' bell hooks asks us, 'when they surface at a historical moment when many subjugated people feel themselves coming to voice for the first time' (hooks 1993: 515).

9 See Susan Hekman's respectful discussion of Foucault in her *Gender and Knowledge: Elements of a Postmodern Feminism* (1990). Hekman's very useful book examines more feminist responses to the postmodern than I have room for here (see the chapter entitled 'The possibilities of a postmodern feminism'). In order not to cover the same ground, I have concentrated on some of the most recent contributions.

10

THE POSTMODERN AS A NEW SOCIAL FORMATION

INTRODUCTION

Daniel Bell's mid-1970s attempt to sketch the sociological background of postmodernism – at that point still exclusively defined as postmodern art, the 'spirit' of the 1960s, or both – was not immediately followed up by other sociologists. With a few exceptions, the social sciences ignored the debate on the postmodern until the mid-1980s, when (mainly British) sociologists began to see postmodernism as something worthy of serious attention.[1]

Not surprisingly, this interest owed less to the new visibility of philosophy in the debate than to those elements in the work of Baudrillard and especially Jameson that were recuperable in sociological terms – in particular the links between consumerism and the postmodern that had been suggested by both. As Mike Featherstone, one of the sociologists who entered the debate in the second half of the 1980s, put it: 'my interest in postmodernism was the outgrowth of the problems encountered in attempting to understand consumer culture, and the need to explore the direct links made between consumer culture and postmodernism by Bell, Jameson, Baudrillard, Bauman and others' (1991: viii-ix). Sharon Zukin straightly points at Jameson as the major influence: 'largely by means of Jameson's essay, the issues he identified and the examples he described gained currency in social analysis' (1988: 432). This is not to say that sociologists, social geographers, and political economists had up till the point that Jameson's influence made itself felt been blind to the restructuring of capitalism that had been underway since the early 1970s. There is an impressive body of literature dealing with so-called post-Fordist capitalism and with the global ramifications of its attempts to cope with the crisis of the early 1970s. Jameson's essay, however, offered a model that seemed to connect those developments to cultural phenomena. Besides, it also offered a useful model of fragmentation within hegemonic unity – in other words, spatialization – and it offered an equally useful new vocabulary. As Zukin puts it: 'Jameson's linking postmodernism to a current state of capitalism complemented the tendency to connect urban and regional developments to the global reorganization of capital' (432). One might add to this that the sociological interest of the later 1980s cannot be separated from the traditional left's realization that the idea of the postmodern was here to stay and that serious leftist perspectives on postmodernism were sorely needed (a realization in which Jameson also played his part).

Much of the new sociological interest was British, and if it wasn't it often went public via British channels, such as Featherstone's influential journal *Theory, Culture & Society*, which started publication in 1986. As I have just noted, up till then the British left had mainly kept its distance from the debate on the postmodern. The surprising about-turn of the mid-1980s was an indirect result of the long-standing interest of a number of critics on the British left in the politics of mass or consumer culture, an interest symbolized by the activities of the University of Birmingham's famous Centre for the Study of Contemporary Culture. When the expanded version of Jameson's 'Postmodernism and consumer society' was published in the *New Left Review* in 1984 the attention of those who were engaged in the study of consumer culture from a leftist perspective was inevitably focused upon postmodernism. That Jameson – a respected critic of impeccable political credentials, at least in leftist circles – functioned as a catalyst is obvious to anyone who looks at the footnotes to the sociological response. (It is only later, after his work becomes more widely known, that Baudrillard's seminal role is recognized and acknowledged, as in the Featherstone quotation. Even then, however, Jameson usually gets top billing.) The reorientation that became possible with Jameson's linking of consumer culture with the postmodern was no doubt facilitated by the weakening of the Althusserian orientation of the avant-gardist British left. And perhaps those who associated themselves with the Birmingham approach to consumer culture, in which subjects are not merely the will-less victims of an overwhelmingly powerful culture industry, but can actually be more or less indifferent to its hegemony and use its flotsam and jetsam to create subversive identities, felt it necessary to meet the challenge that was posed by Jameson's linkage. Indeed, part of the sociological response was provoked by the omnipotence that Jameson seemed to attribute to the culture industry and sought to defend the Birmingham position.

Since an exhaustive discussion of postmodernism and the social sciences is well beyond the scope of this book, I have selected a number of book-length sociological studies that together more or less cover the field. Mike Featherstone's *Consumer Culture and Postmodernism* (1991), as its title indicates, follows up on Jameson's 'Postmodernism and consumer society'. It also draws on the work of Scott Lash, another contributor to the impressive 'Special issue on postmodernism' of Featherstone's *Theory, Culture & Society* (5, 2–3; June 1988), who has collected his essays on the postmodern in his *Sociology of Postmodernism* (1990), the second study that I will consider here. My third selection is the most wide-ranging – and the most properly sociological, or social geographical – study that has so far been published: David Harvey's *The Condition of Postmodernity: An Enquiry into the Origins of Cultural Change* (1989). In my discussion of Harvey's book I will also pay attention to a similarly oriented and simultaneously conceived study, *Back to the Future: Modernity, Postmodernity and Locality* (1990) by Philip Cooke, again another contributor to the 'Postmodernism' issue of *Theory, Culture & Society*. I will then end this chapter with Zygmunt Bauman's essay collection *Intimations of Postmodernity* (1992). Bauman – indeed another contributor to that seminal special issue – is interested in both a sociology of the postmodern and a distinctively postmodern sociology, a vantage point from which the others look like modernist rather than postmodernist social scientists – a claim that they probably would not want to dispute.

POSTMODERN CONSPICUOUS CONSUMPTION

Postmodernism, Mike Featherstone tells us,

> has to be understood against the background of a long-term process involving the growth of a consumer culture and expansion in the number of specialists and intermediar-

> ies engaged in the production and circulation of symbolic goods. It draws on tendencies in consumer culture which favour the aestheticization of life, the assumption that the aesthetic life is the ethically good life and that there is no human nature or true self, with the goal of life an endless pursuit of new experiences, values and vocabularies.
>
> (1991: 126)

This is not to deny that postmodernism may simultaneously refer to 'an antifoundational stance in philosophy and cultural theory' – which is anyway implied in the privileging of the aesthetic – and to other 'frequently cited characteristics' (98). However, from a sociological point of view the expansion of this consumer culture and the accompanying aestheticization of life are of paramount importance:

> we should focus upon the actual cultural practices and changing power balances of those groups engaged in the production, classification, circulation and consumption of postmodern cultural goods, something which will be central to our discussion of postmodernism below.
>
> (5)

For Featherstone, postmodernism as a sociological concern is to be identified with the 'lifestyle' of what he calls the 'new middle class', which he here defines as the 'new cultural intermediaries' and the 'helping professions'. Drawing on the work of Pierre Bourdieu, he argues that this life style 'can best be understood in relation to the habitus of the new petite bourgeoisie, who, as an expanding class fraction centrally concerned with the production and dissemination of consumer culture imagery and information, is concerned to expand and legitimate its own particular dispositions and lifestyle' (84). According to Lash, who is more explicit on this point, we are witnessing a struggle between the settled bourgeoisie, 'the new middle classes of *industrial* capitalism' whose tastes run towards high modernist art, and the new postindustrial bourgeoisie that is intent upon asserting itself and as part of that process seeks to replace the older allegiance to high modernism (to, for instance, modernist architecture and painting) with its own postmodern culture (Lash 1990: 250–1).

But to return to Featherstone. The postmodern life style is not so much one particular style as a whole range of styles that have common denominators in their privileging of the aesthetic and in their eclecticism. To pursue such life styles, the new middle class, or petite bourgeoisie, must of course have 'the necessary dispositions and sensibilities that would make them more open to emotional exploration, aesthetic experience, and the aestheticization of life' (45). This postmodern sensibility is intimately linked to the contemporary city, which does, however, not mean that the city in its entirety is postmodern. Featherstone is careful to draw attention to 'the persistence of classification, hierarchy and segregation within the city' and suggests that 'the new middle class and new rich live in enclaved areas of gentrification and redevelopment which are designed to exclude outsiders' (110). However, the postmodern life style is by no means limited to the city and the new middle class: 'consumer culture publicity suggests that we all have room for self-improvement and self-expression whatever our age or class origins' (86).

The essentially urban and aestheticized character of the postmodern life style suggests an interesting pedigree: the world of Walter Benjamin's *flaneur*, the stroller through late nineteenth-century Paris.

> In this aestheticized commodity world the department stores, arcades, trams, trains, streets and the fabric of buildings and the goods on display, as well as the people who stroll through these spaces, summon up half-forgotten dreams as the curiosity and memory of the stroller is fed by the ever-changing landscape in which objects appear divorced from their context and subject to mysterious connections which are read on the surface of things. The everyday life of the big cities becomes aestheticized.
>
> (23)

Benjamin's notion of allegory – 'which points only to kaleidoscopic fragments which resist any coherent notion of what it stands for' (23) – thus foreshadows the eclectic and aestheticized postmodern sensibility. Seen from this perspective, the rise of postmodernism has been a long-term process that has its roots in the mid-nineteenth-century aestheticization of the metropolis. In the course of that development towards the fully-fledged postmodern, more and more sites have been made available as centers of aesthetic consumption. Shopping malls, (revamped) museums, theme parks, and even (renovated) parts of cities now offer themselves as spaces in which, in Featherstone's words, 'consumption and leisure are meant to be constructed as "experiences" ' (103).

This aestheticization of the quotidian has had the (unintentional) effect of undermining the rigorous distinction that has traditionally been made between high art and mass culture; as a result, the boundary between the two has become blurred, a process aided and abetted by those artists who have gone, and still go, into industrial design, advertising, and the various 'image production industries'. The aestheticizing process can thus draw on the whole repertory of art through the ages; everything is up for grabs, available to be recycled.

But there is room for optimism; Featherstone never allows himself to fall into the trap of wholesale condemnation. First of all, the decentering of the postmodern subject, which is the inevitable result of the new openness toward experience, the willingness to enter into – possibly threatening – emotional and aesthetic experiments, does not necessarily imply a rejection of controls. Carefully keeping Norbert Elias's theory of the civilizing process intact, Featherstone speaks of the 'controlled de-control' involved in the postmodern life style. Postmodern hedonism is a 'calculating hedonism' (59), and 'the shift to aesthetic criteria and local knowledge may just as possibly lead to mutually expected self-restraint and respect for the other' (126). There is, moreover, no need to follow Baudrillard, and, to a somewhat lesser extent, Jameson, in positing an undifferentiated, all-powerful postmodernism. Featherstone repeatedly stresses that postmodernism as he conceives of it is the prerogative of a specific class – well educated, affluent, urban – even if a watered-down version is available to the larger population in the experience/consumption of theme parks and similar goodies. Moreover, consumer culture does not necessarily lead to the death of the subject and to totalitarian control: 'research into the practice of watching television has shown that a whole host of different activities in different groups takes place. . . . Furthermore the actual reception and reading of programmes is also filtered through a particular class habitus' (57–8).

Featherstone's postmodernism, or at least its hard core, is a rather strictly circumscribed social phenomenon. Its controlled hedonism may strike more orthodox fellow citizens as basically irresponsible, but it presents no direct threat to representational practices or traditional politics. It may raise eyebrows but could easily be accommodated by the right-of-center politics that constituted its original backdrop.

MODERNIST *DISCOURS*, POSTMODERN *FIGURE*

Like *Consumer Culture and Postmodernism*, Scott Lash's *Sociology of Postmodernism* does not see postmodernism in terms of a 'condition' or as a 'type of society'. It is, instead, 'confined to the realm of *culture*' (1990: 4); it is a cultural paradigm, a '*regime of signification*' in which 'only *cultural* objects are produced' (5). Lash approaches that cultural postmodernism – which is not to be equated with contemporary culture as a whole – by way of three 'interrelated' theses. The first thesis claims that while modernization was 'a process of cultural differentiation . . . *post*modernization is a process of cultural "*de*-differentiation" '. The second thesis proposes that while modernism was a ' "discursive" cultural formation . . . postmodernism is a "figural" cultural formation'. The third thesis is the sort of thesis one would expect from a sociologist and concerns 'social stratification'. It suggests that 'the producers and relevant audience of modernist and postmodernist culture are found in particular declining and emergent social classes' (ix-x).

To begin with this last thesis, the audience for postmodern culture is the 'newer, post-industrial middle classes, with their bases in the media, higher education, finance, advertising, merchandising, and international exchanges' (20). Postmodernism can thus be seen 'in terms of a set of symbols and legitimations which promote the ideal interest of this new, "Yuppified" post-industrial bourgeoisie' (21). Apart from telling us that this bourgeoisie is too massive to qualify as an elite, Lash has little to say about it, except that it is one of the driving forces behind the process of postmodernization.

The postmodern culture that these 'post-industrial middle classes' produce and consume is, Lash tells us, de-differentiated. Whereas modernization can be seen in terms of an ever-increasing differentiation, along the lines originally suggested by Weber (and more recently, as we have seen, taken up by Habermas), postmodernism is a matter of de-differentiation, of *Entdifferenzierung* instead of *Ausdifferenzierung*. Lash points to the 'famous disintegration of the author celebrated by poststructuralists'; to 'the merging of the author into the cultural product as in the late 1980s biographical novels or performance art from Laurie Anderson to Bruce MacLean'; to the attack on the distinction between literature and criticism; and to the postmodern problematization of the distinctions between signifier, signified, and referent, which involves a de-differentiation of reality and representation. (Hassan, who is not mentioned in Lash's bibliography, could have provided him with more and better examples.)

Furthermore, although Lash does not mention it, the aestheticization of everyday life noted by Featherstone would also seem to support his thesis in its de-differentiation of art and life. Here, however, we touch upon a basic duality in Lash's view of the postmodern. As we have just seen, the examples of postmodern culture that Lash offers suggest that what he has in mind is intellectualist art rather than the aestheticization of the quotidian. It is because he is thinking of avant-gardist artforms that he can claim that the most significant distinction between modernism and postmodernism is that '*modernism conceives of representations as being problematic whereas postmodernism problematizes reality*' (13, his italics), a claim that places this postmodernism firmly within a deconstructionist, anti-representational framework. Whereas modernism with its ever more refined exploration of the possibilities of the various artistic disciplines and with its concentration on problem-solving as a central artistic activity ignored the problem of representation in favor of art's autonomy (and thus differentiated art and life), postmodern de-differentiation, like the best deconstructionist scenario, shakes our faith in our representational schemes and 'puts chaos, flimsiness, and instability in our experiences of *reality* itself' (15). Postmodernism may have given up on experimentation and returned to narrative and figuration (as in the work of *neue Wilden* such as Baselitz and Kiefer), but not to revive a reassuring nineteenth-century realism. Instead, it confronts its audience with the problematic status of the real itself, with the fact that basically the world is unrepresentable. However, this surely cannot be the postmodernism produced and consumed by the 'new, "Yuppified" post-industrial bourgeoisie' which, if anything, gives the confident appearance of having more solid, representational, ground under its feet than the average modernist intellectual ever dreamt of. The postmodernism that Lash presents here is a version of deconstructionist postmodernism and falls almost completely outside the purview of his sociologically targeted group (which to a large extent may be equated with Featherstone's 'new middle class').

Lash is not wholly unaware of this contradictory state of affairs, and in a later chapter offers some sort of a solution, although he simultaneously complicates matters further (*Sociology of Postmodernism* is a collection of overlapping essays with at times irritatingly shifting perspectives). In that later chapter he distinguishes between two postmodernisms: 'mainstream postmodernism', which 'privileges . . . the implosion of the cultural and the commercial and the eclipse of the avant-garde' and a second postmodernism that 'privilege[s] the problematization of the real as image' (37). Mainstream postmodernism is all but identical with Featherstone's consumer postmodernism. It 'furthers the hegemonic project of the new middle classes' and 'promotes the values of consumer capitalism inside the working class' while 'position[ing] subjects in fixed places and foster[ing] social hierarchies based on cultural objects functioning as status symbols and the principles of "distinction" '. The other postmodernism seems at first sight of the anti-representational variety. If so, it has, however, already moved beyond the purely deconstructionist stage and entered the field of micropolitics, since it 'tends to foster radical-democratic and decentralized worker resistance' (37). This is a postmodernism in which various anti-hegemonic, oppositional forces apparently find themselves side by side in a privileging of the local and the community-based (33).

Lash's suggestion of a mainstream postmodernism solves the problem I noted above: his failure to connect his postmodernism with the sociologically relevant group. One has no trouble in linking this postmodernism with the new middle classes. But that leads to an inevitable conflict with Lash's claim that postmodernism destabilizes the real. Mainstream postmodernism clearly reaffirms the real as experienced by the new middle classes. Only oppositional postmodernism would then 'privilege the problematization of the real as image', but since it simultaneously 'foregrounds a strong sense of locality' and organizes itself around political issues ('the new social movements' and 'decentralized worker resistance') the assumption would seem to be warranted that those involved in its diverse political projects have rather strong feelings about the real – at least about their utopian versions of the real. In other words, the radically anti-representational postmodernism that Lash defined earlier would seem to have no place in the dualistic scheme that is offered here.

But I will leave these and other problems in Lash's theory of postmodernism for what they are and move on to the most completely argued of his theses: the thesis that the 'figural' cultural formation of postmodernism has replaced an earlier modernist 'discursive' formation. For Lash, 'the postmodern is inextricably bound up with a theory of desire' (79). Postmodernity means 'a break with formalisms', both on the aesthetic level, where it leads to 'the supersession by the unconscious and the bodily of the hegemony of the symbolic', and on the theoretical level, where it spells a Nietzschean 'divorce with *structuralisms*' (80–1). Its prophets in the field of theory are therefore Foucault, Deleuze and Guattari, and Lyotard (and *not* such 'moderns and structuralists' as Barthes, Lacan, and Derrida, 'whose inspiration is Saussurean' (81)), with a clear emphasis on Lyotard, that is, the early Lyotard.

The 'desire' that Lash sees as inextricably bound up with postmodernity is Freud's libido seen from a Nietzschean perspective. For Deleuze and Guattari, for instance, '[i]t consists of flows of energy created by the id' (66) but is also 'the equivalent of Nietzsche's will to power' (67). These flows of libidinal energy, or desire, which in Freud 'solidify' to make up a psychic apparatus, are for Lyotard 'embodied in libidinal (or "pulsional") "dispositives" ', and whereas Freud mainly considered 'variation in the qualities of the psychic apparatus in terms of individual patients in the here and now', Lyotard casts a much wider net – and this is his essential contribution – in his concern with 'types of cultural practice', as a result of which 'his libidinal dispositives vary mainly between spheres of culture and over history' (90). It is this theory of cultural and epochal – in contrast to individual – differentiation of libidinal dispositives that enables Lash to arrive at his own theory of the postmodern as a primarily figural cultural formation.

For Lyotard, a 'work of art – and its corresponding dispositive – has value . . . in proportion to the intensity of energy it transmutes to the consumer of art' (90). For Lash, postmodern art meets Lyotard's requirements:

(1) Postmodern art draws on the uncoded and semi-coded libido in the unconscious to produce a literature and fine

> arts that break with the classical aesthetics of representation and with the formalism of modernity. It penetrates to underneath the signifier, to the real, the material, to sensation, to what Barthes many years ago described as the 'degree-zero of writing'. Postmodern art not only draws on desire, and operates from a position of sensation; it also embodies desire. The intensity of libido embodies [sic] in a work of art – hence transmitted to the consumer – increases proportionally with the extent to which it departs from the representational. Moreover, the form and content of postmodern art, for instance in the theatre of Peter Brook, is bodily and, in some sense, of the unconscious.
> (2) The effect on the consumer, the spectator, the 'public', is equally by means of the unconscious. The flows of libido embodied in the book, painting, or piece of music produce forces that give rise to 'sensation' when they strike the bodies of consumers, through the now polyvalent eye or ear.
>
> (99–100)

Lash's reminder that this libidinal postmodernity has critical potential and that for its theorists – Foucault, Deleuze and Guattari, Lyotard – 'postmodern culture is directly political' and 'often understood in quite concrete connection with the "micro-politics" of the various social movements' (100), suggests that once again he is primarily thinking of deconstructionist postmodernism and not, surprisingly enough, of Susan Sontag's 'erotic' postmodernism – which was anti-representational for wholly different reasons – or of the equally 'erotic' consumer postmodernism to which all of this eminently applies. Yet, elsewhere, he again shows himself aware of a postmodern 'middle-brow culture (*art moyen*)' (251). In any case, Lash sees the postmodern as an essentially figural cultural formation, both in its anti-representational, avant-gardist form, and in its middle-brow, consumerist form.

Lash connects postmodern culture, with its privileging of the image and the spectacle (and of the ensuing 'sensation' in the spectator), with a new 'libidinal dispositive' that has liberated the direct libidinal energy that modernist representation and formalism had repressed. In terms borrowed from Lyotard's *Discours, figure,* Lash argues that modernism 'signifie[d] in a largely "discursive" way, while postmodernist signification is largely "figural" ' (174). Discursive signification gives priority to words over images; it privileges form while in texts it simultaneously stresses (discursive) meaning; it has, since it is 'a sensibility of the ego rather than of the id', a rationalist view of culture; and it creates distance between the artistic object and its audience. Figural signification, in contrast, privileges the visual over the discursive, is dismissive of formalism, rationalism, and didacticism, is interested in the (sensuous) impact rather than the (discursive) meaning of texts, and 'operates through the spectator's immersion, the relatively unmediated investment of his/her desire in the cultural object' (175). This, then, is the postmodern cultural formation, which, to return to an earlier point, is also one of de-differentiation: modernism's exclusive orientation upon the discursive has been replaced by what one could call a mixed economy of the discursive and the figural. With Lash, postmodernism loops back to the mid-1960s and the early theoretizations of Sontag and Fiedler.[2]

POSTMODERN TIME-SPACE

As the subtitle of his wide-ranging *The Condition of Postmodernity: An Enquiry into the Origins of Cultural Change* (1989) suggests, David Harvey focuses explicitly on what Featherstone and Lash discuss only tangentially: the socio-economic factors responsible for the transition from modernity to postmodernity, which is indeed what one would expect from a social geographer who, according to a colleague, 'more than any other geographer, has shaped and continues to shape the course of Marxist geographical inquiry' (Soja 1989: 64). This is not to say that Harvey is dismissive of the cultural theorizing that I have reviewed earlier. His intellectual debts obviously include Baudrillard, and Jameson, but he is on the whole refreshingly skeptical of hyperbole. Hence his remarks that Baudrillard, in unwitting complicity with the postmodern, replicates postmodern 'time-space compression' in his own 'frenetic writings' and that Jameson, 'for all his brilliance, likewise loses his hold on both the reality he is seeking to represent and on the language that might properly be deployed to represent it in his more protean writings' (351).

Since he draws on sources that I have already examined (even Hassan, who is otherwise ignored by the sociologists), Harvey's postmodernism should not surprise us, although he is more specific as to its actual beginnings than most other theorists. For Harvey, postmodernism emerges 'as a full-blown though still incoherent movement out of the chrysalis of the anti-modern movement of the 1960s' (38). That anti-modernist movement is composed of numerous strains. There is Thomas Kuhn's trailblazing deconstruction of scientific 'progress' in his *The Structure of Scientific Revolutions* of 1962; there is Foucault's 'emphasis upon discontinuity and difference in history and his privileging of "polymorphous correlations in place of simple and complex causality" ' (9); there is Jane Jacobs's attack on modernist architecture and urban planning in *The Death and Life of Great American Cities* of 1961, followed by Robert Venturi's *Complexity and Contradiction in Architecture* of 1966; there is the rise of Derridean deconstruction as 'a powerful stimulus to postmodernist ways of thought' (49), and so on and so forth. This proto-postmodern movement then culminates in 'the global turbulence of 1968' which, although failing to bring the expected revolution, must be 'viewed . . . as the cultural and political harbinger of the subsequent turn to postmodernism' (38).

The postmodernism that emerges after 1968 is, to a large extent, continuous with the modernism that precedes it, departing from modernism most radically with respect to its conception of space:

> Whereas the modernists see space as something to be shaped for social purposes and therefore always subservient to the construction of a social project, the postmodernists see space as something independent and autonomous, to be shaped according to aesthetic aims and principles which have nothing necessarily to do with any overarching social objective, save, perhaps, the achievement of timeless and 'disinterested' beauty as an objective in itself.
>
> (66)

It is, consequently, in the fields of architecture and urban design that postmodernism breaks most radically with modernism. Modernism's 'large-scale, metropolitan-wide, technologically rational and efficient urban *plans*, backed by absolutely no-frills architecture (the austere "functionalist" surfaces of "international style" modernism)', have given way to a postmodernist 'conception of the urban fabric' as 'fragmented', as a ' "palimpsest" of past forms superimposed upon each other' and a ' "collage" of current uses'

(66). Technological innovation has made '[d]ispersed, decentralized, and deconcentrated urban forms' feasible and computer modeling and other new technologies have led to the development of personalized designer architecture and made a non-homogeneous mass-production possible: 'The postmodern architect and urban designer can, as a consequence, more easily accept the challenge to communicate with different client groups in personalized ways, while tailoring products to different situations, functions, and "taste cultures" ' (76).

Apart from this radical shift in architecture and urban planning, postmodernism is best seen as a particular kind of crisis within modernism, one that 'emphasizes the fragmentary, the ephemeral, and the chaotic . . . while expressing a deep scepticism as to any particular prescriptions as to how the eternal and immutable should be conceived of, represented, or expressed' (116). However, with 'its emphasis upon the ephemerality of *jouissance*, its insistence upon the impenetrability of the other, its concentration on the text rather than the work, its penchant for deconstruction bordering on nihilism, its preference for aesthetics over ethics', postmodernism takes matters 'beyond the point where any coherent politics are left, while that wing of it that seeks a shameless accommodation with the market puts it firmly in the tracks of an entrepreneurial culture that is the hallmark of reactionary neoconservatism' (116). In its rejection of metatheories that could grasp 'the political-economic processes (money flows, international divisions of labour, financial markets, and the like)' (117), even deconstructionist postmodernism plays into the hands of the reactionary enemy. Like so many other theorists Harvey distinguishes between a progressive and a reactionary version of postmodernism, even if his language often suggests otherwise: 'Postmodernism then signals nothing more than a logical extension of the power of the market over the whole range of cultural production' (62). As this quotation, and the earlier reference to postmodernism's 'shameless accommodation with the market' make clear, Harvey sees postmodernism largely in terms of an aestheticized and eclectic consumer culture. Indeed, in an interesting addition, he expands Featherstone's palette of postmodern consumer possibilities with the 'heritage industry'.

Following Andreas Huyssen, Harvey also recognizes an oppositional postmodern politics which 'has been particularly important in acknowledging "the multiple forms of otherness as they emerge from differences in subjectivity, gender and sexuality, race and class, temporal (configurations of sensibility) and spatial geographic locations and dislocations" ' (113). (It must be said, though, that just as in Jameson postmodernity's positive aspects get remarkably short shrift. Harvey acknowledges them almost with reluctance, as if unhappy that they effectively prevent a blanket condemnation.) Harvey's theory of the postmodern thus seeks to draw all post-1968 developments within one grand explanatory scheme. What is more important, he seeks to anchor them in a macro-theory of socio-economic change, as a 'transition in the *regime of accumulation* and its associated *mode of social and political regulation*' (121). In doing so, he makes use of the conceptual framework of the French so-called 'Regulation School' of economic theory (Palloix, Aglietta, and Lipietz), while there is also the marked influence of Henri Lefebvre's *La Production de l'espace* (1974) which argues, in Edward Soja's summary, that

> The very survival of capitalism . . . was built upon the creation of an increasingly embracing, instrumental, and socially mystified spatiality, hidden from critical view under thick veils of illusion and ideology. What distinguished capitalism's gratuitous spatial veil from the spatialities of other modes of production was its peculiar production and reproduction of geographically uneven development via simultaneous tendencies toward homogenization, fragmentation, and hierarchization.
>
> (1989: 50).

Post-Fordist capitalism

For Harvey the postwar economic boom, that lasted from the immediate postwar years to 1973, was built upon a stable, even rigid, Fordist–Keynesian regime of accumulation (that is, a form of profit maximization). It is the break-up of this configuration that 'since 1973 has inaugurated a period of rapid change, flux, and uncertainty' (1989: 124).[3] New systems of production and marketing, characterized by 'more flexible labor processes' than Fordism allowed, and aimed at more flexible markets, have taken over. Geographical mobility has increased and consumption is subject to 'rapid shifts'. Although Harvey is not sure that these changes actually 'warrant the title of a new regime of accumulation' or that 'the revival of entrepreneurialism and of neo-conservatism, coupled with the cultural turn to postmodernism, warrant the title of a new mode of regulation', he argues that 'the contrast between present political-economic practices and those of the post-war boom period are sufficiently strong to make the hypothesis of a shift from Fordism to what might be called a "flexible" regime of accumulation a telling way to characterize recent history' (124). This 'flexible accumulation'

> is marked by a direct confrontation with the rigidities of Fordism. It rests on flexibility with respect to labour processes, labour markets, products, and patterns of consumption. It is characterized by the emergence of entirely new sectors of production, new ways of providing financial services, new markets, and, above all, greatly intensified rates of commercial, technological, and organizational innovation.
>
> (147)

As a result of this shift towards flexible accumulation, and of the unemployment caused by 'two savage bouts of deflation' (147), the labor market has been radically restructured: 'Faced with strong market volatility, heightened competition, and narrowing profit margins, employers have taken advantage of weakened union power and the pools of surplus (unemployed and underemployed) labourers to push for much more flexible work regimes and labour contracts' (150). On the consumption side, the 'relatively stable aesthetic of Fordist modernism' – elsewhere Harvey speaks of the 'more solid values implanted under Fordism' (171) – has been replaced by the instability of a postmodern aesthetic that 'celebrates difference, ephemerality, spectacle, fashion, and the commodification of cultural forms' (156). This shift in consumption patterns, combined with 'changes in production, information gathering and financing' might well underlie 'a remarkably proportionate surge in service employment since the early 1970s' (156), although another reason might be that 'the need to accelerate turnover time in consumption' has led to a shift away from the production of durable goods to the production of 'events (such as spectacles that have an almost instantaneous turnover time)' (157).

Philip Cooke and Edward Soja also describe the reorganization of capital that we have witnessed in the last two decades in terms of an increased flexibility. Cooke points to the way that large corporations have moved 'from a bureaucratic hierarchy to a matrix structure' in order to 'derigidify the organizational system' (1990: 144); to their 'forming contracts of limited life with each other or with innovative smaller firms' (146); to the ' "just-in-time" stock handling and "total quality control" systems' (147) developed in Japan; to the flexibility that 'is increasingly built into the technology used in contemporary workplaces'; and to the new 'numerical flexibility' of a labor force that is partly hired on short-term contracts or hired for part-time jobs (154–61). Soja tells us that 'management structures are often less centrally controlled and more flexible, while the core production processes have increasingly been broken into separate segments operating, unlike the integrated Fordist assembly line, at many different locations'. He speaks of 'further flexibility through parallel production' and through 'more extensive subcontracting'; of 'sprawling spatial systems of production linking centres of administrative power over capital investment to a constellation of parallel branches, subsidiaries, subcontracting firms, and specialized public and private services'; of 'an increasingly "footloose" and mobile capital' that has created a whole new, fragmented, configuration: 'Never before has the spatiality of the capitalist city or the mosaic of uneven regional development become so kaleidoscopic, so loosened from its nineteenth-century moorings, so filled with unsettling contrariety' (1989: 185–7).[4]

This new flexibility, and the accompanying shift towards services, do not necessarily imply that capitalism, in Scott Lash and John Urry's phrase, has become disorganized.[5] On the contrary, because of its new flexibility – its dispersal, its geographical mobility, its flexible responses *vis-à-vis* labor markets, consumer markets, and labor processes, its 'institutional, product, and technological innovation' (Harvey) – capitalism is becoming ever more tightly organized and centralized. Cooke ingeniously reconciles capitalism's simultaneous centralizing and decentralizing tendencies:

> One of the most important changes in setting has been the emergence in the late modern period of an increasingly integrated global economy, dominated by the most advanced forms of capitalist production and exchange. This

> development could be thought to run counter to the theme that has been developed thus far, namely the trend towards decentralism. Yet it is not, because the global system has no centre. It is a decentred space of flows rather than a clearly hierarchically structured space of production.
>
> (1990: 141)

This decentralized centralization, coupled with the volatility of the postmodern consumer (and financial) markets, makes access to and control over information of paramount importance.

Harvey is careful not to overstate his case and does not claim a monopoly position for the 'flexible technologies and organizational forms' of this 'flexible accumulation'. Instead, he sees a constant interaction between the new flexibility and the older, more stable, Fordism:

> We can, I think, trace back many of the surface shifts in economic behaviour and political attitudes to a simple change in balance between Fordist and non-Fordist systems of labour control, coupled with a disciplining of the former either through competition with the latter (forced restructurings and rationalizations), widespread unemployment or through political repression (curbs on union power) and geographical relocations to 'peripheral' countries or regions and back into industrial heartlands in a 'see-saw' motion of uneven geographical development.
>
> (1989: 192)

He is therefore tempted to see the new flexibility in production, labor markets, and consumption, 'more as an outcome of the search for financial solutions to the crisis-tendencies of capitalism, rather than the other way round' (194). This would, he suggests, 'imply that the financial system has achieved a degree of autonomy from real production unprecedented in capitalism's history, carrying capitalism into an era of equally unprecedented financial dangers' (194). Harvey, too, has a taste for hyperbole if the issue is the ways of capital.

At an earlier stage, Harvey had seemed unsure what to make of 'the problem of the ways in which norms, habits, and political and cultural attitudes have shifted since 1970, and the degree to which such shifts integrate with the transition from Fordism to flexible accumulation' (170–1). These changes in the culture at large – which Daniel Bell had situated much earlier in time – are evidently of great importance and they would seem to parallel the transition toward flexible accumulation (at least for Harvey), but at that point it was unclear which took precedence, the cultural or the socio-economic shift: 'the direction (if any) of causality is not [clear]' (171). Now, however, Harvey seems satisfied that it is capitalism that is the prime mover. After a first suggestion that 'the crisis of Fordism was in large part a crisis of temporal and spatial form' (196), he informs us that he will follow Jameson in 'attribut[ing] the postmodern shift to a crisis in our experience of space and time' – 'In what follows I shall accept these statements at their face value' (201) – in other words, to an underlying crisis in representation.

Time-space compression

Introducing the term 'time-space compression', Harvey tells us that the term implies 'processes that so revolutionize the objective qualities of space and time that we are forced to alter, sometimes in quite radical ways, how we represent the world to ourselves' (1989: 240). Compression signals here two related effects of capitalism: the way in which it speeds up the pace of life and the way it overcomes spatial barriers so that the world seems to implode, to use Baudrillard's term. Harvey argues that

> we have been experiencing, these last two decades, an intense phase of time-space compression that has had a disorienting and disruptive impact upon political-economic practices, the balance of class power, as well as upon cultural and social life. While historical analogies are always dangerous, I think it no accident that postmodern sensibility evidences strong sympathies for certain of the confused political, cultural, and philosophical movements that occurred at the beginning of this century (in Vienna, for example) when the sense of time-space compression was also peculiarly strong.
>
> (284)

Time-space compression is the result of attempts to cope with 'the grumbling problems of Fordism–Keynesianism that erupted into open crisis in 1973' (284). Harvey is not explicit on the nature of these problems, but Cooke, who dates the advent of the postmodern from these problems of the late 1960s and early 1970s rather than from the crisis of 1973, is more forthcoming:

> the source of the productivity crisis lay within the Fordist production process itself. The removal of expertise from the shopfloor worker and the centralization of strategic information within an increasingly bureaucratized hierarchy of control meant that problems arising at shopfloor level took an increasingly long time to resolve. This was exacerbated by the increasingly sophisticated technology used in the manufacturing process. . . . The limits of Fordist technology and labour organization were being reached.
>
> (1990: 80)

Capital's answer to these problems – accelerated turnover time in production made possible by organizational shifts, electronic control, etc. – has led, in Harvey's words, to 'parallel accelerations in exchange and consumption' (285) that were actively promoted by a faster circulation of commodities, and to a turn towards ever more ephemeral services in consumption. The advent of the computer likewise facilitated faster action with respect to financial services and markets. It is this space-time compression that leads to the schizophrenic disorientation that Jameson sees as characteristic of the postmodern experience:

> we can link the schizophrenic dimensions to postmodernity which Jameson emphasizes . . . with accelerations in turnover times in production, exchange, and consumption that produce, as it were, the loss of a sense of the future except and insofar as the future can be discounted into the present. Volatility and ephemerality similarly make it hard to maintain any firm sense of continuity. Past experience gets compressed into some overwhelming present. . . . Everything, from novel writing and philosophizing to the experience of labouring or making a home, has to face the challenge of accelerating turnover time and the rapid write-off of traditional and historically acquired values. The temporary contract in everything, as Lyotard remarks . . . then becomes the hallmark of postmodern living.
>
> (291)

Paradoxically, the virtual disappearance of space as a barrier has not led to the homogeneity one might have expected. On the contrary, 'the less important the spatial barriers, the greater the sensitivity of capital to the variations of place within space, and the greater the incentive for places to be differentiated in ways attractive to capital'.[6] And thus we get 'fragmentation, insecurity, and ephemeral uneven development within a highly unified global space economy of capital flow' (295–6).

Postmodernity can thus be seen as a new installment in the 'history of successive waves of time-space compression generated out of the pressures of capital accumulation with its perpetual search to annihilate space through time and reduce turnover time' and is therefore 'accessible to historical materialist analysis and interpretation' (306–7) or, to put it differently, 'capable of theorization by way of the meta-narrative of capitalist development that Marx proposed' (328). The 'crisis of representation in cultural forms' and the 'intense aesthetic concern' (322) that have been generated by this most recent space-time compression thus also find their materialist explanation. For Harvey, as earlier for Jameson, the Marxist representational scheme has remained intact in this turmoil or, rather, outside this turmoil. This is, however, a materialism that is significantly modified. First of all, it sees difference and 'otherness' – in terms of race, gender, religious culture, etc. – not as an element to be added to more fundamental categories such as class and the mode of production, but as equally fundamental to a proper 'historical materialist enquiry'. Secondly, it sees, following Foucault, Baudrillard, and others, the production of discourses and of images as important activities in the reproduction and transformation of symbolic orders. Unfortunately, these modifications at the level of theory are not worked out in Harvey's practice. Harvey's gloomy account pays very little attention to the struggle over discourses and images and virtually ignores the very real achievements of feminism, anti-apartheid, or the ecological movement. One suspects that like Jameson he had rather not acknowledge what is suggested by his own model: that capitalism's crises can as a by-product lead to what by many is regarded as social improvement and a welcome further democratization.

FROM A SOCIOLOGY OF POSTMODERNISM TO A POSTMODERN SOCIOLOGY

Let me now turn to an equally comprehensive but less totalizing view than Harvey's and look at a collection of essays by Zygmunt

Bauman, the last social scientist whose work I will discuss. *Intimations of Postmodernity* proposes a reading of the postmodern that presents a true alternative to Jameson, Baudrillard, and Harvey in that it refuses to see postmodernity as the failure of modernity or as a catastrophic mutation within modernity, but sees it, rather, as the logical outcome of the modern project:

> Postmodernity may be interpreted as fully developed modernity taking a full measure of the anticipated consequences of its historical work. . . . Postmodernity may be conceived of as modernity conscious of its true nature – *modernity for itself*. The most conspicuous features of the postmodern condition: institutionalized pluralism, variety, contingency and ambivalence – have been all turned out by modern society in ever increasing volumes; yet they were seen as signs of failure rather than success, as evidence of the unsufficiency of efforts so far, at a time when the institutions of modernity, faithfully replicated by the modern mentality, struggled for *universality, homogeneity, monotony* and *clarity*. The postmodern condition can be therefore described, on the one hand, as modernity emancipated from false consciousness; on the other, as a new type of social condition marked by the overt institutionalization of the characteristics which modernity – in its designs and managerial practices – set about to eliminate and, failing that, tried to conceal.
>
> (Bauman 1992: 187–8)

Rather than a modernity in ruins, postmodernity is 'a self-reproducing, pragmatically self-sustainable and logically self-contained social condition defined by *distinctive features of its own*' (188). Bauman's postmodernity clearly merits our attention. But there is, as I have noted in the opening remarks to this chapter, another reason to round it off with Bauman's work. Bauman's sociological interpretation of the postmodern questions the sociological project itself and proposes an alternative, postmodern sociology that should replace the 'orthodox' sociology (his term) that still orients itself upon modernity rather than upon its own time and place. Under postmodernity, classical sociology – derived from the models of capitalism, industrialism, and rationalization (and combinations thereof) proposed by Marx, Durkheim, and Weber, and understood, in Anthony Giddens' words, 'as generating knowledge about modern social life which can be used in the interests of prediction and control (Giddens 1990: 15) – has lost its relevance.

Bauman's sociology of the postmodern

In his 'Introduction' Bauman initially creates the impression that for him, too, postmodernity is fraught with disasters: 'The postmodern mind seems to condemn everything, propose nothing. Demolition is the only job the postmodern mind seems to be good at' (ix). But we soon find him siding with postmodernity against the modernist paradigm:

> All in all, postmodernity can be seen as restoring to the world what modernity, presumptuously, had taken away; as a *re-enchantment* of the world that modernity had tried hard to *dis-enchant.* It has been the modern artifice that has been dismantled; the modern conceit of meaning-legislating reason that has been exposed, condemned and put to shame.
>
> (x)

Postmodernity restores to us the world in its pristine indeterminacy. In doing so, it also restores to us 'the fullness of moral choice and responsibility'. This is a more dubious gift, however, since we are simultaneously deprived of 'the comfort of the universal guidance that modern self-conscience once promised' (xxii). We are 'thrown back on [our] own subjectivity as the only ultimate ethical authority' (xxii). This state of affairs has far-reaching consequences, both at the individual level and at what remains of the collective level. Let me first look at the consequences at the level of the collective, that is, the level of politics. For Bauman the inevitable and drastic individualization of what used to belong to the realm of the collective leads directly to a postmodern politics of communities. It is the postmodern 'privatization of fears' that leads us to search for 'communal shelters' (xxi), for 'imagined communities' (xx):

> Having no other (and above all no objectified, supra-individual) anchors except the affections of their 'members', imagined communities exist solely through their manifestations: through occasional spectacular outbursts of

> togetherness (demonstrations, marches, festivals, riots) – sudden materializations of the idea, all the more effective and convincing for blatantly violating the routine of quotidianity. . . . The right of an imagined community to arbitrate is established (though for a time only; and always merely until further notice) in proportion to the amount and intensity of public attention forced to focus on its presence; 'reality', and hence also the power and authority of an imagined community, is the function of the attention. Seeking an authority powerful enough to relieve them of their fears, individuals have no other means of reaching their aim except by trying to make the communities they imagine more authoritative than the communities imagined by others – and this by heaving them into the centre of public attention.
>
> (xix-xx)

The result is a proliferation of communities, all seen, by themselves and the others, as 'agencies', all involved in a Lyotardian agonistics, in a 'rampant tribalism' (xxi), and all threatened with extinction since the 'communal spaces' that they create 'are grounded in their activities only' (36).

Although this might seem to suggest another analysis of postmodernity in terms of the crisis of modernity, Bauman distances himself in no uncertain terms from what he calls the 'crisis theorists'. For those theorists

> the identity of present-day society is fully negative; one describable in terms of absences, failures, declines, erosions – with the classical capitalist society, that archetype of modernity, serving as the benchmark and point of departure for all theorizing. Ours is a disorganized society; and a disorganized capitalism. It is, in other words, capitalism, or the capitalist form of modernity, in crisis.
>
> (47)

For Bauman, however, capitalism, whether late or not, is 'in good health, rather than in crisis' (53). In an argument that offers a theoretical foundation to virtually everything that has so far been said about consumer or mass culture, he connects consumer culture, individual freedom, and the reproduction of the social, i.e., of the capitalist system. Drawing on Marcuse's notion of one-dimensionality and on Bourdieu's suggestion that seduction has replaced repression as the 'vehicle' of social integration, Bauman argues that capitalism, in a masterly strategy, has succeeded in linking individual freedom with the idea of consumption: 'Reproduction of the capitalist system is therefore achieved through individual freedom (in the form of consumer freedom, to be precise), and not through its suppression'. As a result, the new form of social integration is immensely profitable compared to the older, repressive, form: 'Instead of being counted on the side of systemic overheads, the whole operation "social control" may now be entered on the side of systemic assets' (51). The upshot of all this, Bauman argues, is that 'the future of capitalism looks more secure than ever' (51). One can, on the whole, agree with this. To see the recent history of capitalism exclusively in terms of crisis, is to focus on British and American capitalism (as Harvey and Jameson tend to do) or western capitalism at large, but to ignore capitalism's successes, which are largely responsible for that crisis in the first place, outside its original core area.

Under the postmodern condition, then, the reproduction of the social and social integration are based on 'entirely new grounds' that have supplanted modern forms of social reproduction. The implication of this is that such eminently 'traditional mechanisms' as a 'consensus-aimed political legitimation', 'ideological domination', and a 'uniformity of norms promoted by cultural hegemony' have also largely lost their relevance to the reproduction of the capitalist system (51–2). In other words – and this is where Bauman's argument is of course vulnerable in its one-sidedness – the social has been reduced to the economic. If that is the case, then politics that operate via imagined communities or follow a neo-tribalistic pattern do not pose a serious threat to the system, in spite of their fragmentary, centrifugal character; such politics may signal a crisis in traditional politics, but the system, narrowed down to the economic, no longer needs traditional politics to perpetuate itself.

Although Bauman does not theorize the shift from modernist reproduction mechanisms to the consumer freedom reproduction mechanism of postmodernity, he would seem to locate it in the 1950s when critics, alarmed by a burgeoning mass culture, began to predict a deadening uniformity. But such a uniformity never materialized, Bauman tells us (there is obviously room for disagreement here): 'The market thrives on variety; so does consumer freedom and with it the security of the system' (52). And yet, for all its diversity – and paradoxically even *because* of that diversity – postmodernity is an integrated, well-oiled system within which 'individual life-world, social cohesiveness and systemic capacity for reproduction fit and assist each other' (53).

Towards a postmodern sociology, or the problem of sociological representation

In spite of the undeniable 'systemness' of the postmodern world, its systemic character escapes the dragnet of classical, modernist, sociology which finds itself faced with, and baffled by,

> a social space populated by relatively autonomous agents who are entangled in mutual dependencies and hence prompted to interact. These agents . . . are not operating in anything like the 'principally co-ordinated' space, similar to that inside which all traditional sociological categories have been once securely located.
>
> (Bauman 1992: 61)

To make (sociological) sense of the postmodern condition, a postmodern sociology will have to accept that 'the social condition it intends to model is essentially and perpetually *unequilibrated*'; that all order it will find is 'local, emergent and transitory'; and that it will furthermore have to abandon the idea of progress that informed all sociological theories of modernity (189). Such a postmodern sociology will even have to give up on the whole category of 'society', that is, the enabling condition for its own larger representational claims, and with it its legislative and engineering aspirations. Instead, it will have to work with the idea of 'sociality': a category that 'tries to convey the processual modality of social reality, the dialectical play of randomness and pattern (or, from the agent's point of view, freedom and dependence' (190), and that is reluctant to see stable structures in the processes that it describes, preferring to see them as emergent or, as the case may be, residual. One important consequence of this reorientation is that the focus must now be on 'agency' and, more in particular, on 'the *habitat* in which agency operates and which it produces in the course of operation' (190–1).[7] Such habitats do, however, not determine the conduct of the agents in question; they merely offer those agents a setting in which action, the assignment of meaning, and self-constitution – which in postmodern times had better be viewed as 'self-assembly' – are possible.

Let me briefly review some of the main tenets of Bauman's 'theory of postmodernity'. Postmodern habitats are 'complex' systems, in contrast to the 'mechanical systems' assumed by orthodox sociology. They are not only unpredictable, but are also 'not controlled by statistically significant factors' (191–2). Their successive states appear to be 'unmotivated and free from constraints of deterministic logic' (192) and are thus not open to predictive analysis. One reason for this indeterminacy is that habitats are no longer a priori dominated by ' "goal-setting" agencies', so that they can no longer be thought of in terms of organizations. A second reason is that they are populated by great numbers of 'single-purpose' agencies, so that within a habitat no agency can emerge that could bring together and eventually control the others with an eye to an overarching purpose. As a result, habitats 'have no overwhelming reasons for being what they are, and they could be different if any of the participating agencies behaved differently' (193).

The agencies, or agents, that constitute postmodern habitats are – from a sociological point of view – autonomous since their actions 'remain staunchly under-determined' (192). Their 'existential modality' is one of 'insufficient indetermination, inconclusiveness, motility and rootlessness', while their identities are 'neither given nor authoritatively confirmed' (193) but rather the temporary outcome of processes of self-constitution which should not be seen in terms of self-development, but rather in terms of a self-assembly that may be continuous but is not cumulative. The resulting confusion is exacerbated because the orientation points that guide agents in their actions are provided by other agents, and not by any overall goals such as those that served purposes of orientation under modernity. The upshot is that postmodern society cannot be represented by the sociological schemes of modernity that therefore have lost all relevance for what Talcott Parsons, for instance, saw as their objective: to resolve the problem of order.

Under such conditions politics inevitably become 'neo-tribal' politics that, focusing on one issue, bring together 'agents too heterogeneous in other respects to prevent the dissolution of the formation once the desired progress on the issue in question has been achieved' (197). This dissolution is all the more inevitable since no single issue can command the total allegiance of postmodern agents, whose diversity of interests effectively works against complete identification with any single goal, political or otherwise.

The question arises, of course, whether Bauman's description of the postmodern habitat and its postmodern agents does indeed apply to the whole of what he sees as the postmodern world – 'the affluent countries of Europe and of European descent'. One is inclined to accept its validity with regard to certain, fairly well-circumscribed, sectors of the urban population – the politically sensitive sector of the new middle classes of Featherstone and Lash, for instance, and the loose 'neo-tribal' groupings at the heart of the various youth cultures – but these (still) constitute usually small minorities in any given national culture. If there is a postmodernity, in Bauman's sense, it is still engulfed by a much larger modernity, or perhaps is it better to say that a still representable and predictable modernity is shot through with an unrepresentable, unpredictable and indeterminate postmodernism. Similarly, traditional politics have far from disappeared, even though their appeal has undeniably diminished, and they continue to dominate the political scene. Indeed, the traditional politics of modernity as often as not successfully incorporate the moral and existential concerns of the new postmodern micropolitics, in some cases even acquiring a new (and unforeseen) élan. Although Bauman's analysis of our current social formation in terms of the postmodern has its highly illuminating aspects, I will, for the time being, stick with Anthony Giddens's 'radicalised modernity'. But that is for the next, concluding chapter.

Notes

1 One of those exceptions is Vytautas Kavolis, whose 'Revolutionary metaphors and ambiguous personalities: notes toward an understanding of post-modern revolutions' (1969) and 'Post-modern man: psycho-cultural responses to social trends' (1970) deserve honorable mention. Kavolis's articles failed to elicit response, however.

2 Like Featherstone, Lash offers a pedigree that traces postmodern theory via Susan Sontag back to Walter Benjamin – 'the paradigmatic theorist . . . for the postmodern' (1990:11) – and postmodern culture to the various avant-gardes of the interbellum.

3 Edward Soja prefers to 'locate the onset of this passage to postmod-

ernity in the late 1960s and the series of explosive events which together marked the end of the long post-war boom' (1989: 60–1). Philip Cooke also sees earlier tendencies towards a crisis that were then reinforced by the 1973 oil crisis. Harvey's turning-point of 1973 clearly makes it difficult to theorize the anti-modernist overtures of the 1950s and 1960s in terms of underlying socio-economic factors.

4 Albert Borgmann, although a philosopher and not a sociologist or a social geographer, notes the same shift in his *Crossing the Postmodern Divide* (1992). The section devoted to these developments is significantly called 'Flexible specialization'. Especially interesting is that, like Cooke, he sees a revival of certain forms of early capitalist entrepreneurship in postmodern capitalism (and gives some examples drawn from his immediate environment in Montana).

5 See Scott Lash and John Urry, *The End of Organized Capitalism* (1987).

6 One of Philip Cooke's more interesting arguments – which explains, by the way, why he has chosen the rather unlikely title of *Back to the Future* for a book on Fordist and post-Fordist economies – is that we are witnessing

> what is perhaps the most remarkable development of the post-Fordist era, the revival of the eighteenth- and nineteenth-century phenomenon of the *industrial district*. Nineteenth-century industrial districts, as described by Alfred Marshall, were systems of small, craft-based companies specialized in the production of a particular set of products, interlinked by tight networks of sub-contractors, often organized around family relationships, dependent on starting finance raised within the community and capable of producing customized products, often for a luxury market.
>
> (1990: 164)

He sees revivals of such districts in north-central Italy, in Silicon Valley and Orange County in California, and along Route 128 near Boston, and mentions Benetton as a spectacularly successful example of the new entrepreneurial spirit. Under the decentered conditions of the new ' "postmodern" space economy' (164) new 'localities' can spring up anywhere, although they tend to appear in regions that once qualified as industrial districts.

7 Steven Seidman sees such a postmodern sociology in terms of 'local narratives' that should 'analyze a circumscribed social phenomenon in a densely contextual way' while locating it 'spatially and temporally' (Seidman 1992: 70).

11

CONCLUSION

In the American novelist Don DeLillo's *Ratner's Star* (1976), fourteen-year-old genius Billy Twillig, who has just been awarded the Nobel Prize for mathematics, is flown out to a research center somewhere in the desert to join an international effort to decode a numerical message that has come in from the outer darkness of the cosmos. The enigmatic code, which might even contain the mathematical key to the universe itself, has so far baffled all attempts at solving it and has apparently driven the famous mathematician Endor over the edge and into the desert, where he has dug a hole for himself and spends his days meditating, eating worms, and solemnly saying mysterious things to those who visit him.

Billy does indeed succeed in cracking the code, but the result is not exactly glorious: the numbers in the code would simply seem to indicate a time. At this point Billy's findings can be connected with the theories of a fantastic scientist, a certain Mohole, who claims to have discovered zones in the cosmos where the supposedly universal laws of theoretical physics do not apply. As Mohole, who in all modesty has named these zones after himself, points out: 'The essence of my brand of relativity – that in a mohole the laws of physics vary from one observer to another – is at odds with every notion of the universe that displays a faith in nature' (DeLillo 1980: 185). It turns out that the time indicated in the message pinpoints the moment when the planet Earth will enter a mohole. Apparently the message has been sent out from the Earth itself, by an enormously sophisticated human civilization that eons ago has been destroyed by a mohole and, using something out in the cosmos as a reflector, desperately and in what with reason may be called a long shot, has tried to warn a possible future generation against a similar fate.

When Billy has arrived at these startling conclusions the indicated time is near. The novel ends with Billy and his fellow scientists at the research center scrambling in all directions to avoid the impending catastrophe, which is heralded by a theoretically impossible and thus totally unforeseen total eclipse of the sun. Billy himself heads toward Endor's hole, realizing that Endor must have deciphered the code long before he did and had withdrawn into his mystic visions precisely for that reason. The last scene finds Billy moving across the desert on a tricycle – he is only fourteen and it is the only vehicle he can grab – when he is overtaken by the eclipse.

When the Earth enters the mohole, all forms of representation, even those offered by that flagship of the sciences, theoretical physics, come abruptly to an end. A good many theoretizations of the postmodern suggest that for some time now we have been finding ourselves in the middle of a moral, political, and cognitive mohole and, indeed, may never get out on the other side. At the surface, there is much to support that proposition. As in DeLillo's novel, the end of representation – the postmodern mohole – has sent us scrambling in various directions. Baudrillard suggests that as the ultimate defensive strategy we metamorphose ourselves into objects; Jameson offers homeopathic measures as a last-ditch effort at resistance; Hassan counsels the comforts of American pragmatism. Others seek a New Age-like spiritual unity beyond the current malaise. Peter Fuller has suggested 'a Post-Modern renewal of our imaginative and spiritual relationship to the world of nature' (Fuller 1987: 8), while Colin Falck tells us that a 'true post-modernism can now be defined only in terms of a head-on rejection of the nihilism which would reduce literature to the status of a game with itself, or with language' (Falck 1989: 151) and predicts that a 'true post-modernist literature' will move beyond the self-reflexivity of modernism 'to the actual finding of revelatory fictions' (162). All truth, Falck declares, 'is carnal, and that Energy is from the Body is the true meaning of the Word made flesh' (170). In fact, the whole New Age movement itself is a response to our representational crisis, just as are the various forms of fundamentalism, which, far from being out of sync with the times, as Jameson thinks, are perfectly in tune with them: in the West as a reaction to the current, accelerated phase of modernization, elsewhere as a furious act of resistance against both its earlier stages and the current information phase. Finally, there are those, like Lyotard, who actively seek to contribute to the demise of representation and for whom the mohole is a form of the sublime with emancipatory potential.

There are a number of things to be said about this general crisis of representation. Probably the first thing is that it reflects a narrow point of view, primarily that of the humanities. One can agree that morally, and therefore also politically (*pace* the orthodox Marxist view), we lack grounded representations. However, unconditionally to extend non-representation to the cognitive sphere is an imperious maneuver that may seek to serve the purpose of reasserting the power of the humanities over the sciences in an age in which the former have been relegated to the far background, but that convinces none of those it should convince. This is one of the paradoxes at the heart of postmodernity (or, rather, of modernity): one does not want to refute the proposition that knowledge is bound up with the knower, is therefore historically and culturally determined, and operates, as Foucault has demonstrated, always in a field of power. One might even go further and agree with the deconstructionists that knowledge is always under erasure and therefore, properly speaking, never exists (or acknowledge the power of the more traditional arguments against knowledge). And yet we seem to know things. There is one cognitive style, one set of procedural principles that holds the promise of leading us to unconditional knowledge. It is impossible to establish beyond theoretical doubt why these principles work but they would certainly seem to do so: it takes more than the poststructuralist turn to shake the scientific community's belief that we indeed know about, say, the speed of light or the second law of thermodynamics, and for good reasons. Lyotard's privileging of 'paralogy' is a feeble effort to make us think otherwise. The knowledge produced by these cognitive principles – which Ernest Gellner has half-ironically called 'Enlightenment Rationalist Fundamentalism' (Gellner 1992: 80) – would seem to transcend history and culture in a way that arguably is theoretically impossible. Scientific practice is not transhistorical, as Thomas Kuhn's *The Structure of Scientific Revolutions* has convincingly shown us. Yet Kuhn's book implicitly reveals that the principles that underlie scientific practice have become increasingly transhistorical, and that, given the time we all need to adjust to new perspectives, scientists agree on the basis of these principles on what constitutes a better representation of the real than the one that has become inadequate. Because of these principles – which have revealed the inadequacy of a given representation in the first place – scientific knowledge is cumulative; each paradigm, in the Kuhnian sense, absorbs, and improves upon, the one it has dislodged. In short, the idea that the current crisis in representation has revealed to us that knowledge is impossible must be regarded with the strongest suspicion, even though theoretically it makes perfect sense. As Anthony Giddens has remarked with respect to the social sciences, a field that from this point of view is much more controversial than that of the hard sciences: 'Let us first of all dismiss as unworthy of serious intellectual consideration the idea that no systematic knowledge of human action or trends of social development is possible' (Giddens 1990: 46–7). Indeed, the social scientists I have discussed clearly support that view (not surprisingly one should, with the partial exception of Bauman's, classify their models as modern rather than postmodern). So do, for that matter, Best and Kellner in their book on the postmodern:

> Our position is that while it is impossible to produce a fixed and exhaustive knowledge of a constantly changing complex of social processes, it is possible to map the fundamental domains, structures, practices, and discourses of a society, and how they are constituted and interact.
>
> (1991: 260)

What postmodernity discovers (or, rather, rediscovers), is that rationality cannot ground itself, and that therefore modernity cannot be grounded. As a result, the idea of modern knowledge turns out to be a self-defeating proposition. The reflexivity that is at the heart of the modern project is ultimately its undoing since it reveals to us that reflection, in the form of reflection upon reflection, is always the starting-point of an infinite regression. And yet, inexplicably, the same rationalist reflection would seem to lead to universal and transcendent knowledge. Morally and politically, in the field of value, modernity confronts us with a similar dilemma. Here, too, its reflexivity has ultimately undermined its universal moral and political claims. Like modern knowledge, the modern idea of value is inherently paradoxical, as the attempts of Mouffe and Laclau or Best and Kellner to circumvent that paradox, or Lyotard's open admission of its baffling consequences, have illustrated. It is perhaps not so much the case that modernity is 'enigmatic at its core', as Anthony Giddens has remarked (1990: 49), as that it sends out contradictory impulses which have come to constitute the two modes of thought – the one expansionist, transcendent, and omni-representational, the other self-reflexive, inward spiralling, and anti-representational – that in our day and age have come to clash so violently. Their siren songs constantly lead us into the temptation of wanting it both ways, and thus into self-contradiction. Knowing that universals inevitably violate the rights of the particular, we yet want a universal rule to protect the particular from the possibly universalizing aspirations of other particulars. In practice, we oscillate between universalist and particularist positions, in a dialectic which, in the last twenty-five years, has not been unsuccessful in the field of concrete, practical politics – at least not where I live – but that theoretically cannot be resolved. The only option would seem to go beyond reflexivity itself, as suggested in the Colin Falck quotation and by the various anti-reflexive popular movements of the day, but critical reflexiveness is too great an intellectual and moral good to be thrown overboard that way. What Barry Smart has called the 'resurrection of the "sacred" as a sphere of experience pertinent to modern forms of life' (1993: 89) may recently have gained ground as a postmodern circumvention of an equally postmodern paradox, but it is not much more than a sophisticated throwback to the very beginnings of the debate in Olson and to the Heideggerian tradition that Olson worked from.

At this level of abstraction, that of postmodernity as mohole, postmodernism is a resurfacing of the anti-representationalism that has its source in the self-reflexivity of modernity. The vehemence of the attack on representation surely has to do with the stranglehold that representational modernity until quite recently had upon our imagination, not to mention our institutions. It is tempting to think that the radicalism of the positions of older theorists such as Lyotard, Jameson, or Baudrillard, is directly related to their deep (former) commitment to representational modernity: in their case the monolithically representational schemes of Marxism. Radical postmodern theory must be regarded as a transitional phenomenon, as instrumental in the creation of a more moderate new paradigm that is already building upon its achievements while ignoring its more excessive claims.

The causes of the anti-representationalist turn are far from clear. The best one can do is list the factors that have potentially contributed to its amazing international success. In the first place, in the postwar period the representational schemes of the West became increasingly suspect in the light of decolonization, the Civil Rights movement, feminism, and the ever more problematic legitimation of the Marxist alternative (with as its high-point the events of May 1968 in Paris). Collectively, these and other developments led to an unprecedented visibility of what much later came to be called 'the Other' and sometimes revealed – as in the oil crisis of 1973 or the American withdrawal from Vietnam of the same year – a wholly unexpected and therefore all the more threatening vulnerability. Secondly, the second half of the twentieth century has shown us that the Enlightenment assumption that society can be controlled and centrally directed is no longer tenable – if it ever was. We have been increasingly confronted with the fact that 'highly complex systems, like modern economic orders, cannot effectively be subordinated to cybernetic control' (Giddens 1990: 164). The falseness of that assumption is disturbingly revealed in, for example, the failure of the various western economies to provide full employment and in the crime rates that, not coincidentally, have soared in the last twenty-five years. Other major sources of destabilization have been the anxiety produced by Harvey's time-space compression and the somewhat older anxiety, analyzed by Daniel Bell and others, that was generated by the clash between an essentially Victorian morality and the new hedonistic consumer and instant gratification society that seemed to develop almost overnight.

With hindsight, both time-space compression and the emergence of an international consumer society can be situated within the larger framework of the intense globalization that we have witnessed since the mid-1950s. The homogenization that followed in the wake of globalization provoked waves of resistance that emphasized the local and the regional over and against the transnational – that is, difference over and against unity – at the point where under the pressure of international capital, and, somewhat later, of post-colonial immigration, the older boundaries and demarcations had already partially been eroded. Still, the reluctant transformation of subjectivity forced by all these social developments would probably not have generated the current crisis without the instrumental role of another, decisive, factor: the veritable explosion of the universities in the 1960s and the resulting professionalization of a vastly increased teaching staff, whose young, ambitious, and often politically articulate members became increasingly dissatified with the conservative parochialism of the older generation and fielded the prestige of disciplines such as anthropology, linguistics, and philosophy in their struggle for intellectual and political dominance. It is this group that, following the example of Hassan, would eventually link the growing awareness that the West's representations were increasingly untenable with poststructuralism's theoretical attack on that which in practice had already been shaken to the core (witness, for instance, the counterculture of the mid-1960s).

This brief and superficial genealogy brings me back to my earlier point. Western representation was undermined by two simultaneous but contradictory developments, one of them universalist, the other radically anti-universalist. We find the impulse radically to democratize the 'freedom, equality, and fraternity' (read brother/sisterhood) promised by the Enlightenment and to apply those principles, now fully democratized, on a truly universal scale – the attempt to make the Enlightenment live up to its promises – alongside the radicalization of Enlightenment self-reflexivity, leading to a rejection of everything that smacked of universalism. Both impulses derived from the Enlightenment itself, with both parties, the universalists and the anti-representationalists, acting, to the best of their beliefs, on behalf of freedom and emancipation. From this perspective, the radically democratic thrust of postmodernism, no matter which of these two strategies it follows, presents a new round in the realization of the potential of the Enlightenment vision. The story of Enlightenment politics is, after all, one of gradual, not immediate democratization, departing from an elitist electorate that reserved Enlightenment benefits mainly for itself. Although one does not find much of that awareness in postmodern theory, modernity must, apart from all else, also be identified with an ever-developing discourse on human rights, on universal education, on the importance of social justice, and so on, and the pressure of this discourse has been a constantly democratizing factor, leading to various rethinkings, and extensions – by way of the franchise, for example – of Enlightenment democracy. In the current round of democratization, an older Enlightenment dispensation is giving way to a new one in a process in which the Enlightenment is – belatedly – forced by its own momentum to confront the problem of the Other. One can see postmodernism, then, as Enlightenment principles finally coming home to roost, while, paradoxically, that home is simultaneously being subjected to a thorough deconstruction.

This takes place in a confusing social situation that mirrors the universalizing and simultaneously self-destructive tendencies of modernity whose clash we now think of as the postmodern. Postmodern theories on the whole tend towards excessive fragmentarization, even if that fragmentarization is sometimes placed within a globalizing interpretative framework, as for instance by Jameson and Baudrillard. The emphasis is on decenterment and difference, and, more generally, the forces of centrifugality. But that picture is too one-sided. It should be obvious that an indeed impressive fragmentarization is counteracted by a further homogenization. On the international political scene, for instance, the regionalization sought by, say, Flanders, Catalonia, or Northern Italy, is countered by the European Union's stumbling pursuit of further integration. The disintegration of the former Soviet Union leads to the expressed intent of much of Central and Eastern Europe to join NATO and the European Union, which has already negotiated admission terms with a number of other European nations that so far had elected to stay out. Outside Europe, both the NAFTA and the GATT negotiations have led to massive free trade agreements. If anything should be clear, then, it is that international capitalism and its homogenizing force is the overwhelming fact of the world we live in, so overwhelming that the nation-state, that mainstay of an earlier modernity, has in some cases lost its relevance. It is true that western capital may be less absolutely dominating than it used to be, but that in itself is a sign of globalization. It only means that modernity and its institutions have so completely penetrated a number of non-Western societies, that they can now compete successfully with the former centers of modernization. After Ihab Hassan, one of the very few theorists of the postmodern to be interested in such globalizing tendencies, postmodern theory became myopically concerned with fragmentation.

It is because of that strategic blindness that many theorists find it so easy to speak of postmodernity rather than a further development of modernity itself. One does not want to deny the murderous tribalization that we can witness in some regions, or, less spectacularly, the rise of single-issue politics and other developments that are taken as signs of social disintegration. But those signs may be misleading. 'Just as the modern quest for an orderly and certain world called into existence forms of disorder and uncertainty', Barry Smart has noted, 'so the global diffusion of modern Western economic, political and cultural forms of life has precipitated complex accommodations, adaptions, contests and conflicts between the "same" and the "different".' Smart adds that '[i]t is to this unpredictable and uncertain global condition that the idea of postmodernity belongs' (1993: 149). More succinctly, Anthony Giddens has pointed out that globalization 'is a process of uneven development that fragments as it coordinates' (1990: 175), and we should not forget that Marx himself already saw all that was solid melt into air under the pressure of homogenizing modernization. Fragmentarization may very well be a symptom of a less clearly visible homogenization rather than the autonomous process that it is often taken to be. Postmodernity, then, is not so much a 'countermodernity', but 'a way of describing experiences of, relationships to, and struggles with diverse and complex manifestations of a modernity that is still very much with us' (Smart 1993: 141).

This is not to say that nothing has changed; on the contrary, change would seem to face us everywhere, but its nature is by and large familiar. The grand theories of social transformation that tried to capture modernity when it had just hit its stride – Marx's capitalism, Durkheim's industrialization, Weber's rationalization – have not become obsolete now that we have found that none of them can claim transcendent explanatory power. We can see now, as Giddens has argued, that the grand theories are not mutually exclusive and that modernity is 'multidimensional on the level of institutions' (1990: 12). The social field created by modernity is much more difficult to map than we used to believe, the more so since our attempts to map it tend to interfere with whatever balance it has. But that does not mean that it has become as radically different as much postmodern theory wants us to believe. It seems to me, therefore, that Giddens is right to speak of a 'radicalised' or 'high' modernity (1990: 150), although I would not strenuously object to 'postmodernity', as long as we acknowledge the important continuities with (the earlier stages of) modernity. The most significant difference between 'radicalised' modernity, or postmodernity, and the modernity of, say, the 1950s, is that the self-reflexivity inherent in the modern project has come to question modernity at large. In the last twenty years, modernity, as a grand socio-political project, has increasingly been called to account by itself; modernity has turned its critical rationality upon itself and has been forced to reluctantly admit to its costs.

That, in spite of this, so many theorists argue that we have entered a new postmodern era, must be ascribed to their tendency to overrate the importance of the cultural changes of the recent past. Here, too, the humanities perspective that most of them bring to the debate betrays itself. This is not to deny the importance of those changes. It seems to me that both at the level of high culture – which, in spite of all claims that the barrier between high and low culture has disappeared, is still recognizably high culture[1] – and at that of consumer culture as theorized by Featherstone and Lash, postmodern theory has its strongest claims. Postmodernism has deeply affected all artistic disciplines, reenergizing and transforming them, and has in its later stages effectuated a welcome, if rather haphazard, repoliticization of contemporary art.

As for the rest, one might call our period a period of transition if the helpfulness of such a label was not severely undercut by the fact that from one perspective or the other all periods are periods of transition. Let me therefore abuse Thomas Kuhn's notion of scientific paradigms to be a little more precise. What we have been witnessing for some time now is the constitution of a new political paradigm, just as its predecessor based upon the principles of the Enlightenment. The old paradigm, which universalized not only the political aspirations, but also the rationality and the self-image of the North Atlantic bourgeoisie, to borrow Rorty's term again, is giving way to a condition of political plurality in which the politics of difference and of identity are replacing the former politics of repressive unity. However, in their emancipatory ideals and in their inevitably universal horizon the new politics constitute much less of a break with the old paradigm than is often assumed. The old paradigm is not so much completely discarded as it is rethought, refined, and much improved. In spite of deconstructionist postmodernism's furious pursuit of radical dissensus, we would seem to be moving towards a new consensus. 'Could it be', David Harvey asks in a retrospective on the analysis developed in *The Condition of Postmodernity*, 'that we are gradually adjusting to this new sense of time and space?' (1990: 12). It would seem so, even if I would prefer to see that adjustment in somewhat different terms. After an overlong period in which Enlightenment universalist representationalism dominated the scene, and a brief, but turbulent period in which its opposite, radical anti-representationalism, captured the imagination, we now find ourselves in the difficult position of trying to honor the claims of both, of seeing the values of both representation and anti-representation, of both consensus and dissensus. Postmodern or radicalized modern – this is our fate: to reconcile the demands of rationality and those of the sublime, to negotiate a permanent crisis in the name of precarious stabilities.

NOTES

1 To give an example: Brenda K. Marshall's admirable *Teaching the Postmodern* (1992) discusses Italo Calvino's 'A sign in space', J. M. Coetzee's *Foe*, Michel Tournier's *Friday*, Christa Wolf's *Cassandra*, Timothy Findley's *Famous Last Words*, Salman Rushdie's *Midnight's Children*, and Toni Morrison's *Beloved*. There is nothing low-brow about such texts (which, to be fair, Marshall never claims). The erosion of the barrier between high and low culture has in practically all cases led to more high culture, although now decked out with low elements.

BIBLIOGRAPHY

Adorno, Theodor W. and Max Horkheimer(1979) *The Dialectics of Enlightenment.* London: Verso.

Allen, Donald and George E. Butterick eds (1982) *The Postmoderns: The New American Poetry Revised.* New York: Grove Press.

Alloway, Lawrence, Donald B. Kuspit, Martha Rosler, and Jan van der Marck (1981) *The Idea of the Post-Modern: Who Is Teaching It? The Idea: At the Henry* 2. Seattle: Henry Art Gallery.

Altieri, Charles (1973) 'From symbolist thought to immanence: the ground of postmodern American poetics.' *boundary 2* 1, 3: 605–41.

Altieri, Charles (1979) 'Postmodernism: a question of definition.' *Par Rapport* 2, 2: 87–101.

Altieri, Charles (1990) 'The powers and limits of oppositional postmodernism.' *American Literary History* 2: 443–81.

Andre, Linda (1984) 'The politics of postmodern photography.' *Minnesota Review,* n.s. 23: 17–35.

Arac, Jonathan, ed. (1986) *Postmodernism and Politics.* Minneapolis: University of Minnesota Press.

Aronowitz, Stanley (1987) 'Postmodernism and politics.' *Social Text* 18: 99–115.

Auslander, Philip (1987) 'Towards a concept of the political in postmodern theatre.' *Theatre Journal* 39, 1: 20–34.

Banes, Sally (1985) 'Dance.' In Trachtenberg (1985): 81–101.

Banes, Sally (1993) 'Introduction to *Terpsichore in Sneakers.*' In Docherty (1993): 157–71.

Barth, John (1967) 'The literature of exhaustion.' *The Atlantic* 220, 2: 29–34.

Barth, John (1980) 'The literature of replenishment.' *The Atlantic* 245, 1: 65–71.

Barth, John (1988) 'Postmodernism revisited.' *Review of Contemporary Fiction* 8, 3: 16–24.

Barthes, Roland (1977) *Image–Music–Text.* New York: Hill and Wang.

Baudrillard, Jean (1968) *Le Système des objets.* Paris: Denoel-Gonthier.

Baudrillard, Jean (1970) *La Société de consommation.* Paris: Gallimard.

Baudrillard, Jean (1975) *The Mirror of Production.* St Louis: Telos Press.

Baudrillard, Jean (1976) *L'Echange symbolique et la mort.* Paris: Gallimard.

Baudrillard, Jean (1981) *For a Critique of the Political Economy of the Sign.* St Louis: Telos Press.

Baudrillard, Jean, (1982) 'L'Effet Beaubourg: implosion et dissuasion.' *October* 20: 3–13.

Baudrillard, Jean (1983a) 'The ecstasy of communication.' In Foster (1983a): 126–33.

Baudrillard, Jean (1983b) *In the Shadow of the Silent Majorities: or, the End of the Social and Other Essays.* New York: Semiotext(e).

Baudrillard, Jean (1983c) *Simulations.* New York: Semiotext(e).

Baudrillard, Jean (1983d) *Les Stratégies fatales.* Paris: Grasset.

Baudrillard, Jean (1984a) 'Interview: game with vestiges.' *On the Beach* 5: 19–25.

Baudrillard, Jean (1984b) 'On nihilism.' *On the Beach* 6: 38–9.

Baudrillard, Jean (1987) *Forget Foucault.* New York: Semiotext(e).

Baudrillard, Jean (1988) *Selected Writings.* Ed. Mark Poster. Stanford: Stanford University Press.

Bauman, Zygmunt (1986–7) 'The left as the counter-culture of modernity.' *Telos* 70: 81–93.

Bauman, Zygmunt (1988) 'Is there a postmodern sociology?' *Theory, Culture & Society* 5, 2–3: 217–39.

Bauman, Zygmunt (1992) *Intimations of Postmodernity.* London: Routledge.

Bell, Daniel (1973) *The Coming of Post-Industrial Society.* New York: Basic Books.

Bell, Daniel (1976) *The Cultural Contradictions of Capitalism.* London: Heinemann.

Bell, Daniel (1992) 'The cultural wars: American intellectual life, 1965–1992.' *Wilson Quarterly,* 16, 3: 74–107.

Belsey, Catherine (1980) *Critical Practice.* London: Methuen.

Benamou, Michel (1977) 'Presence and play.' In Benamou and Caramello (1977): 3–11.

Benamou, Michel, and Charles Caramello, eds. (1977) *Performance in Postmodern Culture.* Madison, Wis.: Coda Press.

Bernstein, Richard J., ed. (1985) *Habermas and Modernity.* Cambridge, Mass.: MIT Press.

Bertens, Hans (1986) 'The postmodern *Weltanschauung* and its relations with modernism: an introductory survey.' In Fokkema and Bertens (1986): 9–51.

Best, Steven and Douglas Kellner (1991) *Postmodern Theory: Critical Interrogations.* London: Macmillan.

Blake, Peter (1974) *Form Follows Fiasco: Why Modern Architecture Hasn't Worked.* Boston: Little, Brown.

Bordo, Susan (1990) 'Feminism, postmodernism, and gender-scepticism.' In Nicholson (1990): 133–57.

Borgmann, Albert (1992) *Crossing the Postmodern Divide.* Chicago: University of Chicago Press.

Bové, Paul (1990) 'A conversation with William V. Spanos.' *boundary 2* 17, 2: 1–39.

Boyne, Roy and Ali Rattansi, eds (1990) *Postmodernism and Society.* London: Macmillan.

Brodsky, Garry M. (1987) 'Postmodernity and politics.' *Philosophy Today* 31, 4/4: 291–305.

Buchloh, Benjamin H.D. (1982) 'Allegorical procedures: appropriation and montage in contemporary art.' *Artforum* (September 1982): 43–56.

Buchloh, Benjamin H.D. (1984) 'Figures of authority, ciphers of regression: notes on the return of representation in European painting.' In Wallis (1984): 106–35.

Bürger, Peter (1984 [1974]) *Theory of the Avant-garde.* Minneapolis: University of Minnesota Press.

Burgin, Victor (1986) *The End of Art Theory: Criticism and Postmodernity.* London: Macmillan.

Burnham, Jack (1974) *Great Western Salt Works: Essays on the Meaning of Post-Formalist Art.* New York: George Braziller.

Butler, Christopher (1980) *After the Wake: An Essay on the Contemporary Avant-Garde.* Oxford: Oxford University Press.

Calhoun, Craig (1992) 'Culture, history, and the problem of specificity in social theory.' In Seidman and Wagner (1992): 244–88.

Calinescu, Matei (1987) *Five Faces of Modernity: Modernism, Avant-garde, Decadence, Kitsch, Postmodernism.* Durham, NC: Duke University Press.

Callinicos, Alex (1989) *Against Postmodernism: A Marxist Critique.* Cambridge: Polity Press.

Callinicos, Alex (1990) 'Reactionary postmodernism?' In Boyne and Rattansi (1990): 97–118.

Caramello, Charles (1977) 'On styles of postmodern writing.' In Benamou and Caramello (1977): 221–34.

Carroll, Noël (1985) 'Film.' In Trachtenberg (1985): 101–35.

Chambers, Ian (1990) *Border Dialogues: Journeys in Postmodernity. London and New York: Routledge.*

Chodorow, Nancy (1978) The Reproduction of Mothering: Psychoanalysis and the Sociology of Gender. Berkeley: University of California Press.

Clark, Michael (1989) 'Political nominalism and critical performance: a postmodern politics for literary theory.' In Joseph Natoli, ed., *Literary Theory's Future(s)* (Urbana and Chicago: University of Illinois Press, 1989): 221–64.

Collins, Jim (1989) *Uncommon Cultures: Popular Culture and Post-modernism.* New York and London: Routledge.

Connor, Steven (1989) *Postmodernist Culture: An Introduction to Theories of the Contemporary.* Oxford and New York: Basil Blackwell.

Connor, Steven (1992) *Theory and Cultural Value.* Oxford and Cambridge, MA: Blackwell.

Cooke, Philip (1990) *Back to the Future: Modernity, Postmodernity and Locality.* London: Unwin Hyman.

Couturier, Maurice, ed. (1983) *Representation and Performance in Postmodern Fiction.* Montpellier: Université Paul Valery.

Creed, Barbara (1987) 'From here to modernity: feminism and postmodernism.' *Screen* 28, 2: 47–68.

Crimp, Douglas (1977) *Pictures.* New York: Committee for the Visual Arts.

Crimp, Douglas (1979) 'Pictures.' *October* 8: 75–88. Also in Wallis (1984): 175–87.

Crimp, Douglas (1980a) 'On the museum's ruins.' *October* 13: 41–59. Also in Foster (1983a): 43–56.

Crimp, Douglas (1980b) 'The photographic activity of postmodernism.' *October* 15: 91–101.

Crimp, Douglas (1982) 'Appropriating appropriation.' In Paula Marincola, ed., *Image Scavengers: Photography* (Institute of Contemporary Art / University of Pennsylvania Press, 1982): 27–34.

Crimp, Douglas (1987) 'The postmodern museum.' *Parachute* 46: 61–9.

Crowther, Paul (1990) 'Postmodernism in the visual arts: a question of ends.' In Boyne and Rattansi (1990): 237–59.

Davis, Douglas (1987) 'Late postmodern: the end of style?' *Art in America* 75, 6: 15.

Davis, Mike (1985) 'Urban renaissance and the spirit of postmodernism.' *New Left Review* 151: 106–13.

Deleuze, Gilles and Félix Guattari (1983) *Anti-Oedipus.* Minneapolis: University of Minnesota Press.

Delillo, Don (1980) *Ratner's Star.* New York: Vintage.

Derrida, Jacques (1970) 'Structure, sign, and play in the discourse of the human sciences.' In Macksey and Donato (1970): 247–65.

Docherty, Thomas (1993) *Postmodernism: A Reader.* Hemel Hempstead: Harvester Wheatsheaf.

Downes, Rackstraw (1976) 'Post-modernist painting.' *Tracks* (Fall 1976): 70–3.

During, Simon (1987) 'Postmodernism or post-colonialism today.' *Textual Practice* 1, 1: 32–47.

Easthope, Anthony (1988) *British Post-Structuralism Since 1968.* London: Routledge.

Falck, Colin (1989) *Myth, Truth, and Literature: Towards a True Post-Modernism.* Cambridge: Cambridge University Press.

Featherstone, Mike (1991) *Consumer Culture and Postmodernism.* London: Sage.

Federman, Raymond (1973) 'Surfiction: a position.' *Partisan Review* 40, 3: 427–32.

Federman, Raymond (1975) 'Surfiction – four propositions in the form of an introduction.' In Raymond Federman, ed., *Surfiction: Fiction Now...and Tomorrow* (Chicago: Swallow Press, 1975): 5–15.

Fiedler, Leslie (1965) 'The new mutants.' *Partisan Review* 32: 505–25.

Fiedler, Leslie (1975 [1969]) 'Cross the border – close that gap: postmodernism.' In Marcus Cunliffe, ed., *American Literature Since 1900* (London: Sphere Books, 1975): 344–66.

Firestone, Shulamith (1970) *The Dialectic of Sex.* New York: Bantam.

Flax, Jane (1987) 'Postmodernism and gender relations in feminist theory.' *Signs: Journal of Women in Culture and Society* 12, 4: 621–43.

Flax, Jane (1990) *Thinking Fragments: Psychoanalysis, Feminism, and Postmodernism in the Contemporary West.* Berkeley: University of California Press.

Fokkema, Douwe (1984) *Literary History, Modernism, and Postmodernism.* Amsterdam and Philadelphia: John Benjamins.

Fokkema, Douwe and Hans Bertens, eds (1986) *Approaching Postmodernism.* Amsterdam and Philadelphia: John Benjamins.

Foster, Hal (1982) 'Subversive signs.' *Art in America* (November 1982): 88–92.

Foster, Hal, ed. (1983a) *The Anti-Aesthetic: Essays in Postmodern Culture.* Port Townsend, Wash.: Bay Press.

Foster, Hal (1983b) 'Postmodernism: a preface.' In Foster (1983a): ix-xvi.

Foster, Hal (1984a) '(Post)Modern polemics.' *New German Critique* 33: 67–78.

Foster, Hal (1984b [1982]) 'Re: post.' In Wallis (1984): 189–201. Originally in *Parachute* 26 (1982): 11–15.

Foster, Hal (1985) *Recodings: Art, Spectacle, Cultural Politics.* Port Townsend, Wash.: Bay Press.

Foster, Hal (1988) 'Wild signs: the breakup of the sign in seventies' art.' In Ross (1988): 251–69.

Frampton, Kenneth (1983) 'Towards a critical regionalism: six points for an architecture of resistance.' In Foster (1983a): 16–30.

Fraser, Nancy and Linda Nicholson (1988) 'Social criticism without philosophy: an encounter between feminism and postmodernism.' In Ross (1988): 83–105.

Friedberg, Anne (1991) 'Mutual indifference: feminism and postmodernism.' In Juliet Flower MacCannell, ed., *The Other Perspective in Gender and Difference: Rewriting Women and the Symbolic* (New York: Columbia University Press, 1990).

Fuller, Peter (1987) 'Towards a new nature for the Gothic.' *Art & Design* 3, 3–4: 5–10.

Gablik, Suzi (1984) *Has Modernism Failed?* New York: Thames and Hudson.

Gellner, Ernest (1992) *Postmodernism, Reason and Religion.* New York and London: Routledge.

Giddens, Anthony (1990) *The Consequences of Modernity.* Cambridge: Polity Press.

Gitlin, Todd (1989) 'Postmodernism: roots and politics.' In Ian Angus and Sut Jhally, eds, *Cultural Politics in Contemporary America* (New York and London: Routledge, 1989): 347–60.

Goldberger, Paul (1977) 'Post-modernism: an introduction.' *Architectural Design* 47, 4: 256–60.

Graff, Gerald (1973) 'The myth of the postmodernist breakthrough.' *TriQuarterly* 26: 383–417.

Graff, Gerald (1975) 'Babbitt at the abyss: the social context of postmodern American fiction.' *TriQuarterly* 33: 305–37.

Graff, Gerald (1979) *Literature Against Itself: Literary Ideas in Modern Society.* Chicago: University of Chicago Press.

Greenberg, Clement (1980) 'Modern and postmodern.' *Arts Magazine* 54: 64–6.

Grosz, E.A., Terry Threadgold, David Kelly, Alan Chodolenko, and Edward Colless, eds (1986) *Futur*Fall: Excursions Into Postmodernity.* Sidney: Power Institute of Fine Arts and Futur*Fall.

Habermas, Jürgen (1981) 'Modernity versus postmodernity.' *New German*

Critique 22: 3–14. Rpt as 'Modernity – an incomplete project' in Foster (1983a): 3–15.

Habermas, Jürgen (1984–7) *The Theory of Communicative Action.* Boston: Beacon Press.

Habermas, Jürgen (1985) 'Questions and counterquestions.' In Bernstein (1985): 192–216.

Harding, Sandra (1990) 'Feminism, science, and the anti-Enlightenment critiques.' In Nicholson (1990): 83–107.

Hartsock, Nancy (1990) 'Foucault on power: a theory for women?' In Nicholson (1990): 157–76.

Harvey, David (1989) *The Condition of Postmodernity: An Enquiry into the Origins of Cultural Change.* Oxford and Cambridge, MA: Blackwell.

Harvey, David (1990) 'Looking backwards on postmodernism.' *Architectural Design* 88: 10–12.

Hassan, Ihab (1963) 'The dismemberment of Orpheus.' *American Scholar* 32: 463–84.

Hassan, Ihab (1967a) *The Literature of Silence: Henry Miller and Samuel Beckett.* New York: Knopf.

Hassan, Ihab (1967b) 'The literature of silence: from Henry Miller to Beckett & Burroughs.' *Encounter* 28, 1: 74–82.

Hassan, Ihab (1970a) 'Frontiers of criticism: metaphors of silence.' *Virginia Quarterly Review* 46, 1: 81–95.

Hassan, Ihab (1970b) 'Joyce–Beckett: a scenario in 8 scenes and a voice.' In Hassan (1975): 63–73.

Hassan, Ihab (1971a) *The Dismemberment of Orpheus: Toward a Postmodern Literature.* New York: Oxford University Press.

Hassan, Ihab, ed. (1971b) *Liberations: New Essays on the Humanities in Revolution.* Middletown, CT: Wesleyan University Press.

Hassan, Ihab (1971c) 'POSTmodernISM: a paracritical bibliography.' *New Literary History* 3, 1: 5–30.

Hassan, Ihab (1971d) 'Fiction and future: an extravaganza for voice and tape.' In Hassan (1971b): 176–96.

Hassan, Ihab (1973) 'The new gnosticism: speculations on an aspect of the postmodern mind.' *boundary 2* 1, 3: 547–69.

Hassan, Ihab (1975) *Paracriticisms: Seven Speculations of the Times.* Urbana: University of Illinois Press.

Hassan, Ihab (1977) 'Prometheus as performer: toward a posthumanist culture? A university masque in five scenes.' In Benamou and Caramello (1977): 201–21.

Hassan, Ihab (1980a) *The Right Promethean Fire: Imagination, Science, and Cultural Change.* Urbana: University of Illinois Press.

Hassan, Ihab (1980b) 'The question of postmodernism.' *Bucknell Review* 25, 2: 117–26.

Hassan, Ihab (1980c [1978]) 'Culture, indeterminacy, and immanence: margins of the (postmodern) age.' In Hassan (1980a): 91–124.

Hassan, Ihab (1982) *The Dismemberment of Orpheus: Toward a Postmodern Literature,* 2nd rev. edn. Madison: University of Wisconsin Press.

Hassan, Ihab (1983) 'Desire and dissent in the postmodern age.' *Kenyon Review* 5: 1–18.

Hassan, Ihab (1987a) *The Postmodern Turn: Essays in Postmodern Theory and Culture.* Columbus: Ohio State University Press.

Hassan, Ihab (1987b) 'Making sense: the trials of postmodern discourse.' *New Literary History* 18, 2: 437–59.

Hassan, Ihab and Sally Hassan, eds (1983) *Innovation/Renovation: New Perspectives on the Humanities.* Madison: University of Wisconsin Press.

Hekman, Susan J. (1990) *Gender and Knowledge: Elements of a Postmodern Feminism.* Boston: Northeastern University Press.

Heller, Agnes and Férenc Feher (1988) *The Postmodern Political Condition.* Oxford: Blackwell.

Herman, David J. (1993) 'Modernism versus postmodernism: towards an analytic distinction.' In Natoli and Hutcheon (1993): 157–92.

Hoesterey, Ingeborg, ed. (1991) *Zeitgeist in Babel: The Postmodernist Controversy.* Bloomington: Indiana University Press.

Hoffmann, Gerhard (1982) 'The fantastic in fiction: its "reality" status, its historical development and its transformation in postmodern narration.' *REAL (Yearbook of Research in English and American Literature)* 1: 267–364.

Hoffmann, Gerhard, Alfred Hornung and Rudiger Kunow (1977) ' "Modern", "postmodern," and "contemporary" as criteria for the analysis of twentieth-century literature.' *Amerikastudien* 22: 19–46.

Holquist, Michael (1971) 'Whodunit and other questions: metaphysical detective stories in post-war fiction.' *New Literary History* 3, 1: 135–56.

Honneth, Axel (1985) 'An aversion against the universal: a commentary on Lyotard's *Postmodern Condition.*' *Theory, Culture & Society* 2, 3: 147–57.

hooks, bell (1993) 'Postmodern blackness.' In Natoli and Hutcheon (1993): 510–18.

Hornung, Alfred (1983) 'Recollection and imagination in postmodernist times.' In Couturier (1983): 57–72.

Howe, Irving (1959) 'Mass society and post-modern fiction.' *Partisan Review* 26: 420–36.

Howe, Irving (1970) *The Decline of the New.* New York: Harcourt, Brace and World.

Hutcheon, Linda (1980) *Narcissistic Narrative: The Metafictional Paradox.* Waterloo, Ontario: Wilfried Laurier University Press.

Hutcheon, Linda (1988) *A Poetics of Postmodernism: History, Theory, Fiction.* New York and London: Routledge.

Hutcheon, Linda (1989) *The Politics of Postmodernism.* New York and London: Routledge.

Huyssen, Andreas (1981) 'The search for tradition: avant-garde and postmodernism in the 1970s.' *New German Critique* 22: 23–40.

Huyssen, Andreas (1984) 'Mapping the postmodern.' *New German Critique* 33: 5–52.

Huxtable, Ada Louise (1981) 'The troubled state of modern architecture.' *Architectural Design* 51, 1–2: 8–17.

Jacobs, Jane (1961) *The Death and Life of Great American Cities.* New York: Vintage.

Jameson, Fredric (1983) 'Postmodernism and consumer society.' In Foster (1983a): 111–25.

Jameson, Fredric (1984a) 'Postmodernism, or the cultural logic of late capitalism.' *New Left Review* 146: 53–92.

Jameson, Fredric (1984b) [untitled review of Don DeLillo's *The Names* and Sol Yurick's *Richard A.*] *Minnesota Review* n.s. 5, 23: 116–22.

Jameson, Fredric (1984c) 'Foreword.' In Lyotard (1984c): vii-xxi.

Jameson, Fredric (1985) 'Baudelaire as modernist and postmodernist: the dissolution of the referent and the artificial "sublime".' In Chaviva Hosek and Patricia Parker, eds, *Lyric Poetry: Beyond New Criticism* (Ithaca and London: Cornell University Press, 1985): 247–63.

Jameson, Fredric (1986a) 'On magic realism in film.' *Critical Inquiry* 12: 301–25.

Jameson, Fredric (1986b) 'Hans Haacke and the cultural logic of postmodernism.' In Brian Wallis, ed., *Hans Haacke: Unfinished Business* (New York: New Museum of Contemporary Art; Boston, Mass.: Godine, 1986): 38–50.

Jameson, Fredric (1987) 'Reading without interpretation: postmodernism and the video-text.' In Nigel Fabb *et al.*, eds, *The Linguistics of Writing: Arguments Between Language and Literature* (Manchester: Manchester University Press, 1987): 199–233.

Jameson, Fredric (1988) 'Cognitive mapping.' In Cary Nelson and Lawrence Grossberg, eds, *Marxism and the Interpretation of Culture* (Urbana: University of Illinois Press, 1988): 347–60.

Jameson, Fredric (1989) 'Marxism and postmodernism.' *New Left Review* 176: 31–45.

Jameson, Fredric (1991) *Postmodernism, or, the Cultural Logic of Late Capitalism.* Durham, NC: Duke University Press.

Jardine, Alice (1982) 'Gynesis.' *Diacritics* 12, 2: 54–65.

Jardine, Alice (1985) *Gynesis: Configurations of Woman and Modernity.* Ithaca and London: Cornell University Press.

Jay, Martin (1991) 'Habermas and postmodernism.' In Hoesterey (1991): 98–110.

Jencks, Charles (1975) 'The rise of Post-Modern architecture.' *Architecture Association Quarterly* 7, 4: 3–14.

Jencks, Charles (1977a) *The Language of Post-Modern Architecture.* London: Academy.

Jencks, Charles (1977b) 'A genealogy of Post-Modern architecture.' *Architectural Design* 47, 4: 269–71.

Jencks, Charles (1978) *The Language of Post-Modern Architecture*, 2nd rev. edn. London: Academy.

Jencks, Charles (1980) *Late-Modern Architecture.* London: Academy.

Jencks, Charles (1981) *The Language of Postmodern Architecture*, 3rd rev. edn. London: Academy.

Jencks, Charles, ed. (1982) 'Free-style classicism.' *Architectural Design* 52, 1–2.

Jencks, Charles (1986) *What is Post-Modernism?* London: Academy/New York: St Martin's Press.

Jencks, Charles (1987a) *Post-Modernism: The New Classicism in Art and Architecture.* London: Academy.

Jencks, Charles (1987b) 'Interview with Charles Jencks.' *Art & Design* 3, 7–8: 45–7.

Jencks, Charles (1987c) 'The classical sensibility.' *Art & Design* 3, 7–8: 48–68.

Johnson, Philip (1977) 'On style and the International Style: on postmodernism: on architecture.' *Oppositions* 10: 15–19.

Kafalenos, Emma. (1985) 'Fragments of a partial discourse on Roland Barthes and the postmodern mind.' *Chicago Review* 35: 72–94.

Kahler, Erich (1968) *The Disintegration of Form in the Arts.* New York: Braziller.

Kaplan, E. Ann (1987) *Rocking Around the Clock: Music Television, Postmodernism and Consumer Culture.* London and New York: Methuen.

Kaplan, E. Ann, ed. (1988) *Postmodernism and Its Discontents: Theories, Practices.* London: Verso.

Kavolis, Vytautas (1969) 'Revolutionary metaphors and ambiguous personalities: notes toward an understanding of post-modern revolutions.' *Soundings* 52: 394–414.

Kavolis, Vytautas (1970) 'Post-modern man: psycho-cultural responses to social trends.' *Social Problems* 17: 435–9.

Keane, John (1987) 'The modern democratic revolution: reflections on Jean-François Lyotard's *La condition postmoderne.*' *Chicago Review* 35: 4–19.

Kearney, R. 'Ethics and the postmodern imagination.' *Thought: A Review of Culture and Ideas* 62, 244: 39–58.

Kellner, Douglas (1989) *Jean Baudrillard: From Marxism to Postmodernism and Beyond.* London: Polity Press.

Kellner, Douglas, ed. (1989) *Postmodernism/Jameson/Critique.* Washington, DC: Maisonneuve Press.

Kermode, Frank (1966) 'Modernisms again: objects, jokes, and art.' *Encounter* 26, 4: 65–74. Expanded and reprinted as 'Modernisms' in Frank Kermode, *Continuities* (New York: Random House, 1968): 10–26.

Kern, Robert (1978) 'Composition as recognition: Robert Creeley and postmodern poetics.' *boundary 2* 6, 3 and 7, 1: 211–30.

Ketcham, Diane (1992) 'More is more: Robert Venturi and Denise Scott Brown.' *Art News* 91, 4: 90–4.

Kipnis, Laura (1988) 'Feminism: The Political Conscience of Postmodernism?' In Ross (1988): 149–67.

Kirby, Michael (1975) 'Post-modern dance issue: an introduction.' *Drama Review* 19, 1: 3–4.

Klotz, Heinrich (1988) *The History of Postmodern Architecture.* Cambridge, Mass.: MIT Press.

Köhler, Michael (1977) ' "Postmodernismus": ein begriffsgeschichtlicher Überblick.' *Amerikastudien* 22, 1: 8–18.

Kolb, David (1990) *Postmodern Sophistications: Philosophy, Architecture, and Tradition.* Chicago: University of Chicago Press.

Krauss, Rosalind (1979a) 'John Mason and post-modernist sculpture: new experiences, new words.' *Art in America* 67, 3: 120–7.

Krauss, Rosalind (1979b) 'Sculpture in the expanded field.' *October* 8: 31–44.

Krier, Leon (1985) *Albert Speer: Architecture 1932–1942.* Brussels: Archives d'Architecture Moderne.

Kuhn, Thomas (1970) [1962] *The Structure of Scientific Revolutions*, 2nd edn. Chicago: University of Chicago Press.

Kuspit, Donald (1981) 'Postmodernism, plurality and the urgency of the given.' In Alloway *et al.* (1981): 13–24.

Laclau, Ernesto (1988) 'Politics and the limits of modernity.' In Ross (1988): 63–82.

Laclau, Ernesto and Chantal Mouffe (1985) *Hegemony and Socialist Strategy: Towards a Radical Democratic Politics.* London: Verso.

Laclau, Ernesto and Chantal Mouffe (1987) 'Post-marxism without apologies.' *New Left Review* 166: 79–106.

Lash, Scott (1990) *Sociology of Postmodernism.* London and New York: Routledge.

Lash, Scott and John Urry (1987) *The End of Organized Capitalism.* Cambridge: Polity Press.

Lauretis, Teresa de (1986) 'Feminist studies/critical studies: issues, terms, and contexts.' In Teresa de Lauretis, ed., *Feminist Studies/Critical Studies* (Bloomington: Indiana University Press, 1986): 1–19.

Lawson, Hilary (1985) *Reflexivity: The Post-modern Predicament.* London: Hutchinson.

Lea, Kenneth (1987) ' "In the most highly developed societies": Lyotard and postmodernism.' *Oxford Literary Review* 9, 1–2: 86–104.

Lefebvre, Henri (1974) *La Production de L'espace.* Paris: Anthropos.

Lethen, Helmut (1986) 'Modernism cut in half: the exclusion of the avant-garde and the debate on postmodernism.' In Fokkema and Bertens (1986): 233–8.

Levin, Kim (1980) 'Farewell to modernism.' *Arts* 54: 90–2.

Lipsitz, George (1986–7) 'Cruising around the historical bloc: postmodernism and popular music in East Los Angeles.' *Cultural Critique* 5: 157–77.

Lovibond, Sabina (1990) 'Feminism and postmodernism.' In Boyne and Rattansi (1990): 154–86.

Lyotard, Jean-François (1971) *Discours, figure.* Paris: Klinksieck.

Lyotard, Jean-François (1973) *Dérive à partir de Marx et Freud.* Paris: Union générale d'éditions.

Lyotard, Jean-François (1974) *Economie libidinale.* Paris: Minuit.

Lyotard, Jean-François (1977) 'The unconscious as mise-en-scène.' In Benamou and Caramello (1977): 87–98.

Lyotard, Jean-François (1978) 'Notes on the return of capital.' *Semiotext(e)* 3, 1: 44–53.

Lyotard, Jean-François (1979) *La Condition postmoderne: rapport sur le savoir.* Paris: Minuit.

Lyotard, Jean-François (1983a) 'Answering the question: what is postmodernism?' In Hassan and Hassan (1983): 329–41.

Lyotard, Jean-François (1984a) *Driftworks.* Ed. Roger McKeon. New York: Semiotext(e).

Lyotard, Jean-François (1984b) 'Interview: Jean-François Lyotard.' Conducted by Georges Van Den Abbeele. *Diacritics* 14: 16–21.

Lyotard, Jean-François (1984c) *The Postmodern Condition: A Report on Knowledge*. Minneapolis: University of Minnesota Press.

Lyotard, Jean-François (1984d) 'The sublime and the avant-garde.' *Artforum* 22, 8: 36–43.

Lyotard, Jean-François (1985) *Just Gaming*. With Jean-Loup Thébaud. Minneapolis: University of Minnesota Press.

Lyotard, Jean-François (1986) 'Complexity and the sublime.' In Lisa Appignanesi, ed., *Postmodernism: ICA Documents 5* (London: ICA, 1986): 10–12.

Lyotard, Jean-François (1988a) *The Différend: Phrases in Dispute*. Minneapolis: University of Minnesota Press.

Lyotard, Jean-François (1988b) 'An interview with Jean-François Lyotard.' Conducted by Willem van Reijen and Dick Veerman. *Theory, Culture & Society* 5, 2–3: 277–309.

McGowan, John (1991) *Postmodernism and its Critics*. Ithaca, NY: Cornell University Press.

McHale, Brian (1987) *Postmodernist Fiction*. London and New York: Methuen.

Macksey, Richard and Eugenio Donato, eds (1970) *The Structuralist Controversy: The Languages of Criticism and the Sciences of Man*. Baltimore: Johns Hopkins University Press.

McRobbie, Angela (1986) 'Postmodernism and popular culture.' In Lisa Appignanesi, ed., *Postmodernism: ICA Documents 5* (London: ICA, 1986): 54–7.

Mandel, Ernest (1978) *Late Capitalism*. London: New Left Books.

Marshall, Brenda K. (1992) *Teaching the Postmodern: Fiction and Theory*. New York and London: Routledge.

Martin, Wallace (1980) 'Postmodernism: Ultima Thule or seim anew?' *Bucknell Review* 25, 2: 142–54.

Meyer, Leonard B. (1963) 'The end of the Renaissance?' *Hudson Review* 16: 169–86.

Moi, Toril (1988) 'Feminism, postmodernism and style: recent feminist criticism in the United States.' *Cultural Critique* 9: 3–22.

Morris, Meaghan (1993) 'Feminism, reading, postmodernism.' In Docherty (1993): 368–89.

Morrisette, Bruce (1975) 'Post-modern generative fiction: novel and film.' *Critical Inquiry* 2: 253–62.

Mouffe, Chantal (1988) 'Radical democracy: modern or postmodern?' In Ross (1988): 31–45.

Mulvey, Laura (1975) 'Visual pleasure and narrative cinema.' *Screen* 16, 3: 6–18.

Natoli, Joseph and Linda Hutcheon (1993) *A Postmodern Reader*. Albany: State University of New York Press.

Nicholson, Linda J., ed. (1990) *Feminism/Postmodernism*. New York and London: Routledge.

Norris, Christopher (1985) *The Contest of Faculties: Philosophy and Theory After Deconstruction*. London and New York: Methuen.

Norris, Christopher (1990) *What's Wrong with Postmodernism: Critical Theory and the Ends of Philosophy*. London and New York: Harvester Wheatsheaf.

O'Doherty, Brian (1971) 'What is post-modernism?' *Art in America* 59: 19.

Oliva, Achille Bonito (1982) 'The international trans-avantgarde.' *FlashArt* 104: 36–43.

Olsen, Lance (1989) 'The next generation in fiction.' *Virginia Quarterly Review* 65, 2: 277–87.

Olson, Charles (1967) *Human Universe and Other Essays*. Ed. Donald Allen. New York: Grove Press.

Owens, Craig (1979) 'Earthwords.' *October* 10: 120–30.

Owens, Craig (1980a) 'The allegorical impulse: toward a theory of post-modernism. Part I.' *October* 12: 67–86.

Owens, Craig (1980b) 'The allegorical impulse: toward a theory of post-modernism. Part II.' *October* 13: 59–80.

Owens, Craig (1983) 'The discourse of others: feminists and postmodernism.' In Foster (1983a): 57–82.

Palmer, Richard (1976) 'The postmodernity of Heidegger.' *boundary 2* 4: 411–32.

Palmer, Richard (1977a) 'Postmodernity and hermeneutics.' *boundary 2* 5, 2: 363–93.

Palmer, Richard (1977b) 'Toward a postmodern hermeneutics of performance.' In Benamou and Caramello (1977): 19–33.

Paoletti, John T. (1985) 'Art.' In Trachtenberg (1985): 53–81.

Patton, Paul (1986) 'Ethics and post-modernity.' In Grosz *et al.* (1986): 128–46.

Pavis, Patrice (1986) 'The classical heritage of modern drama: the case of postmodern theatre.' *Modern Drama* 25, 1: 1–22.

Perloff, Marjorie (1980) 'Contemporary/postmodern: the "new" poetry.' *Bucknell Review* 25, 2: 171–9.

Perloff, Marjorie (1981) *The Poetics of Indeterminacy: Rimbaud to Cage*. Princeton: Princeton University Press.

Perloff, Marjorie (1982) 'From image to action: the return of story in postmodern poetry.' *Contemporary Literature* 23, 4: 411–27.

Perloff, Marjorie (1985) *The Dance of the Intellect: Studies in the Poetry of the Pound Tradition*. Cambridge and New York: Cambridge University Press.

Portoghesi, Paolo (1983) *Postmodern: The Architecture of the Postindustrial Society*. New York: Rizzoli.

Portoghesi, Paolo (1993) 'Postmodern.' In Docherty (1993): 308–15.

Poster, Mark (1988) 'Introduction.' In Baudrillard (1988): 1–9.

Poster, Mark (1989) *Critical Theory and Poststructuralism: In Search of a Context*. Ithaca and London: Cornell University Press.

Probyn, Elspeth (1987) 'Bodies and anti-bodies: feminism and the post-modern.' *Cultural Studies* 1, 3: 349–60.

Probyn, Elspeth (1990) 'Travels in the postmodern: making sense of the local.' In Nicholson (1990): 176–90.

Rorty, Richard (1980) *Philosophy and the Mirror of Nature*. Princeton: Princeton University Press.

Rorty, Richard (1982) *Consequences of Pragmatism (Essays 1972–1980)*. Minneapolis: University of Minnesota Press.

Rorty, Richard (1983) 'Postmodernist bourgeois liberalism.' *Journal of Philosophy* 80, 10: 583–9.

Rorty, Richard (1985) 'Habermas and Lyotard on postmodernity.' In Bernstein (1985): 161–75.

Rorty, Richard (1989) *Contingency, Irony, and Solidarity*. Cambridge: Cambridge University Press.

Rose, Margaret A. (1991) *The Post-modern and the Post-industrial: A Critical Analysis*. Cambridge: Cambridge University Press.

Rosenberg, Harold (1966) *The Anxious Object: Art Today and Its Audience*. New York: Horizon Press.

Rosler, Martha (1981) 'The system of the postmodern in the decade of the seventies.' In Alloway *et al.* (1981): 25–51.

Ross, Andrew, ed. (1988) *Universal Abandon? The Politics of Postmodernism*. Minneapolis: University of Minnesota Press.

Rossi, Aldo (1989) *The Architecture of the City*, rev. edn. Cambridge, MA: MIT Press.

Rothenberg, Jerome (1977) 'New models, new visions: some notes toward a poetics of performance.' In Benamou and Caramello (1977): 11–19.

Russell, Charles (1974) 'The vault of language: self-reflective artifice in contemporary American fiction.' *Modern Fiction Studies* 20, 3: 349–59.

Russell, Charles (1980) 'Individual voice in the collective discourse: literary innovation in postmodern American fiction.' *Sub-Stance* 27: 29–39.

Russell, Charles (1982) 'Subversion and legitimation: the avant-garde in postmodern culture.' *Chicago Review* 33, 2: 54–9.

Ryan, Michael (1988) 'Postmodern politics.' *Theory, Culture & Society* 5, 2–3: 559–76.

Schechner, Richard (1982) *The End of Humanism: Writings in Performance*. New York: Performing Arts Journal Publications.

Seidman, Steven (1992) 'Postmodern social theory as narrative with a moral intent.' In Seidman and Wagner (1992): 47–81.

Seidman, Steven and David G. Wagner (1992) *Postmodernism and Social Theory: The Debate over General Theory*. Oxford and Cambridge, MA: Blackwell.

Silverman, Kaja (1986) 'Fragments of a fashionable discourse.' In Tania Modleski, ed., *Studies in Entertainment: Critical Approaches to Mass Culture* (Bloomington and Indianapolis: Indiana University Press, 1986): 139–54.

Smart, Barry (1992) *Modern Conditions, Postmodern Controversies*. London and New York: Routledge.

Smart, Barry (1993) *Postmodernity*. London and New York: Routledge.

Smith, C. Ray (1977) *Supermannerism: New Attitudes in Post-Modern Architecture*. New York: E.P. Dutton.

Soja, Edward W. (1989) *Postmodern Geographies: The Reassertion of Space in Critical Social Theory*. London: Verso.

Solomon-Godeau, Abigail (1984a) 'Photography after art photography.' In Wallis (1984): 75–85.

Solomon-Godeau, Abigail (1984b [1983]) 'Winning the game when the rules have been changed: art photography and postmodernism.' *Screen* 25, 6: 88–102.

Solomon-Godeau, Abigail (1988) 'Living with contradictions: critical practices in the age of supply-side aesthetics.' In Ross (1988): 191–214.

Sontag, Susan (1964a) 'Against interpretation.' In Sontag (1967): 3–14.

Sontag, Susan (1964b) 'Godard's *Vivre Sa Vie*.' In Sontag (1967): 196–208.

Sontag, Susan (1964c) 'Notes on "camp".' In Sontag (1967): 275–92.

Sontag, Susan (1965) 'One culture and the new sensibility.' In Sontag (1967): 293–304.

Sontag, Susan (1967) *Against Interpretation and Other Essays*. New York: Dell.

Sontag, Susan (1969 [1967]) 'The aesthetics of silence.' In Susan Sontag, *Styles of Radical Will* (London: Secker and Warburg, 1969): 3–34.

Spanos, William V. (1972) 'The detective and the boundary: some notes on the postmodern literary imagination.' *boundary 2* 1, 1: 147–68.

Spanos, William V. (1976) 'Heidegger, Kierkegaard, and the hermeneutic circle: towards a postmodern theory of interpretation as dis-closure.' *boundary 2* 4: 455–88.

Spanos, William V. (1978) 'The un-naming of the beasts: the postmodernity of Sartre's *La Nausée*.' *Criticism* 20: 223–80.

Spanos, William V. (1979) 'De-struction and the question of postmodern literature: towards a definition.' *Par Rapport* 2, 2: 107–22.

Spanos, William V. (1987) *Repetitions: The Postmodern Occasion in Literature and Culture*. Baton Rouge: Louisiana State University Press.

Starenko, Michael (1983) 'What's an artist to do? a short history of postmodernism and photography.' *Afterimage* 10, 6: 4–5.

Stephanson, Anders (1988) 'Regarding postmodernism – a conversation with Fredric Jameson.' In Ross (1988): 3–31.

Stern, Robert (1969) *New Directions in American Architecture*. New York: Braziller.

Stern, Robert (1977) 'At the edge of Post-Modernism.' *Architectural Design* 47, 4: 274–88. [The magazine's table of contents lists the article as 'At the edge of modernism.']

Stern, Robert (1980) 'The doubles of post-modern.' *The Harvard Architecture Review* 1: 75–87.

Suleiman, Susan (1986) 'Naming a difference: reflections on "modernism versus postmodernism" in literature.' In Fokkema and Bertens (1986): 255–70.

Suleiman, Susan Rubin (1991) 'Feminism and postmodernism: a question of politics.' In Hoesterey (1991): 111–30.

Thiher, Allen (1976) 'Postmodern dilemmas: Godard's *Alphaville* and *Two or Three Things That I Know About Her*.' *boundary 2* 4, 3: 947–65.

Thiher, Allen (1984) *Words in Reflection: Modern Language Theory and Postmodern Fiction*. Chicago: University of Chicago Press.

Thornton, Gene (1979) 'Postmodern photography: it doesn't look modern at all.' *Art News*, April: 64–8.

Tomkins, Calvin (1965) *The Bride and the Bachelors: The Heretical Courtship in Art*. London: Weidenfeld and Nicholson.

Touraine, Alain (1969) *La Société postindustrielle*. Paris: Denoël.

Trachtenberg, Stanley, ed. (1985) *The Postmodern Moment: A Handbook of Contemporary Innovation in the Arts*. Westport, CT and London: Greenwood Press.

Turim, Maureen (1991) 'Cinemas of modernity and postmodernity.' In Hoesterey (1991): 177–91.

Turner, Bryan S., ed. (1990a) *Theories of Modernity and Postmodernity.* London: Sage.

Turner, Bryan S. (1990b) 'Periodization and politics in the postmodern.' In Turner (1990a): 1–13.

Venturi, Robert (1965) 'A justification for a Pop architecture.' *Arts and Architecture* 5 (April 1965): 22.

Venturi, Robert (1977 [1966]) *Complexity and Contradiction in Architecture.* London: The Architectural Press.

Venturi, Robert and Denise Scott Brown (1968) 'A significance for A&P parking lots, or learning from Las Vegas.' *Architectural Forum* 128, 2: 37–43, 89–91.

Venturi, Robert and Denise Scott Brown (1970) 'Co-op city: learning to like it.' *Progressive Architecture,* February: 64–72.

Venturi, Robert and Denise Scott Brown (1971) 'Ugly and ordinary architecture, or the decorated shed.' Pt I, *Architectural Forum,* November: 64–7; Pt II, December: 48–53.

Venturi, Robert, Denise Scott Brown and Steven Izenour (1972) *Learning from Las Vegas: The Forgotten Symbolism of Architectural Form.* Cambridge, MA.: MIT Press.

Venturi, Robert, Denise Scott Brown and Steven Izenour (1977) *Learning from Las Vegas,* 2nd rev. edn. Cambridge, MA: MIT Press.

Wallis, Brian, ed. (1984). *Art After Modernism: Rethinking Representation.* Boston: David R. Godine/New York: New Museum of Contemporary Art.

Wasson, Richard (1969) 'Notes on a new sensibility.' *Partisan Review* 36: 460–77.

Wasson, Richard (1974) 'From priest to Prometheus: culture and criticism in the post-modern period.' *Journal of Modern Literature* 3, 5: 1188–202.

Waugh, Patricia (1984) *Metafiction: The Theory and Practice of Self-Conscious Fiction.* London and New York: Methuen.

Waugh, Patricia (1989) *Feminine Fictions: Revisiting the Postmodern.* London and New York: Routledge.

Wellmer, Albrecht (1985) 'On the dialectic of modernism and postmodernism.' *Praxis International* 4: 337–62.

Welsch, Wolfgang (1987) *Unsere postmoderne Moderne.* Weinheim: Acta Humaniora.

West, Cornel (1993) 'Black culture and postmodernism.' In Natoli and Hutcheon (1993): 390–7.

Wilde, Alan (1976) 'Barthelme unfair to Kierkegaard: some thoughts on modern and postmodern irony.' *boundary 2* 5: 45–70.

Wilde, Alan (1980) 'Irony in the postmodern age: toward a map of suspensiveness.' *boundary 2* 9, 1: 5–46.

Wilde, Alan (1981) *Horizons of Assent: Modernism, Postmodernism and the Ironic Imagination.* Baltimore: Johns Hopkins University Press.

Wilde, Alan (1982) ' "Strange displacements of the ordinary": Apple, Elkin, Barthelme, and the problem of the excluded middle.' *boundary 2* 10, 2: 177–99.

Wolff, Janet (1990) 'Postmodern theory and feminist art practice.' In Boyne and Rattansi (1990): 187–208.

Woodward, Kathleen, ed. (1980) *The Myths of Information: Technology and Post-Industrial Culture.* Madison: Coda Press.

Wyver, John (1986) 'Television and postmodernism.' In Lisa Appignanesi, ed., *Postmodernism: ICA Documents 5* (London: ICA, 1986): 52–4.

Zukin, Sharon (1988) 'The postmodern debate over urban form.' *Theory, Culture & Society* 5, 2–3: 431–46.

INDEX

DUNDEE DISTRICT LIBRARIES